GENDER ACTIVISM AND STUDIES IN AFRICA

I0113062

Signe Arnfred
Babere Kerata Chacha
Amanda Gouws
Josephine Ahikire
Ayodele Ogundipe
Charmaine Pereira
Mansah Prah
Charles Ukeje
Felicia Arudo Yieke

CODESRIA Gender Series 3

COUNCIL FOR THE DEVELOPMENT OF
SOCIAL SCIENCE RESEARCH IN AFRICA

CODESRIA

ISBN: 2-86978-140-7

Typeset by Djibril Fall

Cover image designed by Andre Nel, UNISA Press

Printed by Lightning Source

Distributed in Africa by CODESRIA

Distributed elsewhere by
African Books Collective, Oxford, UK
Web site: www.africanbookscollective.com

CODESRIA would like to express its gratitude to the Swedish International
Development Cooperation Agency (SIDA/SAREC), the International
Development Research Centre (IDRC), Ford Foundation, MacArthur Foundation,
Carnegie Corporation, the Norwegian Ministry of Foreign Affairs, the Danish
Agency for International Development (DANIDA), the French Ministry of
Cooperation, the United Nations Development Programme (UNDP), the
Netherlands Ministry of Foreign Affairs, Rockefeller Foundation, FINIDA,
NORAD, CIDA, IIEP/ADEA, OECD, IFS, OXFAM America, UN/UNICEF
and the Government of Senegal for supporting its research, training and publication
programmes

Contents

Contributors

Signe Arnfred is a sociologist, gender researcher and associate professor at the Institute of Geography and Development Studies at Roskilde University, Denmark. Since 2000 she has been attached to the Nordic Africa Institute in Uppsala, Sweden, as coordinator of a research programme on Sexuality, Gender and Society in Africa.

Babere Kerata Chacha is an assistant lecturer and a doctoral student in the department of History at Egerton University Njoro, Kenya, he teaches agricultural and environmental history as well as women history and sexuality. Previously he had taught at the University of Eastern Africa, Baraton and Kamagambo Adventist College as an adjunct lecturer in history and development studies.

Amanda Gouws is Associate Professor and Head of the Department of Political Science at the University of Stellenbosch in South Africa. Her research deals with women and citizenship. She is the Chair of the Women's Forum at the University of Stellenbosch as well as the Chair of the Advisory Committee on Sexual Harassment.

Josephine Ahikire obtained an MA in Development Studies from the Institute of Social Studies in The Hague, specialising in Women and Development. For several years, Josephine has worked as a lecturer at Makerere University in the Department of Women and Gender Studies. She is also a Senior Research Fellow at the Centre for Basic Research. She has published in a range of fields including labour, gender and governance.

Ayodele Ogundipe teaches at the Department of Sociology and Anthropology, University of Benin, Benin City, Edo State, Nigeria. He is the current president of the Nigerian Association of Anthropologists.

Charmaine Pereira is an independent scholar based in Abuja, Nigeria. Her research interests include feminism and women's struggles, the state and civil society, and sexual harassment in Nigerian universities. She has taught at universities in Britain and Nigeria, and is currently the National Co-ordinator of the Network for Women's Studies in Nigeria.

Mansah Prah is Associate Professor, Department of Sociology, Faculty of Social Sciences, University of Cape Coast, Ghana. Currently she is the Vice-Dean. Her main experience is in teaching and research. Drawing on her experience in teaching courses on Women in Development she has also been involved in policy-making. She has published widely in refereed journals on gender violence and contributed chapters in many books. Her research interests are on gender issues.

Charles Ukeje is a Faculty member in the Department of International Relations of the Obafemi Awolowo University, Ile-Ife, Nigeria, where he has just completed a doctoral dissertation on 'Oil Capital, Ethnic Nationalism and Civil Conflicts in the Niger Delta of Nigeria'.

Felicia Arudo Yieke has a PhD in Applied Linguistics from the University of Vienna. She currently teaches at Egerton University in Kenya. Her areas of specialisation include Discourse Analysis and Sociolinguistics, especially in the field of Gender analysis and language. She has published considerably in applied linguistics and other areas.

Preface

Over the years since its founding in 1973, gender research and training activities have assumed a progressively important role and place in the work of the Council for the Development of Social Science Research in Africa (CODESRIA). Within the framework of the Council's strategic plans for the period 2002–2007, a decision was made to carry the existing institutional commitment one step further by launching a *CODESRIA Gender Series* that would also serve the goal of creatively extending the frontiers of the institution's publications programme. The hope was that through the *Series*, not only would the Council take a lead role in showcasing the best in African gender research but also provide a platform for the emergence of new talents to flower. The thematic variety and analytic quality of contemporary debates and research in Africa around gender issues is testimony to the mileage that has been successfully covered since the early days when African feminists struggled hard to make their voices heard. Today, few are the social scientists who are not aware of the basic issues in gender research and the community of those who apply the gender approach is growing. But as several of the participants at the CODESRIA-sponsored April 2002 Cairo international symposium on new directions in African gender research also observed, the challenges that remain in engendering the social sciences and the policy process are numerous, and addressing them requires the mustering of the capacities and convening powers of institutions like CODESRIA. The Council stands ready to play its part in meeting these challenges and the new *Gender Series* is designed as a modest contribution which in full bloom will capture current debates and deepen the African contribution to reflections on the theme of gender, feminism and society.

As indicated earlier, CODESRIA's commitment to the goal of engendering the social sciences and humanities in Africa dates back a long time. Some of the early research which the Council supported was instrumental in the development of new perspectives in African gender research while an investment has also been made in recent years in the provision of opportunities for training younger scholars in gender methodologies. In this connection, the CODESRIA Gender Institute has run every year since its inception in 1998, covering a variety of themes and gaining in respect and recognition among female and male scholars alike. The path-breaking 1992 international conference which the Council hosted on the theme of engendering the social sciences stimulated a series of initiatives and debates, and also generated some of CODESRIA's best-selling publications. The emergence of an active and networked community of gender researchers in Africa in which CODESRIA has played a frontline role underscores the point that a positive wind of change has blown across the social research community, and there is no turning back the clock of the struggle for gender equality. This notwithstanding, the term 'feminist' still generates fear among some male (and female) researchers, and as Fatou Sow observed in her keynote address at the CODESRIA 10th General Assembly, it is still not completely given that women can fully enjoy their rights without let or hindrance (*'les femmes ont le droit d'avoir les droits'*).

Through its gender-related scientific activities and the launching of its *Gender Series*, CODESRIA acknowledges the need to challenge the masculinities underpinning the structures of repression that target women. It is to be hoped that the *Series* will be kept alive and nourished with insightful research and debates that challenge conventional wisdom, structures and ideologies that are narrowly informed by caricatures of gender realities. While much research has been done in this regard by feminist scholars elsewhere, in Africa, sustained research remains to be initiated in ways that are sensitive to the predicaments of women at different levels of society within and across national and regional boundaries. CODESRIA is committed to encouraging research along these lines. However, the rigour with which such research is conducted is of utmost importance, if gender studies and feminist scholarship are not to fall prey to the same myopia that accounts for the insensitivities of mainstream male-centred perspectives or the irrelevancies of western approaches masquerading as a universalism that takes no cognisance of the African historical context or which is ill-adapted to African concerns.

Most of the papers that have been selected to launch the *CODESRIA Gender Series* were initially presented at the April 2002 Cairo symposium which was organised around five main objectives, namely, to: (a) provide a space/platform for an exchange of ideas as well as a sharing of visions on gender-related themes and issues from pan-African perspectives; (b) prioritise areas of gender research that have a potentiality to transform social relations; (c) encourage gender-based knowledge production which is informed by African realities and give a 'voice' to younger African scholars; (d) identify ways and means of improving advocacy and consolidating linkages between knowledge production and activism for the advancement of women interests; and (e) work towards a cross fertilisation of ideas, methodologies and epistemologies, as well as consider ideas for the creation of comparative research networks on issues affecting women and their livelihoods. The first four publications chosen to launch the *CODESRIA Gender Series* bear testimony to the diversity of interests in the field of gender research, diversities which are necessary for a healthy debate that advances knowledge. The Council hopes that readers will be sufficiently stimulated as to consider contributing manuscripts for consideration for publication in the *Series*.

Adebayo Olukoshi   Francis B. Nyamnjoh
Executive Secretary   Head of Publications

GENDER ACTIVISM AND STUDIES IN AFRICA

Signe Arnfred
Babere Kerata Chacha
Amanda Gouws
Josephine Ahikire
Ayodele Ogundipe
Charmaine Pereira
Mansah Prah
Charles Ukeje
Felicia Arudo Yieke

CODESRIA Gender Series 3

COUNCIL FOR THE DEVELOPMENT OF
SOCIAL SCIENCE RESEARCH IN AFRICA

CODESRIA

1

Locating Gender and Women's Studies in Nigeria: What Trajectories for the Future?*

Charmaine Pereira

Women's and gender studies

From a time when it was considered 'normal' that intellectual discourse in Nigeria should remain silent on the experiences, concerns and activities of women, or else only address women in stereotypical and restricted ways, such discourse is more likely to be challenged today. New intellectual arenas have opened up that are more critical in their aims. Women's studies is a key example of such an arena, having emerged as a field of teaching, research and scholarship in Nigerian universities since the 1980s. Orthodox ways of producing knowledge have left out not only women but also most groups of men, those who are not white, who do not belong to the dominant class, ethnic, religious groups and so on. Whilst recognising this, women's studies focuses on ensuring that women's lives, realities and concerns are central to the content of knowledge production.

Overlapping the field of women's studies is that of gender studies. Both fields originate in a common concern with the status and conditions of women. However, gender studies focuses on the socially constructed ways in which women, as well as men, are located and differentiated in a given context. Gender studies spans a wide spectrum of work. At one end are those studies that appear to be primarily motivated by a desire to appear neutral and inclusive—analyses of men's relations with women, for example, may not even acknowledge the possibility of men's domination or even abuse of women. At the other end of the spectrum are analyses that recognise inequalities and the operations of power in the social relations of gender. Scholarship within women's studies and gender studies is also differentiated by the extent to which research is aimed primarily at *describing* the relevant phenomena concerning women and/or gender relations, as opposed to *subverting* oppressive gender hierarchies. The latter is more likely to address issues of change and transformation, and in the process, to challenge the conceptual framework for organising what traditionally counts as knowledge.

The feminist agenda in gender and women's studies entails the production of knowledge that would empower women in the struggle for liberation in the context of social transformation. Within feminism, a wide variety of schools of thought exist (see e.g. Roberts 1983; Stamp 1989; Mbilinyi 1992; Kemp et al. 1995). A range of concepts and methodologies are used that directly engage the overall project of understanding social realities in order to change them in the direction of gender justice. Recognising the agency of women as well as men, and the existence of structures and processes that are gendered, feminist scholarship asks different questions from those conventionally asked. As such, it has the potential to radically transform social knowledge, including knowledge that is otherwise viewed as progressive (see e.g. Pereira 2002a).

In this paper, I have chosen to refer to gender and women's studies in the aggregate, partly because differentiating one from the other is not always a straightforward matter and partly because scholars more often refer to their work as falling into one of either of these arenas, as opposed to feminist studies (even when their work is explicitly feminist). In Nigeria, the formation of the Network for Women's Studies in Nigeria (NWSN) in 1996 underscored the wishes of participants to introduce concerns about women as well as gender in their teaching and research. The formation of the Network also contained within it the desire to transcend traditional paradigms, many of which were inappropriate in the Nigerian context (Mama 1996a).

The first comprehensive review of African scholarship in gender and women's studies was carried out by Mama in 1996 (Mama 1996b). Her review captures a number of detailed developments across disciplines and a range of themes under the broad umbrellas of women, politics and the state; cultural studies; work and the economy. Since then, the richness and sheer volume of scholarship has increased dramatically. Lewis's (2002) sequel to Mama's review follows themes and debates in the literature, highlighting diverse theoretical models and methodological approaches in addition to regional and conceptual dialogues and comparisons. The significance of such a review is pointed to below:

> My reading has alerted me to fascinating interventions and exchanges, and especially to the significance of connections between disciplines and the reciprocal and energizing linkages between activism and research ... My impression is of a field that is dynamic, receptive to new directions and findings, and vitally attuned to priorities for transformation and justice in Africa (Lewis 2002: 3).

In view of the above, one may well ask what the status of gender and women's studies in Nigeria is today. The current scenario is one marked by the continuing dominance of First Ladyism in Nigeria, from military to civilian rule. Many among the general public find it difficult to distinguish First Ladies' pronouncements on women from women's studies. A similar scenario obtains when it comes to the public distinguishing national machineries for women from women's autonomous organisations. Moreover, religious, ethnic and 'traditional' chauvinisms of diverse kinds have been fueled by increasing poverty, corruption and mismanagement and by the failure of the state to address longstanding inequities and injustices. What is particularly disturbing here is the apparent inability of gender and women's studies, so far, to further the strategic interests of women, for gender justice. Whilst much work within gender and women's studies has this potential, it has so far not been harnessed effectively. In the context of rapid social change and global restructuring, the consolidation of conservative, anti-feminist gender politics makes it an imperative for scholars to be more critical and more reflexive about the substance of knowledge production and the interests being served by such work. This essay is part of a larger project addressing this central aim. Given the lack of attention paid to the development of women's studies in Africa and the prospects for its future growth (Lewis 2002), such a project is indeed timely.

I begin by locating gender and women's studies in the context of international, regional and national feminisms, as well as the influences of the development industry, the political and economic conditions induced by neo-liberal policies and state structures for women (see Mama 1996a). Since universities are currently a principal site of the production of gender and women's studies in the country, it is also necessary to locate these fields in the changing institutional landscape of higher education.

The aim of this essay is not so much to focus on trends in the literature, theoretical orientations or methodological considerations, important as these are. Rather, my aim is to do something that is less often done, which is to begin a process of relating intellectual content in gender and women's studies to its political agenda, with a view to outlining potential trajectories for the future. The paths of these trajectories will trace the extent to which the knowledge produced enhances or restricts the possibilities of a project of social transformation and gender justice. Theoretical orientations and methodological considerations are addressed to the extent that they impinge on this process of making explicit the links between the content of scholarship and its agenda. In my discussion, I draw considerably on my experience in the Network for Women's Studies in Nigeria (NWSN), as one of the 36 founding members who gave it life in January 1996, and currently as the National Co-ordinator.

The paper is presented in three parts. The first examines the context of gender and women's studies in Nigeria. The second part explores the relations between intellectual content and political agenda. Here, I address conceptualisations of women and gender as well as the content of one of the most developed fields in women's studies in Nigeria – women's history, biography and autobiography. The last part of the paper outlines potential trajectories for the future.

The context of gender and women's studies in Nigeria

International, regional and national feminisms

By the 1970s, an upsurge in feminist organising across the world was becoming increasingly evident (see e.g. Mohanty et al. 1991; Basu 1995). For African women organising against the failure of 'development' strategies, the broader international women's movement offered a forum for articulating their perspectives. Intervening in international fora from the early 1980s onwards, leading African feminists became increasingly aware of the need to voice their distinct concerns and interests within the international women's movement. Tensions in the latter were manifested around the misrepresentations of Africa and African women's lives and realities that prevailed in the Western media and amongst Western feminists alike (see e.g. Ogundipe-Leslie 1994; AAWORD 1985).

The first regional institution set up by African women on the continent to facilitate African women researchers working on questions of gender and development was the Association of African Women for Research and Development (AAWORD). Formed in 1977, one of AAWORD's central aims was to set the agenda for feminism in Africa by facilitating research and activism by African women scholars. Some of the workshops held by AAWORD were on themes such as methodology (1983), the crisis in Africa (1985), development assistance (1989), reproduction (1992), and gender theories and social development (2001). AAWORD remains an important institutional site even though its influence and reach has declined over the years. This, in itself, is an indication of the fraught economic and political conditions under which women's organizations on the continent struggle to sustain themselves, particularly if their scope is intended to be Africa-wide. Nationally-based initiatives and centers are playing increasingly significant roles in the wake of difficulties in sustaining regionally-based sites for gender and women's studies. At the same time, understandings of place and site must necessarily be complicated by the interplay of international conferences, the movement of scholars across national and continental boundaries, and an increasing use of electronic technology (Lewis 2002).

Within the country, the organisation Women in Nigeria (WIN) was founded in 1982 at a conference held at Ahmadu Bello University, Zaria. WIN emerged during the 1980s as a significant force in challenging the subordination of women on the basis of class and gender. WIN's basic philosophy was that women should organise to struggle for their rights but in order to do this, it was necessary to work from a knowledge base that would provide an understanding of how women's and men's lives were structured by the socio-economic and political conditions under which they lived. WIN's objectives included research, advocacy, policy-making and the dissemination of information, viewed as an integrated complex of activities. The proceedings of WIN's annual conferences from 1982 to 1987 are notable contributions to the field (Awe 1996). WIN did not describe itself as feminist, and many of the members may not have identified themselves in that way. However, key figures in its leadership were feminist and WIN's organisational focus and practice, at least in the early days, were recognised as such.

By 1990, resistance to a feminist agenda within WIN became increasingly evident. Gender conflict in WIN was never resolved but was played out in the form of internal power struggles. This took the form of leadership battles, mistrust over funds raised for projects, and allegations of corruption against opposing factions (see Salihu 1999). Not surprisingly, WIN's stature and effectiveness deteriorated during the 1990s. Many of those formerly in the leadership of WIN in its early days, left to form their own, smaller organisations. By the mid-1990s, what used to be an organised, national forum for challenging women's subordination had had its strength diffused.

A number of the newer networks and organisations combine research and activism in their pursuit of gender equity. They include, for example, the International Reproductive Rights Research Action Group (Osakue et al., 1995), and Girl Power Initiative, working on sexuality and reproductive health and rights; the Women and Laws project on Muslim laws (Pereira 1997a), which formed the basis for Baobab for Women's Human Rights. More recent formations that are not primarily the result of a fallout from WIN, include Gender and Development Action (GADA) and Agenda 2003, both working on increasing women's political participation; the National Coalition on Violence Against Women and the Legislative Advocacy Coalition on Violence Against Women (LACVAW Interim Working Group 2001).

I return to the international level, this time to the United Nations. The declaration of the UN Decades for Women (1975–1984, 1985–1994) reflected the UN's response to the pressure exerted upon it by women's groups around the world. Once created, the UN platforms were enthusiastically pursued by women's organisations in Nigeria, largely because the political space available for addressing violations against women at the national level was so restricted. This was the consequence of prolonged military rule and women's serious marginalisation from public life and politics under authoritarian rule, whether civilian or military. The UN requirement for regular reporting on the implementation of international agreements ratified by a country, such as the Convention on the Elimination of All Forms of Discrimination Against Women (CEDAW), provided women-centred organisations with the opportunity not only to monitor governmental reports but to provide alternative accounts through Shadow Reports when necessary, as was the case in 1999 (NGO Coalition 1999). The veritable explosion in research and activism in gender and women's studies in the last two decades has been largely an outcome of the organising that has gone on at various levels during the decades.

Another way in which the UN responded to the pressure from women's groups was by calling on governments to set up structures mandated to address women's participation in development – the National Machinery for Women. Africa had already pioneered the establishment of regional structures for women. This was when the UN Economic Commission for Africa, located in Addis Ababa, had set up a programme on women and development and subsequently established the African Training and Research Centre for Women, in 1975. Under the Abacha regime (1993–1998), a Federal Ministry for Women Affairs and Social Development was set up. Already in existence were the National Commission for Women and National Centre for Women Development. Overall, the National Machinery has done little to further gender equity (Mama 2000) and this continues to be the case even now that there has been a handover from military to civilian rule.

Between the development industry and state structures for women

The dominant current in mainstream development thinking and policy – WID or Women in Development – has posited that development had 'neglected' women and that the solution to this would be to ensure that women were no longer 'left out'. The gender insensitivity and male bias inherent in such 'development' policies have been challenged by feminists internationally (see e.g. AAWORD 1985; Sen and Grown 1988; Elson 1991). AAWORD's (1985) Nairobi Manifesto had pointed to the destructive effects of 'development' strategies that depended on external finance, technology and advice. The damage as a result of structural adjustment and restrictive monetary policies tied to loan conditionalities, had resulted in a deepening of poverty, food crises, unemployment, massive displacement of populations and a rise in political and religious fundamentalisms. Rising poverty in the context of globalisation has been linked to an upsurge in violence against women (Pereira 2002).

The period during which the first Structural Adjustment Programmes (SAPs) were implemented in many African countries was also the period when state structures for women were first developed on a visible scale. Both processes coincided with the first UN Decade for Women (1975–1984). Political regimes were increasingly short of funds during this period; donors, however, were willing to provide money for WID structures and projects. Accordingly, many regimes found it expedient to either create new structures (Mama 1998), co-opt existing structures (Pereira 2000), or combine the two in authoritarian efforts to increase their legitimacy and their access to resources. In Nigeria, the atmosphere regarding women's advancement is only superficially supportive. State discourses on gender have championed a 'better life for rural women' and 'economic advancement for families', through the medium of female power structures deploying the wives of the military Head of State and state governors (see Mama 1998). First Ladies at different levels have experienced greater visibility and improved material conditions than most other categories of women.

For the vast majority of Nigerian women, however, gender inequity and women's subordination continue to pervade their lives – a phenomenon that is widespread across the continent and indeed, internationally. In Nigeria, this takes the form of pervasive beliefs that women are (men's) 'property', and by extension, minors, whose adult status is mediated via men, primarily the father or husband, but also uncle, brother and so on. In addition, there is the widespread denial of education, land and property rights, and access to credit. In defiance of these oppressions, Nigerian women have continued to organise against a range of oppressive and inhumane practices that do violence to women's bodily integrity and their humanity - such as the battery of women, widowhood rites, child marriage and female genital mutilation – each justified in differing ways by recourse to a complex that variously combines 'Culture/Tradition/Religion' (see e.g. NGO Coalition 1999; WIN [Kaduna] 1999; Pereira 2001a; LACVAW Interim Working Group 2001).

The changing institutional landscape of higher education

Since universities comprise one of the major sites at which scholarship in gender and women's studies is produced, it is appropriate to ask under what institutional conditions this has taken place. At its inception, the university system in Nigeria was conceived of as a means of producing 'high-level manpower (sic) for the nation'. National Development Plans have continually reiterated the linkage between universities and 'high-level manpower', although the modalities for implementing the Plans have rarely matched the pronouncements. More serious is the non-recognition of the fact that most groups of women have rarely had any say in how 'national' needs are determined and how priorities are set. Even if this were to be officially recognised, there is no guarantee that women's marginalisation would be treated as a serious problem. It is clear from the Plans that an understanding of the realities of the lives of diverse groups of women was not viewed as necessary to planning. Hence, no attention was paid to gender divisions of labour, gender segregated labour markets, and the ubiquity of gender violence in social relations and institutions (Pereira 2001b).

Knowledge production in the university system has been seriously undermined by the generalised underfunding of university education, coupled with the politicisation of the higher education system. *How* the economic resources of a nation are used is fundamentally determined by *who* governs the polity. This fusion of politics and economics – the politics of funding – has repercussions for the kind of university education that is on offer, in other words, its quality. Yet, even in the absence of under funding and politicisation of the system, the question of what kind of knowledge is produced, by whom and for what purposes, remains.

From the 1990s to date, the paradigms of knowledge production (Imam and Mama 1994), the pedagogies used, the formation of the institution and the ways in which it is reproduced, have all come under scrutiny. The conception of universities as the breeding ground for the grooming of the nation's elite – leaders who are presumed to be men – is fundamentally at odds with the notion of the university as a site for deconstructing the contradictions in the society at large. The contested nature of the purpose of the university is highlighted by Morley et al., (2001), as are the possibilities of change.

> [T]he notion of the purpose of the university [is] contested in different periods and in different regions of the Commonwealth. On the one hand the university has been viewed as ungendered, a site for knowledge to serve national interests and ungendered notions of citizenship. In this guise it is open to primarily quantitative change with regard to including certain formerly excluded groups. On the other hand, the university may be viewed as an institution complicit with the social divisions of the society, but nonetheless open to qualitative change and transformations concerning gendered and other forms of inequity (Morley et al. 2001: 11).

Relations between intellectual content and political agenda

This section addresses some of the ways in which the content of intellectual work and its links to social change may be made explicit. The first part explores the question of relating gender and women's studies to women's interests, and some of the relevant considerations. The second part of the section examines the links between intellectual content and political agenda in two key thematic areas: i) conceptualisations of 'women' and 'gender'; and ii) women's history, biography and autobiography.

Linking Women's Studies to women's interests?

Outlining the development of women's studies in Nigeria, Bolanle Awe (1996) provides an overview of changes during the ten-year period beginning in the mid-1980s. Her account attempts to convey the complexities underlying the growth of women's studies and indicates areas for further work and attention. She points to important antecedents in international and regional meetings, such as the Wellesley Conference of 1976 and the 1983 AAWORD Conference on African women and methodology. In Nigeria, the first Women and National Development seminar was held at the University of Ibadan in 1976, to launch the United Nations International Women's Year. During the 1980s, two important seminars on the subject were held. In 1987, the Institute of African Studies at the University of Ibadan held a seminar on Women's Studies: The State of the Art Now in

Nigeria. In 1988, a workshop on Theoretical and Methodological Issues in Women's Studies was held at Obafemi Awolowo University, Ile-Ife. These early activities point to the emergence of a field that has since grown considerably in scope. The role of WIN during this period was referred to earlier.

The question of how feminism has been received within the academy is an important one. As an intellectual project that is explicit about its relationship to social transformation, feminism simultaneously combines political as well as intellectual practice. In this respect, it is similar to Marxism. Unlike Marxism, however, feminism has been treated with pronounced hostility within the academy. This hostility has compelled women to create additional institutional sites from which to further the development of feminist knowledge, as we saw earlier in the formation of AAWORD. Even when scholars in gender and women's studies have been unwilling to call themselves feminist, there has been a keen interest in setting up new centres and networks as platforms for information sharing, networking and support.

Within the academy, several institutional structures have been formed, primarily centres for gender and women's studies. They are listed below along with their principal aims:

- Women's Research and Documentation Centre (WORDOC), University of Ibadan – focus for women's studies, documentation, links to other centres
- Centre for Gender and Social Policy Studies, University of Ile-Ife – capacity building in gender, social policy and development
- Women's Studies Unit, University of Nigeria, Nsukka – documentation, teaching and research
- Documentation and Analysis of Women's and Gender Studies Unit, Nnamdi Azikiwe University, Awka – documentation
- Network for Women's Studies in Nigeria (NWSN)– building capacity for teaching and research in gender and women's studies
- Ahmadu Bello University, Gender and Women's Studies Group, Zaria - documentation, capacity building in gender and women's studies.

All the above are local centres, except for NWSN which is a national network. Virtually all of these sites are struggling with a lack of funds and institutional support, and apart from NWSN, a lack of autonomy in decision making (see Mama 1996). At the 1996 NWSN workshop on 'Concepts and Methodologies for Gender and Women's Studies in Nigeria', Mama (1997a) posed the question of whether research efforts in this field were advancing Nigerian women's interests, and what specific aspects of such endeavours made them succeed or fail. The notion that 'women' were a homogenous group and all shared the same interests needed to be critiqued. A more appropriate approach, she pointed out, might be to consider the effects of research on different groups of women in Nigeria – 'rural women', 'market women', 'women farmers', 'women factory workers', 'business women', 'domestic servants', 'women doctors' and so on. The South African experience highlights the complexity of defining 'women's interests' and forging common interests in the context of considerable heterogeneity in historical experiences of oppression, whether on the basis of gender, race or class (Kemp et al., 1995). Moreover, building consensus in this sphere requires considerable organisational skill and experience.

Addressing questions such as the extent to which gender and women's studies can further women's interests or gender equity requires an engagement with the legacies of Nigeria's political, economic and social history. One of the key dimensions here is militarism and the militarisation of the state. In her analysis of the implications of the militarisation of the state for women, Nina Mba (1989: 86–7) had this to say about the divides among women in the country:

> The gap between urban and rural women, between the 'formal' and 'informal' sectors, and between the 'elite' and the 'masses' is very wide. Urban, educated middle-class women have the national leadership potential but not the mass support needed for effective political action. Besides, the majority of such women insist on the depoliticisation of 'women's issues' and operate within the framework of voluntary associations which cannot enforce sanctions on their members. Urban market women and rural community-based women have the potential for mass mobilization and can enforce effective sanctions, but they lack the national leadership and political objectives.

Faced with divides such as these that still prevail today among Nigerian women, some of the challenges for gender and women's studies appear to be: to produce the kind of knowledge that will strengthen the agency of diverse categories of women, particularly those impoverished and disempowered within the status quo; to support women's existing efforts to produce knowledge outside the academy; to facilitate women's recognition of diverse forms of oppression across social divides; and to strengthen women's collective efforts to organise effectively across such divides, in support of gender equality and social justice. As an agenda for change, the above intentions will only be effective if consensus is built around their validity, which implies related processes of consensus- and constituency-building.

Relating intellectual content to political agenda

Although gender and women's studies has a long history in Nigeria, by the mid-1990s there was no national forum at which the contemporary situation could be reviewed, experiences shared and future plans developed. The Network for Women's Studies in Nigeria, NWSN, held its inaugural workshop, 'Setting an Agenda for Gender and Women's Studies in Nigeria' in January 1996, with the aim of addressing these concerns (Mama 1996a). A key aspect of those concerns was to set up a process for developing a national agenda on research that would be oriented to the growth and development of gender and women's studies in the country. This paper is intended to contribute to this larger aim.

In this section, I address two key thematic areas: i) conceptualisations of 'women' and 'gender'; and ii) women's history, biography and autobiography. The choice of themes is clearly selective, being limited by time and resources. However, the selection of these two themes as starting points for this project are shaped, firstly, by the significance of conceptualisation for intellectual as well as political concerns. How social realities are understood will determine the strategies used by interested parties, to change these realities. Greater effectiveness at transforming the realities affecting women and gender relations requires critical analysis of how such concepts are being used in the literature, their strengths and limitations. Secondly, since the literature on women's history, biography and autobiography is rich in Nigeria, and has moreover, been drawn on as a contemporary source of inspiration to women in difficult times, it calls out for focused attention.

Conceptualisations of 'women' and 'gender'

At the second NWSN workshop, held in November 1996, the need to re-examine the basic terms and concepts used in gender and women's studies in Nigeria was raised. Instead of assuming the content of these terms and concepts, Mama pointed out that it would be necessary to do the work of developing our own usages of basic terms and concepts, grounding them in local realities. The idea would be to develop existing concepts, thereby making them 'more meaningful and effective tools for analyzing and comprehending the oppression and subordination of women and the nature of gender relations in Nigeria' (Mama 1997b: 3). This discussion took place at a workshop at which participants deliberated upon the following concepts: 'woman' and women's struggles, 'gender', 'feminism' and feminist theory.

One of the key texts in research on gender is *Female Husbands, Male Daughters* by Ifi Amadiume (1987). Working in the South East of Nigeria, Amadiume examined the ideology of gender in the socio-cultural systems of Nnobi from the nineteenth century through to the post-independence period. The author also studied the effects of gender ideology on the structural position of women in the society. Her research indicates that the dual sex principle behind social organisation in the indigenous society was mediated by a flexible gender system of traditional culture and language. Biological sex was not synonymous with ideological gender. Amadiume points out that this flexibility allowed women to play roles usually monopolised by men, or to be classified as 'males' in terms of power and authority over others. Since such roles were not rigidly cast as either masculine or feminine, breaking gender rules did not result in stigma. The acceptance of women as having roles of authority and power, and the status associated with such roles was supported by an all-embracing goddess-focused religion.

Whilst Amadiume's work usefully destabilises conceptualisations of sex and gender by showing that gender is not shaped by sex in a unilinear fashion in Nnobi, she does not interrogate the ways in which flexibility and relations of domination were configured. For example, flexibility *per se* did not allow women the same degree of power relative to men of the same social standing. Women who were classified as 'male daughters' required the consent of men in the father's patrilineage to be so recognised or, if not, recognition could only be attained through the statutory legal process. Female husbands were women who acquired wives by virtue of their economic strength and thereby controlled the labour and services of their wives. Woman-to-woman marriage was literally translated as 'buying a slave'. Amadiume assures us that the term referred only to woman-to-woman marriage and not man-to-woman marriage, and that the woman who was bought had the status and customary rights of a wife. Amadiume makes no comment on the apparent overlap in meaning between 'wife' and 'slave' (or some wives and slaves), nor does she explore the perceived benefits of woman-to-woman marriage to the women married to female husbands, even as she regrets the demise of such 'pro-female' institutions with the onset of colonialism and Christianity.

The author's perspective on the relations between intellectual content and political agenda are nonetheless stated quite clearly:

> Any work by Third World women must therefore be political, challenging the new and growing patriarchal systems imposed on our societies through colonialism and Western religious and educational influences. We cannot afford to be indifferent researchers, glossing over the local struggles in which women in our countries are involved. As well as looking into the socio-cultural systems which guaranteed women power ... African and other Third World women still have a role to play in exposing the contradictions in their societies, recording their own social history with a view to challenging where necessary, discrimination against women and positively aiming for more power for women and more egalitarian societies for everyone (Amadiume 1987:9).

In Northern Nigeria, the invisibility of women and with it, the whole question of gender relations has been 'refracted through the prism of seclusion' (Imam 1994: 26). This scenario has framed Imam's choice of seclusion itself as a focus of research attention. She argues that the focus of analysis should be the social relations of gender, that is, the relations between women and men as they are manifested in terms of power, economics, ideology and so on. Moreover, gender relations need to be understood as they interact with other dimensions of social and economic relations, such as class and ethnicity, to impinge on the positions of women as well as men.

Imam's research shows that the generalisation of women's seclusion during colonialism developed as a result of complex interactions between the religious and political ideologies that were mobilised against the colonial state, and the economic changes brought about by capitalism. These economic changes catalysed changes in the gender division of labour and social relations within Hausaland. It was not Islam *per se* that produced seclusion in Northern Nigeria, as is often argued, but the ways in which particular Muslim discourses were elaborated and became dominant whilst being structured into divisions of labour, relations of production and other social practices. Ideologies of seclusion cut across and overlapped those of femininity and masculinity, the nature of marital relations, ethnicity, religion and status, none of these being uniform or uncontested (Imam 1994).

Imam is quite explicit about the relationship between intellectual content and political agenda, as she sees it:

> ...I want to draw together the threads of the discussion so far. But, I want to do so with a specific purpose in mind – to see what the implications of this study are for informing practice aimed at change. I begin by reviewing the understandings reached about seclusion, past and contemporary. Then I outline the theoretical underpinnings of the relationships between ideological processes, social relations and historical change that implicitly sustain my analysis. Finally, I conclude with some speculations on praxis and the future of seclusion (Imam 1994: 199).

At the national level, the ways in which hegemonic discourses of womanhood have been constructed and deployed in an urban sphere have been of some interest (Pereira 2000). This sphere is the one occupied by the official umbrella women's organisation in Nigeria, the National Council of Women's Societies (NCWS), in its relations with the military state. Whilst the NCWS has effectively reified women as wives and mothers within the existing social order, this has been done primarily to legitimise women's incursion into masculinist, formal public spheres. The actual construction of motherhood evident in NCWS pronouncements and actions reflect different currents underlying its ideology and organisation. These include elements derived from missionary and colonial discourse constructing the mother as the ultimate line of defence against the disruptive forces of modernity alongside elements from the developmentalist legacy inherited from the nationalist period (see Pereira 1997b).

However, allusions to motherhood have had the effect of naturalising and universalising conceptions of appropriate ways of being for women, and appropriate relations with men. This obscures the heterogeneity amongst women in their social positioning, their experiences of motherhood (for those who are mothers), and their interests. It also obscures the extent to which the discursive elements of womanhood utilised by the NCWS have been shaped by the history and politics of the organisation, the class interests of the dominant groups of women within it, and their relations with the state (Pereira 2000). The political agenda in this research was twofold: i) to illustrate how hegemonic and conservative conceptions of 'the way women should be' have been socially and historically constructed; and ii) to destabilise the widespread notion that such ways are either 'natural' or 'universal'.

Writing from a different perspective, Oyewumi (1997) questions the assumption that African societies are structured by gender, as are Euro-American societies. Oyewumi advances the thesis that it is seniority, rather than gender, that orders and divides Yoruba society. Her argument rests on two planks: one, that the Yoruba language is not marked by gender; second, that Yoruba social institutions and practices do not make social distinctions in terms of anatomical differences. On the basis of this argument, Oyewumi goes on to state that the concept of gender is not useful for understanding Yoruba society.

Oyewumi's argument needs to be evaluated against its own claims. Yusuf (2002) provides a useful critique, identifying three major weaknesses in the methodology that Oyewumi uses in order to make her claims. The first is the importance ascribed to language as revealing a cultural essence - the idea that the original meanings of words lie beneath the surface of colonial distortions and can be discerned if only the appropriate methods were used. A more accurate account of how words convey their meaning would take account of the multiple changes and instabilities in the way words are used over time. Otherwise, the political danger is one of supporting an approach to language and culture that claims authenticity (for some), as tyrants such as Mobutu have felt free to do.

The second weakness is the privileging of seniority as the only significant dimension of power. In line with feminist and post-structural approaches to power, Yusuf suggests that different modes of power are interwoven and always working in concert. Oyewumi's lack of consideration of the intersections of diverse modes of power means that she cannot account for the complexity of micro-politics or the nuances of seniority as they actually operate and are experienced by different social categories of people. The political significance here is that the ways in which the ideology of seniority can be, and often is, used to mask abusive forms of power relations, is obliterated from the account.

Finally, Yusuf shows how Oyewumi reduces social reality – the different ways in which seniority is negotiated in practice – to the explicit discourse privileging seniority. In the process, the difference between regulatory frameworks and what actually happens in practice is eliminated, as is the possibility of tracing the workings of ideology. Yusuf refers to the need to place discourse *within* the context of practice and make visible the ways in which the relations between the two are negotiated and manipulated. If this is not done, the political danger is that of repressing differences and silences, whilst being trapped within the terms of the very ideology that is the focus of study.

Efforts to conceptualise gender need to go beyond showing that gender has not been constructed historically in the same ways in Africa, specifically Nigeria, compared to the West. One would indeed expect that this would be the case. What is of greater interest, however, is the significance of particular conceptualisations of gender, in terms of how this expands or restricts the possibilities for diverse categories of women and men, given the social conditions of their time. It is on terrain such as this that the question of the relations between the intellectual content produced by researchers and the political agenda/s associated with that content, is located.

Nigerian women's experiences are structured by multiple lines of power and division other than gender, such as class, age, ethnicity, religion, region and so on, each of these being foregrounded and changing in differing ways according to time, place and so on. It is also the case historically that this multiplicity has often been collapsed into singular divisions such as ethnicity or religion, defined in masculinist terms. The interplay between co-existing lines of division, the implications of all this in terms of how diverse categories of women understand their experiences, and the differences between their living conditions and those of other categories of women and diverse categories of men – all these are yet to be theorised and understood. One may surmise that as intellectual content becomes more nuanced, so too should the political agenda and the strategies required to realise that agenda.

Women's history, biography and autobiography

The rest of this section explores the relations between intellectual content and political agenda in the thematic area of women's history, biography and autobiography. The convergence of these three areas in women's studies in Nigeria is a reflection of developments in the field, such as the push for 'herstories' in historiography as a means of compensating for the invisibility of women in the discipline (Awe 1991).

By the early 1970s, the contours of African historiography were expanding to include women's experiences and engagements as well as the analysis of the role of gender in African history. The first identifiable text on Nigerian women was written by Oshunsheye in 1960. The fact that the article was written by a man prompted some interest in women as a focus of research among male historians. Other landmark works were Afigbo's (1972) analysis of the 1929 Women's War, Okonjo's (1976) study of the dual sex system in Eastern Nigeria, Alagoa's oral history of Queen Kambasa, which remained unpublished until it was included in Awe's (1992) edited collection, and more recently, Denzer's (1998) work on the Iyalode in South Western Nigeria.

The only book on women's history remains Nina Mba's (1982) classic text, which documents and analyses women's political activity in Southern Nigeria from 1900 to 1965. In the context of twentieth century Nigerian political history relegating the role of women to footnotes, the focus on women as a separate category has been necessary to redress the imbalance. Mba also situates the validity of her research on the existence of role differentiation based on sex, which existed to varying degrees in the pre-colonial, colonial and post-colonial societies of South Eastern and South Western Nigeria. Her research focuses on the motivations and self-images of women engaged in political activity, as well as the objectives, organisation, leadership and effectiveness of women's protest movements and political associations. Mba was particularly interested in the effects of historical change on the political positions and roles of women in Southern Nigeria.

There is a rich vein of biographical writing in women's studies in Nigeria. Importantly, biographies and autobiographies have registered an emphasis on social history and processes. Full-length biographies include those of Funmilayo Ransome Kuti (Johnson-Odim and Mba 1997), Lady Kofoworola Ademola (Rosiji 1996), Hafsatu Ahmadu Bello (Adamu 1995), Margaret Ekpo (Effah-Attoe and Jaja 1993), Gambo Sawaba (Shawulu 1990). A number of autobiographies are also available, such as those of Sulia Adedeji (1995) and Irene Ighodaro (1994). Shorter biographical accounts include those of Nana Asma'u (Koko and Boyd 2001), Iyalode Efunsetan Aniwura (Awe 2001), Charlotte Olajumoke Obasa (Olusanya 2001a), Olaniwun Adunni Olawole (Olusanya 2001b), Lady Oyinkan Abayomi (Johnson-Odim 2001). In addition, several student projects at graduate and undergraduate levels exist (see Denzer 1995: xviii-xix).

The focus of much biographical work in Nigeria has largely been the leadership of women who succeeded in achieving public prominence. Rosiji's (1996) biographical portrait of Lady Kofoworola Ademola, growing up as a member of a privileged Lagos family in the 1920s, depicts her subsequent engagement in voluntary work and promotion of the educational advancement of women. Lady Ademola was a founder member of organisations such as the National Council for Women's Societies and the National Association of University Women, both prominent, if not radical, organisations in the following decades.

Unlike many of the women above who were prominent in their time, Hafsatu Ahmadu Bello, the first wife of the Premier of Northern Nigeria, Sir Ahmadu Bello, lived her life far from the public eye. Hafsatu's distinctive qualities, according to those who knew her, were patience and submissiveness - qualities considered ideal for a 'good woman'. She was killed along with her husband in the first of Nigeria's military coups, on the night of January 14–15, 1966. Based on oral recollections, interviews and archival sources, Adamu's (1995) account documents Hafsatu Bello's life in the context of her family background and marriage in Hausaland. The events of the night of the coup are recalled from the point of view of several different actors.

Studies of the lives and activities of prominent Nigerian women have generally been motivated by a desire to create alternative role models for women in the present as well as registering women's presence in the official accounts of history. Awe (2001: xi) states that 'An understanding of women's activities in historical perspective ... provides one useful avenue for an understanding of the possibilities of their involvement in modern development'. Johnson-Odim (2001: 187) refers to 'the great variety of roles which women in Nigeria have played in the shaping of their nation and people', and that awareness of this can serve as 'an inspiration to the women of the present'. From this, the emphasis in biographical work on past female leaders may be viewed as a reflection of their dearth in the post-colonial state in particular, as well as in the broader society. Implicit in the perspectives articulated by Awe and Johnson-Odim is the notion that women's biographies suggest possibilities for social change. An understanding of the lives of women who have been leaders in the past provides pointers to women aspiring to leadership in the present and to women in their struggles to change contemporary gender relations.

The political role of biographies is thus clearly foregrounded, with the emphasis on the *content* of women's lives and the ways in which a more informed understanding of history could serve the present. Whilst these are clearly important dimensions of both the intellectual content and the political agenda of this strand in women's studies, other important dimensions are less often considered. These are questions such as those of interpretive authority and representation – whose voice interprets experience and is recognised as the voice of authority in the text, and clarifying the basis for speaking on behalf of someone else. Also significant is the question of agency, specifically the agency of the woman whose biography is being written – her choices, her decisions, in the context of her interpretations of the options before her (see Lewis 2002).

The carefully researched biography of Funmilayo Ransome-Kuti by Cheryl Johnson-Odim and Nina Mba (1997) is an example of a biography where considerable attention was paid to the relations between subjectivity and history. Cheryl Johnson-Odim and Nina Mba (1997: xiv) refer to Funmilayo Ransome-Kuti as 'a strong personality who helped make history'; in their biography they hoped to convey 'both the personal and political aspects of her life and of her role in history'. The authors sensitively portray the agency of Funmilayo Ransome-Kuti in the nuances of motivation, intention and action, immersed as these were in the social context of her time.

Biographies and life histories of women in the public eye have provided alternative depictions of womanhood from those typically encountered in hegemonic constructions of gender relations, not only in their own time but also in the present. Women such as Funmilayo Ransome-Kuti, Gambo Sawaba, Margaret Ekpo, Olaniwun Adunni Olawole and others outside Nigeria, like Constance Cummings-John, were not only leaders of women but active in the masculinist sphere of national politics. As such, they were living proof that women need not confine themselves to the domestic sphere, as colonialist gender ideology would have it, but could exercise leadership on multiple fronts. Clearly, knowledge of the lives of such women provides a point of departure for countering the widespread tendency to derogate as 'foreign' or 'Western' any form of women's activism that subverts conventional understandings of appropriate gender relations.

At the same time as they destabilise hegemonic constructions of womanhood, biographies of prominent women such as Gambo Sawaba, Constance Cummings-John, Irene Ighodaro, Lady Kofoworola Aina Ademola, also depict the porous character of the boundaries of nations, ethnic and cultural groups. Intermarriage, migration and the return of ex-slaves to the African continent are some of the means of straddling these borders, revealing the differing ways in which collectivities are characterised less by stasis or clear-cut lines of division than by indeterminacy and flux. Whilst this particular thread in women's biographies could be taken further to challenge masculinist orientations towards the study of 'the nation' and ethnicity in Nigeria, this has not yet happened in an explicit manner. Understanding the ways in which the personal relations of African women were shaped by the dynamics of nation, ethnicity, cultural groupings and so on would benefit from further analysis of the relations between biography, social history, politics and women's struggles.

Trajectories for the future

Several possible trajectories may be discerned, not necessarily exclusive, which vary according to the political direction that intellectual work takes. I have distinguished two broad spheres in which such trajectories may be located: i) de-radicalising the agenda, and ii) retaining a feminist vision. Some of the possibilities within these spheres are outlined briefly below.

De-radicalising the agenda

This is by far the most likely trajectory. This section outlines three spheres in which scholars and activists may find themselves engaging with deradicalised agendas concerning women and gender relations.

Servicing the state

There is considerable diversity in the ways in which researchers and activists may have their energies spent in service of the state. The significant feature here is the determination of the interaction and the agenda by the relevant state agency, as opposed to engagement of state institutions by civil society organisations with their self-determined agendas in a process of negotiation.

Servicing the state may involve interactions differentiated by diverse forms of service, with any one of a range of institutions, over varied time spans. Some examples will suffice here. Scholars may be invited to 'participate' in governmental tasks, such as a request by the Ministry of Women's Affairs to complete long-overdue reports on CEDAW within a fortnight, when the reporting cycle is expected to be carried out over years. Alternatively, they could be asked by the Women's Centre to validate reports of projects they played no part in designing or monitoring. Some might be asked to implement WID projects without being previously involved in their formulation. Scholars may be given a few days' notice to present a paper at high-profile meetings intended to promote the image of the Minister of Women's Affairs, where media coverage and the presence of 'big men' and 'big women' matter more than intellectual and political substance. International Women's Day provides a good opportunity for such meetings. A non-governmental organisation may be involved in supporting a female legislator in her preparations for a Public Hearing at the National Assembly, and never get paid for the work months after it has been successfully executed.

Driven by donors

The most likely scenario is that of short-term consultancies, usually with restricted terms of reference, concerning a range of aspects to do with gender and/or women. The key point here is the remarkable obsession on the part of donors with 'quick fix', technical solutions, unmarred by considerations of power relations or political complexities. Recurrent characteristics in the approaches taken include the tendency to define both the problem and the most likely sources of change *externally* i.e. by the donor, who often has less experience and understanding of the problems concerned than those on the ground. In addition to this, there is the tendency to focus on singular strategies and courses of action, all to be implemented within the funding cycle of the particular donor agency concerned, in order to count as success. There is a formidable lack of concern with developing nuanced and grounded understandings of what are usually multi-faceted, complex problems that interlock with several other structures and processes. In this context, it takes some ideological clarity and willingness to go against the grain in order to withstand the pressures to carry out the 'quick and dirty' depoliticised servicing that is called for.

Professionalising gender and women's studies?

The Social Science Academy of Nigeria (SSAN) recently set up a two-week Gender Institute modeled on the lines of the CODESRIA Gender Institute. The motivation for this initiative is rooted largely in the high demand for gender training among researchers and scholars in Nigeria, as evident in the large number of applications from Nigerians for CODESRIA's Gender Institute. As a result, the Academy decided to replicate a similar programme in Nigeria (SSAN 2000). The following questions are of particular salience for what appears to be a process of professionalisation of gender studies: What informs participants' reasons for applying to the Gender Institute? Will the fact that gender studies is being embraced by the Social Science Academy of Nigeria result in its depoliticisation? Or was the depoliticisation of gender studies a condition for its acceptance in the first place?

In addition, two new centres have been set up with the support of the Academy, each with their own journal. One of the centres is the Women Resource Centre (WOREC) at Imo State University, which has published the first edition of the WOREC *Journal of Gender Studies*. The second centre is the Centre for Gender Studies at Benue State University, which has come out with the first issue of the *Review of Gender Studies in Nigeria*. The quality of each of these journals leaves much to be desired. One may well ask what considerations informed the choice of institutions to support, and how the decision to support centres in gender and women's studies at each of the above universities, was arrived at. Both universities are state universities, which are even more poorly funded than federal universities. What place does the role of income generation for the universities play in their inception? Why should institutions be supported to carry out poor quality work? Or will it be argued that this could not have been foreseen? What standards are being set for gender and women's studies, and by whom? Are these standards 'lower' than for other intellectual fields? Where does this leave us regarding an apparent process of 'professionalisation'?

Retaining a feminist vision

Holding on to a feminist vision that can inspire action for change is something that feminists continue to do in Nigeria, often in isolation and under hostile conditions. Changing this situation will not be easy but some of the conditions required for doing so include a strengthening and diversification of institutional bases as well as the formation of organic links between research and activism. I outline each of these dimensions below.

Creating autonomous spaces

Autonomous spaces for gender and women's studies in Nigeria are rare. Of the six organisational sites referred to earlier, the only autonomous space is the Network for Women's Studies in Nigeria. The Network engages in capacity building for teaching and research in gender and women's studies. Being autonomous, however, does not guarantee any security in terms of sustaining the Network. Perennial difficulties arise in fund raising, communication and finding a balance between the high numbers of prospective participants in activities that are intended to be carried out in small groups.

The other five centres of gender and women's studies are located in larger institutional structures that exercise overall decision-making powers. This gives the centres very little leeway to determine their own priorities and plans. Developing organisational strategies to strengthen these centres in a direction that is capable of retaining a feminist agenda, would be a key aim. To date, this aim has yet to be realised.

In this context, the support that is available from regional networking, such as the initiatives of the African Gender Institute at the University of Cape Town, cannot be underestimated. These include the Feminist Studies Network organised around a listserve and occasional workshops, the new journal *Feminist Africa*, and the bibliographic reviews such as that produced by Lewis (2002). In addition, the international conferences held in the region in the year 2002, such as the Women's Worlds Congress held at the University of Makerere, Kampala and the KnowHow conference held at the same time, provide invaluable opportunities for the sharing of information, building of networks, purchase of books and other texts, and general support and solidarity.

Strengthening links between gender/women's studies and women's activism

There is a need to address the content of gender and women's studies scholarship, through more systematic analyses of gender politics at various levels and institutional sites. This needs to be integrated into research and teaching. The sites involved include households, communities, community groups, women's autonomous organisations, social movements, political parties, religious and ethnic groups, non-governmental organisations, institutions of the state, international organisations of diverse kinds and so on. It would also be important to analyse sources of complicity among researchers/gender activists and state/donor agency discourses in gender politics.

At the level of forging connections between research and activism, more needs to be done. Whilst recognising that research and activism are part of a continuum rather than being partitioned from one another, it is also the case that not all researchers engage in activism, and the converse is true for activists engaging in research. In any case, there are real difficulties in devoting sufficient time and energy to carrying out research when one is engaged in activism, and vice versa. Combining both activities also requires knowledge of relevant organisations, the forging of organisational links and ongoing networking. Some advocacy organisations include research amongst their activities, as a prelude to action. Less common is the existence of university-based researchers engaging with women-centred organisations beyond the academy. Although this is happening in some instances, it is not the norm. A more concerted effort at understanding women's activism – its content, form and direction – would suggest possibilities and agendas for the mutual honing of research as well as action (see Pereira 2002b).

These difficulties notwithstanding, strengthening the links between women's studies and women's organising can take place in different ways. One way would be to create issue-based platforms that would provide opportunities for a range of groups (activists, researchers, policy makers, and so on) to meet, share ideas and possibly work on collaborative activities. Such efforts need to be planned, sustained and funded, in other words, well organised. Raising the funds for such activities is not easy, given the politics of donor funding and the vagaries of shifting funding priorities. Donor agencies are rarely willing to envisage the coming together of groups (e.g. researchers and women's rights activists) that may be considered quite separately in their funding plans and programmes. Alternatively, activists may take part in fora for building the capacity of researchers to engage in gender and women's studies, as researchers might do for activists. This is easier to do and is happening in a few instances but tends to be individualised. There is no organised forum at present.

Concluding remarks

The larger project, within which this essay is situated, includes review and analysis of the literature addressing a broader range of thematic areas, each to be covered in some depth. These include themes such as development and the policy arena; politics, the state and militarism; violence against women; religion, culture and the state; sexuality, culture and identity.

I end this essay, not with conclusive statements, but with some questions to think about in terms of discerning future directions that gender and women's studies might take in Nigeria, as in other national contexts:

- What are the social, political and cultural parameters that might determine the effectiveness or failure of gender and women's studies?
- What is the contradictory impact of gender and women's studies, that is, their role in legitimising and sanitising the rule of the regime?
- What is the role of political repression or the way in which complicity is secured with state policies?
- What are the political limits that determine what can or cannot be taken up as issues of women's concern?
- What are the limits of gender and women's studies in Nigeria? To what extent is it playing a constructive role in the struggle for democracy, cultural and political pluralism?

It is the overall configuration of responses to questions such as these (which have not conventionally been part of gender and women's studies in Nigeria) that will highlight potential trajectories for the future.

Note

* This is a revised version of a paper presented at the 10th General Assembly of CODESRIA, 'Africa in the New Millennium', 8–12 December 2002, Kampala, Uganda. It is also published online by the African Gender Institute at http://www.gwsafrica.org/knowledge/pereira.html

Bibliography

AAWORD, 1983, 'Seminar on Research on African Women: What Type of Methodology?', *Occasional Paper Series No. 1*, Dakar: Association of African Women for Research and Development.

AAWORD, 1985, 'AAWORD in Nairobi '85: The Crisis in Africa and its Impact on Women', *Occasional Paper Series No. 3*, Dakar: Association of African Women for Research and Development.

AAWORD, 1989, 'Women as Agents and Beneficiaries of Development Assistance', *Occasional Paper No. 4*, Dakar: Association of African Women for Research and Development.

AAWORD, 1992, 'Women and Reproduction in Africa', *Occasional Paper Series No. 5*, Dakar: Association of African Women for Research and Development.

AAWORD, 2001, *Visions of Gender Theories and Social Development in Africa*, Dakar: Association of African Women for Research and Development.

Adamu, L., 1995, *Hafsatu Ahmadu Bello: The Unsung Heroine*, Kaduna: Adams Books.

Adedeji, S., 1995, *Sulia Adadeji: Metamorphosis of a Kid Trader*, GLJ General Services, Ibadan.

Afigbo, A.,1972, *The Warrant Chiefs*, London: Longman.

Alagoa, E., 1992, 'Queen Kambasa of Bonny', in B. Awe, ed., *Nigerian Women in Historical Perspective*, First Edition, Sankore/Bookcraft: Lagos, Ibadan.

Amadiume, I., 1987, *Male Daughters, Female Husbands: Gender and Sex in an African Society*, London, New Jersey: Zed Books.

Awe, B., ed., 1992, *Nigerian Women in Historical Perspective*, First Edition, Lagos, Ibadan: Sankore/Bookcraft.

Awe, B., 1991, 'Writing Women into History: The Nigerian Experience', in K. Offen et al., eds, *Writing Women's History: International Perspectives*, London: Macmillan.

Awe, B., 1996, 'A Brief Overview of Nigerian Women's Studies', in A. Mama, ed., 'Setting an Agenda for Gender and Women's Studies in Nigeria', *Report of the Network for Women's Studies in Nigeria No.1*, Zaria.

Awe, B., 2001, 'Iyalode Efunsetan Aniwura (Owner of Gold)', in B. Awe, ed., *Nigerian Women in Historical Perspective*, 2nd edition Ibadan, Lagos: Bookcraft/Sankore.

Basu, A., ed., 1995, *The Challenge of Local Feminisms*, Boulder: Westview Press.

Denzer, L., ed., 1995, 'Introduction', in *Constance A. Cummings-John: Memoirs of a Krio Leader*, Sam Bookman for Humanities Research Centre, Ibadan.

Effah-Attoe, S. and Jaja, S., 1993, *Margaret Ekpo: Lioness in Nigerian Politics*, Africa Leadership Forum, Abeokuta.

Elson, D., 1990, 'Male Bias in the Development Process: An Overview', in D. Elson, ed., *Male Bias in the Development Process*, Manchester: Manchester University Press.

Ighodaro, I., 1994, *A Life of Service*, Lagos, Oxford: Malthouse Press/Publishing.

Imam, A., 1994, 'If You Won't Do These Things For Me, I Won't Do Seclusion For You': Local and Regional Constructions of Seclusion Ideologies and Practices in Kano, Northern Nigeria', Unpublished PhD dissertation, University of Sussex.

Imam, A. and Mama, A., 1994, 'The Role of Academics in the Restriction of Academics in Africa', in Mamdani, M. and Diouf, M., eds., *Academic Freedom in Africa*, Dakar: CODESRIA.

Johnson-Odim, C., 2001, 'Lady Oyinkan Abayomi', in Awe, B., ed., *Nigerian Women in Historical Perspective*, 2nd edition, Ibadan, Lagos: Bookcraft/Sankore.

Johnson-Odim, C. and Mba, N., 1997, *For Women and the Nation: Funmilayo Ransome-Kuti of Nigeria*, Urbana and Chicago: University of Illinois Press.

Kemp, A., Madlala, N., Moodley, A. and Salo, E., 1995, 'The Dawn of a New Day: Redefining South African Feminism', in A. Basu, ed., *The Challenge of Local Feminisms*, Boulder: Westview Press.

Koko, A. and Boyd, J., 2001, 'Nana Asma'u', in Awe, B., ed., *Nigerian Women in Historical Perspective*, Second Edition, Ibadan, Lagos: Bookcraft/Sankore.

LACVAW Interim Working Group, 2001, *Report of the Interim Working Group of the Coalition on Legislative Advocacy to Eliminate Violence Against Women* Abuja.

Lewis, D., 2002, 'African Women's Studies: 1980-2001', A Review Essay for the African Gender Institute's 'Strengthening Gender Studies for Social Transformation: An Intellectual Capacity-Building and Information Technology Development Project' African Gender Institute, University of Cape Town, Cape Town.

Mama, A., ed., 1996a, 'Setting an Agenda for Gender and Women's Studies in Nigeria', *Report of the Network for Women's Studies in Nigeria No.1*, Zaria.

Mama, A., 1996b, 'Women's Studies and Studies of Women in Africa During the 1990s', *CODESRIA Working Paper Series 5/96*.

Mama, A., 1997a, 'Opening Session', in C. Pereira, ed., 'Concepts and Methods for Gender and Women's Studies in Nigeria', *Report of the Network for Women's Studies in Nigeria No. 2*, Zaria.

Mama, A., 1997b, 'Implications for Research Practice', in C. Pereira, ed., 'Concepts and Methods for Gender and Women's Studies in Nigeria', *Report of the Network for Women's Studies in Nigeria No. 2*, Zaria

Mama, A., 1998, 'Khaki in the Family: Gender Discourses and Militarism in Nigeria', *African Studies Review*, 41 (2), 1-17.

Mama, A., 2000, *Feminism and the State in Nigeria: The National Machinery for Women*, Third World Network-Africa, Accra.

Mba, N., 1982, *Nigerian Women Mobilised*, Institute of International Studies, Berkeley: University of California.

Mba, N., 1989, 'Kaba and Khaki: Women and the Militarised State in Nigeria', in J. Parpart and K. Staudt, eds., *Women and the State in Africa*, Boulder: Lynne Reiner.

Mbilinyi, M., 1992, 'Research Methodologies in Gender Issues', in R. Meena, ed., *Gender in Southern Africa: Conceptual and Theoretical Issues*, Harare: SAPES Books.

Mohanty, C., Russo, A. and Torres, L., eds., 1991, *Third World Women and the Politics of Feminism*, Bloomington: Indiana University Press.

Morley, L., Unterhalter, E., and Gold, A., 2001, 'Managing Gendered Change in Commonwealth Higher Education', Paper presented at 'Conference on Globalisation and Higher Education: Views from the South', Cape Town, March.

Nigerian NGO Coalition, 1999, *NGOs CEDAW Report for Nigeria*, Nigerian NGO Coalition for a Shadow Report to CEDAW, Lagos.

Ogundipe-Leslie, M., 1994, *Re-creating Ourselves: African Women and Critical Transformations,* Trenton, NJ.:Africa World Press.

Okonjo, K., 1976, 'The Dual Sex Political System in Operation: Igbo Women and Community Politics', in N. Hafkin and E. Bay, eds., *Women in Africa: Studies in Social and Economic Change*, Stanford, Calif.: Stanford University Press.

Olusanya, G., 2001a, 'Charlotte Olajumoke Obasa', in Awe, B., ed., *Nigerian Women in Historical Perspective*, Bookcraft/Sankore, Ibadan, Lagos, 2nd edition.

Olusanya, G., 2001b, 'Olaniwun Adunni Oluwole', in Awe, B., ed., *Nigerian Women in Historical Perspective*, Bookcraft/Sankore, Ibadan, Lagos, Second edition.

Osakue, G., Madunagu, B., Usman, H. and Osagie, J., 1995, *Voices!*, International Reproductive Rights Research Action Group (IRRRAG), Nigeria, Benin City.

Oshunsheye, F., 1960, 'The Role and Status of Women in Nigeria', *Presence Africaine 4*.

Oyewumi, O., 1997, *The Invention of Women: Making an African Sense of Western Gender Discourses*, Minneapolis: University of Minnesota Press.

Pereira, C., 1997a, 'The Women and Laws Project', in C. Pereira, ed., 'Concepts and Methods for Gender and Women's Studies in Nigeria', *Report of the Network for Women's Studies in Nigeria No. 2*, Zaria.

Pereira, C., 1997b, 'No Seamless Narrative': A Gender Analysis of Psychology in Africa', in A. Imam, A. Mama, and F. Sow, eds., *Engendering African Social Sciences*, Dakar: CODESRIA.

Pereira, C., 2000, 'National Council of Women's Societies and the State, 1985-1993: The Use of Discourses of Womanhood by the NCWS', in A. Jega, ed., *Identity Transformation and Identity Politics under Structural Adjustment in Nigeria*, Nordiska Afrikainstitutet, Uppsala with Centre for Research and Documentation, Kano.

Pereira, C., 2001a,'Culture, Gender and Constitutional Restructuring in Nigeria', in J. Oloka-Onyango, ed., *Constitutionalism in Africa: Creating Opportunities, Facing Challenges*, Kampala: Fountain Publishers.

Pereira, C., 2001b, 'A Gender Analysis of the Nigerian University System', Final draft for the Case Studies of Nigerian Universities Project.

Pereira, C., 2002a, 'Between Knowing and Imagining: What Space for Feminism in Scholarship on Africa?', *Feminist Africa*, 1, 9-33.

Pereira, C., 2002b, 'Understanding Women's Experiences of Citizenship in Nigeria: From Advocacy to Research', Paper presented at CODESRIA/Arab Research Centre Symposium on 'African Gender Research in the New Millennium: Perspectives, Directions and Challenges', Cairo, Egypt, 7–10 April.

Roberts, P., 1983, 'Feminism *in* Africa: Feminism *and* Africa', *Review of African Political Economy* No. 27/8, 175-184.

Rosiji, G., 1996, *Lady Ademola: Portrait of a Pioneer*, Lagos: EnClair Publishers.

Salihu, A., 1999, 'Gender Politics in WIN: Reflections on a Women's Organisation 1982–1997', Mimeo.

Sen, G. and Grown, C., 1988, *Development, Crises and Alternative Visions*, London: Earthscan.

Shawulu, R., 1990, *The Story of Gambo Sawaba*, Jos: Echo Communications.

SSAN, 2000, Gender Institute Meeting, October 25–26, 2000, Mimeo Social Science Academy of Nigeria.

Stamp, P., 1989, *Technology, Gender and Power in Africa*, Ottawa: IDRC.

Women in Nigeria (WIN), 1999, *Nigeria's Compliance with its Obligations Under the Convention on the Elimination of All Forms of Discrimination Against Women*, WIN Kaduna Chapter.

Yusuf, B., 2002, 'We Don't Do Gender Here? The Blindspot of Denying Gender Distinction', Paper presented at CODESRIA/Arab Research Centre Symposium on 'African Gender Research in the New Millennium: Perspectives, Directions and Challenges', Cairo, Egypt, 7-10 April.

2

Chasing Illusions and Realising Visions: Reflections on Ghana's Feminist Experience

Mansah Prah

Introduction

In organizing my thoughts in preparation for writing this paper, I realised that I too have been chasing illusions. I had naïvely assumed somehow, that the analysis of the trajectory of women's participation in the political, intellectual and cultural life in Ghana would follow a fairly uniform, straight path, characterised by clearly defined steps and phases. But history is not linear, and the course of the feminist agenda may better be viewed as a meandering path than one that moves in a regular pattern of progression.

The path of Ghanaian gender politics – issues relating to gender hierarchies in the state, women's status, influence in politics and social life – the relationship between the state and women's organisations, (which I refer to as Ghana's feminist experience) has gone through various changes since Independence in 1957. The paper traces the feminist experience in Ghana since 1957 and attempts to tease out the main currents in the nature of women's political participation, voice and state responses to it.[1]

A brief description of gender politics in the pre-colonial era may be useful for our understanding of contemporary trends.

Pre-Independence Feminism and Gender Politics

There was no unified state before the imposition of British rule on the country, and the area that is now Ghana consisted of a variety of ethnic communities with distinct systems of descent and social organisation.

Women in pre-colonial Ghana played various roles depending on the particular social organisation and historical circumstances of their society. As in many traditional African societies, a combination of factors determined the allocation of resources, power, status, rights and duties between men and women. These included descent, succession and inheritance, paternity, affiliation, residence rules, and economic potential (Aidoo 1995). Among the matrilineal Akan, for example, women had relatively high economic and legal independence, and in Akan politics, women played a complementary role to men. Other ethnic groups which had systems of patrilineal descent such as the Konkomba, Kusase, Ewe, and Dagomba were much more male dominated, and in those communities that had been influenced by Islam such as the Gonja and Dagomba restrictions on women were more pronounced (Aidoo 1995). Aidoo goes on to say that the traditional emphasis of anthropologists and other scholars on political offices and the position of the chief (who was usually a male) have eclipsed the political role of all but a few African women. In societies like the Ga, Dagomba, Nzima and Aowin where women controlled certain ritual practices and medicines as well as land, stool property and regalia, the political role of women could be considerable. Regarding the Akan, Manuh (1991) discusses the conflicting views on the status of Akan women in pre-colonial society, and cites Mikell (1985) who points out that the male/female complementarity had eroded in Ashanti between the eighteenth and nineteenth centuries.

Crucial for the future trajectory of women's political agency in Ghana, is the fact that culturally and politically, the notion of women in the public sphere was not completely alien even though it was to a large extent, eroded during colonial rule. Women in Ghana had had a long experience of organization and association in a variety of activities (Tsikata 1989; Manuh 1991) and this heralded the extent to which they rallied round the political parties during the anti-colonial struggle and later around the CPP.

The heterogeneous nature of gender hierarchies in traditional Ghanaian society might have had some implications for the future women's front. Cultural, social, class and ethnic factors are important determinants of attitudes towards gender and feminist consciousness. The recognition of group membership and shared interests, prerequisites that are essential to political action, would be more difficult to attain in such a situation. In the light of this, it is not surprising that large-scale mobilisation of women across ethnic and class boundaries occurred mostly in urban areas, sites of rapid social upheaval and dislocation, shortly before Ghana gained political Independence from Britain in 1957.

Manuh (1991) explains the context within which women mobilised in the anti-colonial struggle. The superimposition of Victorian values and morality on the traditional order by colonialism, which defined men as heads of households, allowed poor access of women to health and education, and created discriminatory practices in workplaces, left women, especially those in the towns, with very few spaces within which they could manoeuvre. The prospect of self-government offered such women hope for a better life and the fulfilment of their gender interests. So women, especially those from urban areas, mobilised behind the United Gold Coast Convention (UGCC) and later, massively behind Nkrumah's Convention People's Party (CPP) towards 'self-government now'.

In the anti-colonial struggle, women mobilised mainly around economic issues. For example, as far back as 1917–1918, they were active in cocoa hold-ups, and their participation in those early protests stemmed from their work as retail traders. They felt the threat posed by the monopolistic activities of the European trading firms (Tsikata 1989). The struggle around which they mobilised was not a feminist one. In terms of the situation in the country, it was a universal political problem whose solution they had vested interests in. Women traders became staunch supporters of the Convention People's Party (CPP) led by Dr. Kwame Nkrumah. They contributed generously to its funding and organisation, and it is through their active participation that women's sections of the party were established. In his autobiography, Nkrumah attributed the solidarity, cohesion and success of the CPP in its early days to the efforts of its women members (Nkrumah 1959).

CPP Feminism[2]

The women's sections of the CPP were not organised around women's specific problems or gender issues,[3] they were effectively support pillars of the party. The CPP Women's League, formed in 1951, was charged with duties such as the organisation of rallies, dances and picnics, and a special day for Women, Ghana Women's Day was established. In 1953, non-political women's organisation, the Ghana Federation of Women, was formed. In 1960, the League, Federation and smaller women's groups merged under a proposal by the CPP. A new women's organisation, the National Council of Ghana Women (NCGW) which replaced the women's section of the Party, was inaugurated by Dr. Nkrumah as the only recognised body under which all Ghanaian women were to be organised to contribute their quota to the political, educational social and economic construction of Ghana. It had become an integral wing of the Party and had representation on its Central Committee.

The NCGW established branches throughout the country. It sent its younger members abroad to study, and assisted them in finding employment. The members who were market women controlled the allocation of space and goods there. The NCGW also organised rallies and built day-care centres in the towns for working women (Tsikata 1989). The NCGW was never completely independent as it was controlled by the government and limited by patriarchal attitudes towards women in government circles. The CPP General Secretary, assigned the task of organising it, saw the NCGW as a potential threat to the position of men, and could not hide his resentment (Tsikata 1989; Manuh 1991).

The dominant ideology of the time could not contain attempts at addressing women's issues that might raise feminist consciousness and galvanise women into action, and so the NCGW died a natural death in 1966, following the overthrow of the CPP.

It has been suggested that the organisation of women during the CPP era shows recognition of their contributions to the anti-colonial struggle and the implications for development of a backward population. For the first time in Ghana's post-colonial history, the importance of women's contributions to development was given a measure of recognition. The CPP government's policies consciously encouraged the participation of women in politics and public life with the result that a few women held offices as members of parliament, deputy ministers and district commissioners (Tsikata 1989). Due to the CPP government's concern about the absence of women in politics, 10 seats were reserved for women in parliament (Manuh 1991:132; Public Agenda, February 10–14, 1997:8).

The CPP government responded to women's demands for changes in the law that would improve their status in marriage. It passed a law on the Maintenance of Children, but another one, the Uniform Marriage, Divorce and Inheritance Bill was defeated and could not be enacted as a law.

From the above, it is clear that from 1957 to 1966 under Nkrumah's CPP, the state was sympathetic to the problems of gender inequalities in social and political life, and made the first attempts to legitimise and institutionalise women's and gender issues. However, gender politics was based on actions initiated from the top down on behalf of women, by President Nkrumah, a 'benevolent pro-feminist'.

Because the mass women's organisation of the day had been initiated by government and was dependent on it for financing, it was open to control. Then, as later in Ghana's political history, the mass women's organisation was based on party lines. By allowing members easier access to control of important resources, as happened for example in the markets, membership of the party (and its women's wing) was linked to greater access to productive resources, increasing the likelihood that people would join the party for economic reasons. This has been an important factor for political party membership throughout Ghanaian political history.

Nkrumah had a vision of African womanhood steeped in high moral standards, which would form the basis of African nationhood (Manuh 1991). The coup d'état that overthrew his government in 1966 turned that vision into an illusion.

Ghanaian women had experienced a period of goodwill and state support at a time when, globally, women's work had not yet been recognised. Unfortunately, due to the fact that the women's wing of the CPP was not made into a broad-based, coherent movement, it died with the overthrow of the government that had supported it.

Military Rule

There were several changes of government between the overthrow of Ghana's First Republic in 1966 and the coup d'état led by Flt. Lt. Jerry Rawlings on 31st December 1981. This was a period when political life was dominated by the military. The various regimes are listed below:

1966–1969 - The National Liberation Council (NLC) (military)
1969–1972 - The Progress Party (PP)
1972–1979 - The National Redemption Council (NRC) which later became the Supreme Military Council (SMC) (military)
1979   The Armed Forces Revolutionary Council (AFRC) (military)
1979–1981 - People's National Party (PNP)
1982–1992 - People's National Defence Council (PNDC) (military)
1992–1996 - National Democratic Congress (NDC)
1996–2000 - National Democratic Congress (NDC)
2001 to date   New Patriotic Party (NPP)

Summary: civilian government (21 years, including 1957–1966, under Dr. Nkrumah's CPP); military government (21 years).

Although there were short periods of civilian rule between 1966 and 1982, for the purposes of this paper, I refer to the time as the period of military rule. The period dominated by Flt. Lt. Jerry Rawlings will be treated separately.

It is interesting to note that only two out of the 140 members of the 2nd Republic (1969–1972) were women, the 3rd Republic had only five women out of 140 members. The civilian regimes of this period did not show any particular interest in raising the profile of women as Nkrumah had done.

The period from 1966 to 1981 has been described as an 'apolitical' phase on the women's front (Tsikata 1989), and there is not much research to throw light on the activities of women during this era. Women's organisations during this period were largely non-political. Several professional women's groups were also formed during this time[4]. The frequent changes of government and the domination of the military could explain the low ebb of women's political activities during the period. It has been rightly suggested that militarised states reinforce male domination in political and social life (Enloe 1987; Mama 1985), and the militarised Ghanaian state during this period did not support any mass women's organisations.

While the National Liberation Council had worked towards handing over power to a democratically elected government, the National Redemption Council created a truly military government, reorganising itself as the Supreme Military Council (SMC) from 1975. This government thought the country's problems were due to a lack of organisation and that a dose of a military administration would remedy the situation. Officers were put in charge of all ministries and state enterprises. Junior officers were assigned leadership roles in all government departments and parastatals. There is very little research about the relationship between women and the state, women's voice and ways in which they coped with the militarism of this period. However, anecdotal evidence points to the fact that, during this period, women managed to survive by capitalising on ties of patronage, social networks and their femininity to 'get ahead' in trading activities, to the extent that their control of the distribution sector of the economy was eventually viewed as a threat to male dominance. It appears that large numbers of women went into the informal sector during this period. The distribution sector at the time cannot have been controlled only by the rich market 'queens'; several 'ordinary' women went into trading, but there is no empirical data to support this suggestion. Trading in foodstuffs, then, as now, was organised in networks that included women of different social classes in rural and urban Ghana.

Manuh's (1993) analysis of relations between women and the state under the PNDC is pertinent here. She points to a kind of political fundamentalism in Ghana that views women's economic activities with resentment and would wish to consign them to the home and the care of children. This political fundamentalism, she says, is in turn reinforced by patriarchal ideology within the society and its pre-determined notions of the proper role of women. As a result, Ghanaian women have been accused of immorality, prostitution and other social evils during periods of crises. This is what happened during the first years of the PNDC rule.

The 'woman bashing' that resulted from political fundamentalism actually had its roots in the 1970s during the NRC and SMC Regime under General Acheampong and later General Akuffo. Anecdotal evidence has it that women used their sexual wiles to obtain trading licences and other favours from the military officers. This was the period of 'kalabule', signifying the corrupt practices of the time, during which women were accused by the media and the rumour mill, of using their 'bottom power' to do business. These accusations were the beginning of the female scapegoating and blaming of women for the country's economic problems, which eventually culminated in the brutal assault, vilification and degradation of women traders during the early eighties, at the beginning of the Rawlings Era[5]. The attacks on women were a backlash to their immense success as traders.

The military did not have any specific agenda for women. Unlike the civilian governments, which attempted to maintain power and control over women's voice and activities by co-opting them through the women's wings of political parties, the military understood the use of brute force as a management measure. The coping strategy of women traders was to use their wits, wiles and social capital to cope with military rule; the educated middle class women retreated into professional organisations and private life.

The major landmark in policy during the period that was to have important repercussions for the Ghanaian feminist experience and gender politics, was the establishment in 1975 of the National Council for Women and Development (NCWD) by government decree[6]. The NCWD was set up in response to a UN resolution calling on member-states to establish the appropriate government machinery to accelerate the integration of women in development and the elimination of discrimination against women on grounds of sex.

The NRC Decree establishing the NCWD gave it advisory and research functions as well as a liaison role between government and nation and international organisations. In 1976 the NCWD commissioned a series of studies on various aspects of the existing situation of Ghanaian women: in the family, employment, education and training, laws, customs and inequities in marriage systems and rights, and their position in agriculture and production. As a result of these studies some changes in legislation were proposed by the NCWD, and groundwork was laid for the implementation of projects that were directed at increasing women's incomes.

This account so far has not mentioned outside influences on the feminist experience. The women's liberation movement in the West had gained some momentum by the late Sixties, and the UN Women's Decade did much in raising feminist consciousness globally. This was not lost on Ghanaian women, particularly the professional middle class. It is not very surprising that the Ghana branch of FIDA (International Federation of Women Lawyers) was established in 1974 with the aim of improving the situation of women and children in the country and strengthening their position in the overall developmental process. By 1985 they had established a free legal aid programme for women. Even though the NCWD was set up through a UN resolution, the support and advocacy to see it through came from professional women including some lawyers. Legal feminist activism has continued to grow in Ghana, and will be discussed later.

The role of international donor agencies during the period (and after it) is also significant. With the establishment of the NCWD came the acceptance and implementation of the Women in Development (WID/GAD) paradigm as the main framework within which activities towards the promotion of the improvement of the status of women take place. This was the paradigm within which the donor agencies worked, and it was accepted and institutionalised probably in order that the 'much needed' funding would be obtained. This paradigm continues to dominate much state backed activities and projects for women and children today.

The problems presented by the WID/GAD framework in Ghana and other African countries have been discussed (Tsikata 2000; Mensah-Kutin et.al 2000; Mama 2000), and it has been argued that the framework stresses developmental issues instead of the more political gender equality issues and tends not to link the two.

At the time it was established in Ghana, the NCWD appeared to be a promising, non-partisan vehicle for advancing a feminist agenda, particularly where there was a non-existent political women's front. But it was not able to do this to any significant degree. By 1985, ten years after it was set up, it had been effectively silenced by the next military regime, through the machinery set up by the wife of the leader, which came to be described in the literature as 'the First Lady Syndrome' or the 'femocracy' (Mama 1995).

1982–2000: The Grand 'Feminist' Illusion

In December 1981 Flt. Lt. Jerry Rawlings overthrew the civilian, democratically elected government of Dr. Hilla Limann and declared a revolution. The following year, new mass political organisations such as the June 4 Movement and New Democratic Movement were formed. In response to the directives of the government, Committees for the Defence of the Revolution or CDR's were set up all over the country to express the interests and power of the people and to protect the 31st December Revolution (Tsikata 1989).

These new mass organisations were not directed specifically at gender needs although they occasionally created platforms upon which women's issues were discussed. This created opportunities for the establishment of a women's organisation, and in March 1982 the Federation of Ghanaian Women (FEGAWO) was formed. It is interesting to note that the honorary president of this organisation later became a member of the ruling PNDC, showing the continuation of a tendency that has been prevalent in the history of women's organisations since the CPP days – lack of independence from the government, leading to easy co-optation by the ruling party. The aims of the FEGAWO were clearly directed at women, and included struggling for equal rights and opportunities for women in economic, social and political matters and to fight against the structures, laws, norms and practices that oppress women.

Unfortunately it did not succeed in spreading its influence throughout the country, and was to be completely eclipsed by the 31st December Women's Movement (DWM), which was launched in May 1982. The FEGAWO, an organisation which had its roots in civil society, could not compete with the DWM, led the by First Lady and enjoying the full support of the PNDC government.

The beginning of the Rawlings era was characterised by a massive and brutal assault on certain groups of Ghanaian women, particularly market women and other traders, who were held responsible for the economic problems of the country and were often mishandled and prosecuted. Soldiers publicly beat up the women, shaved off their hair, and sometimes forced them to take off their clothes in public. The main market in Accra, Makola Market[7] was demolished. Interestingly, by late 1983, when the PNDC changed its economic course from a socialist to a market economy orientation and launched the International Monetary Fund (IMF) backed Economic Recovery Programme, women's economic roles were reconceptualized to fit in with the 'women in development' (WID) approaches that had been propagated by the UN and other international agencies. This was accompanied by a more active sponsorship of women's issues and development programmes targeted at them. The Rawlings Government recognised the international institutionalisation of gender, which was taking place globally because a shift in thinking about women's roles triggered by the International Women's Movement had began and most governments seeking aid had to show some commitment to the gender question.

The appropriation of the gender concept by the state under Rawlings was largely facilitated through his wife Nana Konadu Agyeman-Rawlings' leadership of the 31st December Women Movement. The DWM, described as an NGO, was in reality the women's wing of the government.

By 1986 the DWM had 'clipped the wings' of the national machinery for women, by dissolving and replacing it with a management committee which consisted of prominent DWM members and their nominees. From this time forth, control of the NCWD was firmly placed in the hands of the government. It was systematically deprived of resources, so that the DWM was able to eclipse the NCWD. Thus during the era of Rawlings, many people were not clear about the role of the NCWD, the state and the DWM.

Using the DWM as her Platform, the First Lady steadily rose in prominence. From 1985 onwards she was increasingly visible on radio and television. Through the DWM and the women's wing of the ruling party, the NDC, Mrs. Rawlings was active in raising votes for her husband's campaign for office in 1992 and 1996.

By 1994 the DWM claimed to have a membership of 2.5 million women. Having enjoyed strong support from the government since its inception, the DWM had good access to productive resources such as land, attracted funding from external and internal sources, and was been funded by UN agencies. By the nineties, however, some international and bilateral agencies were unwilling to deal directly with it because of its overtly political character (Manuh 1993).

Although the DWM asserted that it had a mass following from the ranks of women and had aims[8] that could be described as pro-woman or feminist, it did not achieve any substantial changes in the status of women. The economic policies of the regime had adverse effects on women (Clarke and Manuh 1999) and the statistics from this period are not encouraging.

In 1990, the illiteracy rates were 49 per cent for women and 30 per cent for men. Under the PNDC Government, women made up 6 percent of the committee of secretaries and 3 per cent of PNDC secretaries. Women were not represented at both levels in 1990. In the first Government of the NDC government (1993–1996) there were 2 women out of 35 ministerial appointments and made up only 8 per cent of Members of Parliament.

Women's representation on the Judiciary was 10 per cent in 1982 and only rose by 1 per cent in 1994. In the 1996 elections, 18 women secured seats in parliament, an increase of 2 seats over the 16 seats women obtained in the 1st Parliament of the NDC government.

The women's front in Ghana, under the long political tenure of Rawlings, was characterised by a grand illusion of activity[9] purported to be in the interests of the broad masses of women and spearheaded by the First Lady and Life President of the DWM. This illusion was the 'femocracy', coherently described and analysed by Mama (1995), as a postcolonial development in African gender politics. She defines it as:

> An anti-democratic female power structure which claims to exist for the advancement of ordinary women, but is unable to do so because it is dominated by a small clique of women whose authority derives from their being married to powerful men, rather than any action or ideas of their own. Femocracies exploit the commitments of the international movement for greater equality while actually only advancing the interests of a small female elite, and in the long term undermining women's interests by upholding the patriarchal status quo. In short, femocracy is a feminine autocracy running in parallel to the patriarchal oligarchy upon which it relies for its authority and which it supports completely.

There were some positive developments for the women's front under the femocracy, such as the ratification of the UN Convention on the Elimination of all Forms of Discrimination against Women (CEDAW), the passing of the Registration of Customary Marriage and Divorce Law, and the law on Intestate Succession. It will be recalled that the CPP government had been unable to pass this law that was meant to raise the status of women in marriage. The laws probably were successfully passed due to a variety of reasons: the posturing of the state as one that recognised women's gender interests (due to international pressure), and a steady rise in legal advocacy fuelled by a global climate that increasingly fostered a 'rights' discourse.

2001 to date: Chasing Illusions or Realising Visions?

President John Agyekum Kufour took over the reigns of government in 2001 after an exciting electoral process. The atmosphere was charged, reminiscent of the heady days of the early post-independence era. God had 'spoken'[10], and Ghanaians were full of thanks and high expectations. Ghana had now shaken off President Rawlings and his wife, and entered a new era; there was a 'new democratic dispensation' as Ghanaians put it. The new regime talked about leading Ghana into a 'golden age of business', the new government would bring about 'positive change', optimism was the order of the day. The media became more vibrant than it had ever been; people felt free to air their opinions and currently many contentious issues are openly discussed on radio and television. Certainly, a fresh breeze has been blowing through the country, and the discourse of rights and democracy are high on all agendas. On the women's front, the new regime established a Ministry of Women and Children's Affairs. The ministry has absorbed the NCWD. So far, despite the glorious vision of a new Ghana, the status of women has not yet changed; women are still not prominent in the decision-making process. After the initial euphoria of the feeling of living under the 'new democratic dispensation' died down and nominations to political office were effected, a journalist registered her disappointment with the government in this way:

> Should it not be a worry that at present, out of the 200 parliamentarians, only 19 are women? Is it fair that only two members of the country's 16 members of Cabinet are women and that there are only four women in the 20-member Council of State and six out of the country's 31 ministers of state are women? Women constitute only 3.5 percent of elected positions of district assemblies, and in the unit committees, they are insignificant. Out of the 15 chief directors in the sector ministries, there is no woman among them! With the directors in these ministries, only 25 women can be counted among the 138 people.

> Clearly, these statistics are an indication of how we, as a country, in our individual actions and inaction, have over the years relegated women issues to the background. (Golda Armah, *Daily Graphic*, 30 August 2001)

Similar articles were published in the *Daily Graphic*, 21 and 28 June 2001, and *Public Agenda*, 30 July–5 August 5 2001.

Feminist Intellectual Experience and Activism

From the seventies onwards, there was a rise in public awareness of the importance of women's issues partly fostered by the International Women's Year and Decade, women's in the international women's conferences and other action, and strengthened by NCWD's activities. This gave feminist research and activism an impetus (Prah 1996). Internally generated research by Ghanaian women was not done much in the Sixties and Seventies; one recalls the work of academics such Miranda Greenstreet and Christine Oppong during that time. By the Eighties and certainly in the Nineties a more substantial body of knowledge had developed.

In 1989 the Development and Women's Studies Programme (DAWS), the only teaching programme in women's studies in Ghana[11] was launched at the Institute of African Studies. During its planning stages there were consultations between academics, NGO's and other interested civil society members. The programme has now settled into a more academic routine but still maintains contacts with activists. Academic feminism and activism appear to have so far had a fairly productive partnership, cooperating with each other over issues such as the national campaign against domestic violence, which saw both activists and academics working together on research reports, (Prah 2000), demonstrations against serial killing of women, and more recently, activities to sensitise the public on the domestic violence bill. The last activity appears to be exposing differences in strategy; some academics would prefer that the public debate on the bill continues over a longer period, due to a contentious point about marital rape, which is being touted by many as a 'Western' cultural construct. Others, mainly activists, would like to see the bill passed soon, before the next election in 2004. Despite such contradictions, the partnership between activists and intellectuals so far seems to be a fairly productive one. This is due perhaps to the fact that feminist researchers are very often activists and vice versa, straddling the two roles.

The partnership between activists and academics appears to have developed naturally, with the main actors sharing a middle class social background and common perceptions about rights. Historically, activism directed specifically feminist issues in Ghana has originated from the legal arena, and has yielded the most tangible results. Local political realities, coupled with the global ideological environment within which the donor community operates have contributed to the current status quo. The 'civil society' essentially has a middle class social character and aspirations, and one of the greatest challenges that face all the parties interested in social transformation, including gender activists, is to transcend the barriers imposed by middle class interests.

Conclusion

In this paper, I have attempted to trace the path of gender politics and women's political participation in Ghana. The account has hopefully shown how from the outset, the civilian regimes have consistently co-opted women and excluded them from political power and decision-making. Some military regimes did not co-opt women but clamped upon their activities with the use of brute force. The femocratic type of government, of the Rawlings Era, also co-opted women's power.

The current Kufour regime appears to be following the path of all other civilian governments but the difference is the existence of a more vibrant civil society, which is constrained by its middle class character. The women's front has chased illusions and is yet to realise its vision. Some of the great challenges faced by Ghanaian feminists is that of transcending its middle class nature and achieving a sustainable movement or capable of achieving change that will transform the lives of women.

End notes

1   I am very conscious of the limitations of this paper, particularly of the fact that the account tends to be oversimplified, leaping over chunks of history and omitting an analysis of global and local economic processes, including women's economic activities. I have relied on anecdotal evidence for the section on military rule. There is a gap in research on women's activities during this period.

2   'Feminism' in this context refers to the recognition of women's specific interests and activities to realise them

3   'Gender issues' refer to the relations between women and men as they are expressed in terms of power, economics or status, within the context of social and economic relations which define the positions of men and women.

4   Issues of the women's magazine 'Obaa Simaa' that appeared in the Seventies abound with reports of   inaugurations of women's groups based in organizations such as banks, insurance companies and parastatals.

5   Interestingly, the National Reconciliation Commission that began operation in 2003, has had several submissions from women who were victims of 'female scapegoating' during that period.

6   Apparently, negotiating the establishment of the NCWD was difficult. It took several meetings and a very strong, unbending position by the women activists before the SMC accepted to have it set up. (Personal communication from the late Justice Annie Jiaggie, a women's activist).

7   See Manuh (1993) for a more detailed discussion on the scapegoating of women traders.

8   Its early objectives were to involve women in the on going revolutionary process (particularly during the PNDC era), to raise women's political consciousness about national and political affairs; and to raise living standards of women by supporting them in their income-generating activities. It lists social issues, health, environmental protection, childcare, education and training of women, income generation, and peace as its concerns (Manuh 1993; Personal communication with former DWM officials;) see also its Internet website (www.africaonline.com.gh/31dwm/programme.html).

9   At the conference, Zenebeworke Tadesse rightly remarked that what I term a 'grand illusion of activity' is also actually a situation in which the broad masses of women are made to put in more and more work while deriving little for their efforts.

10 This is a reference to an Akan hymn that became a symbol of the NPP campaign '*Ewurade Kasa*' literally meaning 'God, speak'.

11 The University of Cape Coast will shortly launch an undergraduate concentration in Gender Studies in the Department of Sociology.

References

Aidoo, Agnes Akosua, 1995, 'Women in the History and Culture of Ghana', in Mansah Prah, ed., *Women's Studies With a Focus on Ghana: Selected Readings*, Schriesheim, Germany: Books on African Studies.

Clarke, G., and Manuh, T., 1991, 'Women Traders in Ghana and the Structural Adjustment Programme' in C. Gladwin, ed., *Structural Adjustment and African Women Farmers*, Gainesville: University of Florida Press.

Enloe, Cynthia, 1987, 'Feminists Thinking about War, Militarism and Peace', in Beth B. Hess and Myra Marx Ferree, eds., *Analyzing Gender: A Handbook of Social Science Research*, California: Sage.

Mama, Amina, 1995, 'Feminism or Femocracy? State Feminism and Democratisation in Nigeria', *Africa Development* Vol. XX, No. 1:37-58.

Mama, Amina, 2000, *National Machinery for Women in Africa: Towards an Analysis*, Accra: Third World Network.

Manuh, Takyiwaa, 1991, 'Women and their Organisations during the Convention Peoples' Party Period', in Kwame Arhin, ed., *The Life and Work of Kwame Nkrumah*, Accra: Sedco Publishing.

Manuh, Takyiwaa, 1993, 'Women, State and Society under the PNDC'. In, E. Gyimah-Boadi, ed., *Ghana Under PNDC Rule*, London: CODESRIA Books.

Mensah-Kutin, Rose, Alima Mahama, Sarah Ocran, Esther Ofei-Aboagye, Vicky Okyne and Dzodzi Tsikata, 2000, *The National Machinery for Women in Ghana: An NGO Evaluation*, Accra: Third World Network.

Nkrumah, Kwame, 1959, *Ghana: The Autobiography of Kwame Nkrumah*, London: Thomas Nelson and Sons.

Prah, Mansah, 1996, 'Women's Studies in Ghana', in *Women's Studies Quarterly*, Vol. XXIV, Nos. 1 and 2.

Prah, Mansah, 2000, 'Violence Against Women: Experiences from Ghana', in *Ife Psychologia*, Vol. 8. No.1, pp.1-29.

Tsikata, Edzodzinam, 1988, 'The First Lady Syndrome', *Public Agenda*.

Tsikata, Edzodzinam, 1989, 'Women's Political Organisations 1951–1987', in E. Hansen and K. Ninsin, eds., *The State, Development and Politics in Ghana*, London: CODESRIA Books.

Tsikata, Edzodzinam, 2000, *Lip-Service and Peanuts: The State and National Machinery for Women in Africa*, Accra: Third World Network.

3

Establishing Gender Studies Programmes in South Africa: The Role of Gender Activism

Amanda Gouws

Introduction

This chapter provides a critical engagement with the idea of gender activism and its role in the establishment of Gender and Women's Studies in South Africa. It also looks at how the institutionalization of gender has changed the nature of activism in the absence of a strong women's movement post-1994.

The aim of gender activism and its link with Gender and Women's Studies (GWS) has always been to create a better society for women and to enhance democracy. We need to ask ourselves to what extent we have succeeded in this mission when greater corporatization of universities undermines transformation initiatives and agendas.

The Uncomfortable Relationship Between Activism and the Academy

The relationship between women who are political activists and women in the academy (some of whom were also activists) has been an uncomfortable one, but from the perspective of struggle, a mutually beneficial one. Both sides played an important role in putting gender on the agenda during the transition to democracy in South Africa and keeping it there. The activists were responsible for the mobilization of thousands of women, especially when the Women's National Coalition (WNC) was formed.[1] The academics articulated the terms in which gender had to be taken up in government policy documents, legislation and demanded the inclusion of women in parliament.

Tensions between the two groups stemmed from (1) issues of representation and racism, (2) the perceived schism between academics and activists, (3) issues of experience.

The representation debate and racism

A large amount of literature has been generated by the representation debate[2] that has at its core the problem of some white women academics who, when representing black women or doing research on them, silenced their voices and disempowered them. This led to arguments about who can do research on whom and a period of unproductive accusations on both sides. These conversations also begin to address the under representation of black women in the academy – a consequence of larger discriminatory forces in South Africa at the time, such as the lack of access to education or inferior education for black South Africans and discriminatory educational policies.

White women academics who were sensitive toward the issue of representation were often lumped together with women academics guilty of representing the "other" in an unthinking and insensitive way, aggravating the tension between academics and activists.

Due to the privileged position of white women, many had patronising attitudes toward black women in the women's movement, the majority of whom had lower levels of education. In meetings on a grassroots level many black women did not speak English, often requiring the presence of a translator. These patronising attitudes of white women can be viewed as a consequence of the internalization of racism in the South African context. It was easy for white women to deny their own racism or to blame it on structural forces (Hassim and Walker 1993: 527-528). This often led to angry outbursts by black activists.

Schism between grassroots women and academics

Very often, especially during women's conferences in the 1990s, it became apparent that grassroots women perceived academic women as more privileged and disconnected from the lives of women who do not work in the academy. Academic women were perceived as talking on an abstract level without the necessary experience to "understand" the lives of grassroots women. Issues of experience became central to the debate about representation.

Experience

Some black activists insisted that their experience of oppression could not be understood by whites. Experience, therefore, became the platform from which to engage in activism. This absolutist stance on experience foreclosed debate about the engagement of black and white women in each others' experience and prevented the emergence of a debate on class (see Funani 1992 and 1993). In this regard a switch took place from gender to race as the category of analysis. Academics argued that in order to understand experience it has to be mediated through such concepts and theorized accordingly (See Gouws 1996).

Universities as Sites of Struggle

The universities, however, became important sites of struggle as the gender struggle was taken into the academy. Gender and Women's Studies were viewed as the academic arm of the women's movement. Already in 1993, Hassim and Walker suggested a feminist agenda for academic women. They argued that feminism has to encompass a political project to challenge the subordination of women and feminist research had to be part of the process of empowering women. As they (1993:531) argued the relationship between feminist academic work and the women's movement is a complex one and one that requires academics to consider carefully activists' demands for greater accountability. It could never be a one to one relationship – it could not only represent the ideas of the women's movement; it needed to include critique as well. As they put it: (ibid.) "This requires a context of relative autonomy from immediate political imperatives, even though the work may be informed by broader political commitments".

They also argued that one of the important achievements of feminist academics has been to give credence to Women and Gender Studies programmes in the university and they warn that feminist academics should be careful that these programmes do not become a reason for university administration to ignore gender discrimination in the universities. They urged that the women's movement should acknowledge the legitimacy and the limits of academic work and feminist academics should construct a *political project* to further the gender struggle in society (Hassim and Walker 1993:533).

The universities as a site of struggle required that feminist academics destabilize relationships of unequal power and inequality in the academy but maintain the crucial link between activism and the academy.

After the 1994 election with the ANC's commitment to a one third gender quota some of the most competent female activists went into parliament and became active politicians. This depleted the women's movement of some of their most vocal and articulate activists. While this opened some spaces of access for research on women in government for academics, it is far from clear to what extent women in government support the feminist project in the academy. Transformation in higher education requires that academics and activists scrutinize the transformation agenda for its impact on the feminist project.

In the West, the institutionalization of Women's Studies grew out of second wave feminism and the close link between the women's movement and feminist academics.[3] In South Africa, feminist academic work and activism developed separately and had an uncomfortable relationship, as discussed above, but with the advent of women's conferences in the early 1990s, a discourse developed between them that was taken into the academy with the institutionalization of Gender and Women's Studies.

Institutionalization of Gender and Women's Studies in Higher Education

Of the total number of students at higher education institutions in South Africa, 53 percent are women (Council of Higher Education Annual Report 2000/2001). This percentage is much higher than other countries in Africa.[4] Still, fewer women study on a post-graduate level than men.

At many of the higher education institutions, the institutionalization of Gender and Women's Studies (GWS) is a result of tireless struggle by women who persisted this is a legitimate field of study and a necessity in higher education. Not only did the gender-blind teachings of tertiary institutions come under scrutiny, but the door was opened to a debate among South African women scholars about what the content of gender courses/programmes should be. Even whether it should be called Women's Studies or Gender Studies resulted in a protracted discourse[5].

Gender and Women's Studies in the African context

The introduction of Gender and Women's Studies in South Africa has been contested for various reasons including: the challenge that it posed to the existing curriculum, perceived competition for resources in the institutions, and debate about what the content of women's studies or gender studies courses should be. The idea of Women's Studies as taught in the West has been viewed with suspicion because of its Western origins and its neglect of the particularities of other geographical contexts, like Africa.

Women's Studies is a more recent phenomenon in Africa – mainly since the 1980s. Mama's 1996 review shows that Women's studies in Africa is not necessarily linked to the broader women's movement but was motivated by other forces such as development initiatives, national and sub-regional political conditions and the crisis in African education. There has also been an urgency about the importance of studying gender as a central concept in social science in Africa (see Salo 2000:5), the neglect of which Salo refers to as social science's "perpetual deafness".

To escape being only the objects of study by Western scholars with Western research concerns Women's/Gender Studies has been institutionalized all over Africa. As Mama (1996:8) notes "[T]he push for institutionalization of women's and gender studies is remarkable in view of the impoverished and declining condition of so many African academic institutions".

Discontent with being the objects of study has led to African feminist critiques of racist and imperialist knowledge production and a rejection of the hegemony of Western scholars and of the unequal power relations between Western and African women scholars. This has also contributed to a premature rejection of important contributions by female scholars of foreign origin (Mama 1996:9).

While feminist scholars have established an independent body of literature and have challenged gender-blind theories and methodologies, the extent to which this body of knowledge has penetrated or influenced the study of women in Africa is unclear (Mama 1996:4).

South Africa has not been immune to these discontents. Most GWS programmes are under resourced, lacking undergraduate feeder programmes to enable post-graduate programmes to recruit students. The teaching in GWS programmes also runs the risk of becoming undermined in the "gender industry" in South Africa. This industry was created through the need to train people in gender studies for positions in the state and national machinery but also to comply with the agendas of Western aid and development organizations. Manicom (2001:9) in her critical analysis of "gender in governance" has shown that the unquestioning way in which gender is taken up in the governance discourse has led to an uncontextual and formulaic use of gender redress and not the strong theoretical analysis that GWS programmes support.

The main question that needs to be asked here is how GWS is contributing to the political project and a feminist praxis that will liberate women. Some institutions have had more success than others. In this regard the African Gender Institute (AGI) at the University of Cape Town's feminist political project can be singled out as making a unique contribution to South Africa and the African continent.

One of the missions of the AGI is the creation of African gender knowledge and this commitment shows very clearly in its course content and research agenda. As was stated very clearly in the workshop proceedings of the "Strengthening of Gender and Women's Studies in African Contexts" (p.6) organized in 2002 by the AGI "GWS needs to place greater emphasis on independent knowledge production; the internationalization of feminism can easily degenerate into another form of colonisation". Activism thus needs to be focused not only on the South African context but also on the broader African context, emphasising the theoretical connection between gender oppression and its eradication.

At other institutions where GWS is not organized in a separate institution problems abound. Because of their interdisciplinary nature, GWS programmes often do not have departmental or disciplinary homes. For teaching purposes expertise is drawn from different departments and those committed to the teaching of gender subjects do so on top of their regular teaching load—what Berlant (1997:148) calls "the bureaucratic violence of work", even though this is no different from many Western countries in the world where gender is taught. Nevertheless, the lack of funding for gender work, the exploitation of the time and expertise of gender scholars (who very often have to contribute to designing gender change policies) can be viewed as a benign institutional neglect through which institutions do not seriously engage with gender knowledge but can still claim to be teaching gender courses. In this regard Shefer (2003:4) for example says the following about the Women and Gender Studies Programme at the University of the Western Cape:

WGS still functions on a contract basis, with no permanent posts, and still struggles, as appears to be the fate of gender studies across the globe, for basic infrastructural and material resources. Furthermore, the multiplicity of our orientation and the imperative to link the academic programme with 'work on the ground' means that the unit is increasingly overloaded and faces dilemmas of what to prioritise and where to most strategically place one's limited time and energies.

In the African context Tamale and Oloka-Onyango (2000) also argue that gender or women's studies departments have remained outside the mainstream. As they state "In essence, gender studies have become ghettoized, confined principally to women, and making only a limited impact on the overall struggle against gender bias" (Tamale and Oloka-Onyango 2000:11). It is left to women to raise gender consciousness, earning them the labels of "bitches" in the academy when they try to disrupt the patriarchal power relations in educational institutions. (ibid: 11).

We should, however, not underestimate the consciousness of gender inequality that GWS programmes in South Africa and elsewhere in Africa have raised in educational institutions, and what they have achieved in terms of establishing it as a legitimate field of study. It has also been highly effective at changing academic institutions.

Changing the Institution

The university as a site of struggle linked to the broader women's movement gives legitimacy to academic feminists' political work (Hassim and Walker 1993:532).

The institutionalization of GWS has far-reaching consequences for the institutions into which it is introduced. Institutions cannot be left untouched by the subversive nature of women's/gender studies because teachers and students of these programmes are usually change agents who want to transform institutions so they may eradicate gender inequality and discrimination.[6]

Tertiary institutions, specifically universities, are no different from any other institutions where discrimination against women is embedded in the norms of the institution. In a certain sense, the University is more discriminatory in terms of gender because of its hierarchical and competitive nature and its status orientation, which is based on merit.

Gender relations *constitute* institutions so that they reproduce gendered inequities to varying degrees. Gendered preferences are embedded in the norms, structures and practices of institutions – they are not irrational choices on the part of individuals, unintended oversights in policy or deliberate policy outcomes (Goetz 1997:5). Gender Studies programmes intentionally or unintentionally challenge the legitimacy of social forms of organization that discriminate against women.

As Goetz argues, gender differentiation in institutions is the outcome of institutionalized patterns of distributing resources and social values, public and private power. Institutional rules protect and promote the interests of those for which they were designed in the first place. Goetz (1997:7) points out that once "the other" (in the case of universities women and people of colour) enter these institutions they find themselves without voice.

Institutions also shape identities and experiences through their dominant discourses. In the case of universities women are forced to internalize male norms and values. As Luke and Gore (1992:202) have argued there are few other places that show patriarchal rule better than a university – in how women are underrepresented in decision making positions on committees and senior academic positions. Melanie Walker's (1997) case study of the Executive Committee of Senate of the University of the Western Cape is a good indication of not only the visible under representation of women but also the invisible discursive practices that silence women.

Changing the Canon

The even greater challenge of Gender and Women's Studies to the academy is to the canon – through the subversive nature of feminist teaching. Questions are posed as to what is a legitimate body of knowledge to be taught and why certain knowledge, when not produced by white men, is not accepted as valid knowledge but marginalized instead. (For example, how is it possible that students can go through a three year philosophy curriculum without having been taught the work of a single woman philosopher?). This challenge goes to the heart of the academy because as Berlant (1997:157) points out, interdisciplinary knowledge, such as gender studies, undoes orthodox training and "defamiliarizes traditional objects of knowledge and norms of evidence and argument".

Berlant (1997:153) expresses the contribution of feminist scholarship as follows:

> The promise was that the counterknowledge and donated activity of feminists would create a new meritocracy, somehow without the violence of hierarchy, fear of difference, and disciplinary defensiveness that frequently serve as a bar to recognition of subaltern talents, knowledge, language, and experience.

Gender and Women's Studies want to deliver on the promise of making learning personal and socially transformative (Berlant 1997:153). Luke and Gore (1992:196) talk of the ongoing opposition to sexist, patriarchal and phallocentric knowledge systems. Feminists make the relations and conditions in which knowledge is produced visible (Luke and Gore 1992:193-194).

Berlant, as well as Luke and Gore write about the Western context, but in the African context feminist scholarship carries an even heavier burden because it has to destabilize Western feminist scholarship and link feminist interventions to the complexity and diversity of African societies, to bring about a new body of knowledge that is both African and transformative of oppressive gender relations on the continent.

Education and Transformation: The Lack of Institutional Support

On all levels education in South Africa has gone through changes aimed at redressing the past inequalities of apartheid education. Schools and tertiary institutions have become racially integrated. Curriculum changes to incorporate outcomes based education in primary and secondary schools have been introduced. Greater diversity in the classroom has brought about needs to develop each individual's intellect regardless of race, gender, age and other forms of difference as suggested in the National Commission on Higher Education's *A Framework for Transformation*. In the face of a context of transformation created by the transition to democracy, feminist academics expected to find an institutional context that would open spaces to strengthen the rather weak institutionalization of Gender and Women's Studies, where the search for gender justice would find an institutional home. Unfortunately, quite the opposite occurred as the teaching of Gender and Women's Studies became seriously undermined.

Ten years after the official end of apartheid in 1994, the higher education landscape in South Africa has changed dramatically. In the face of greater corporatization of universities on a global level, the South African Department of Education has also made policy shifts to accommodate these changes. While some changes have added benefits to the universities others have been detrimental to the contributions that Gender and Women's Studies can make to societal and institutional change.

Greater central control of higher education has increasingly eroded institutional autonomy that has effected the distribution of resources, choices about what to teach and the internal quality control thereover. As Figaji (2003) has recently pointed out

> What has been happening in South Africa over the past four years, as reflected in the series of amendments to the Higher Education Act of 1997, is a clear indication that central control of higher education institutions has increased and that institutional autonomy and academic freedom are being seriously undermined.

The trends in education to position national and regional economies for global success, prompting Figaji's remarks are succinctly summarized by Singh (2001:10):

- The requirement of higher education to demonstrate efficiency, effectiveness and value for money by integrating it in to public finance management accounting systems, external quality assurance systems etc,
- Declining investments of public funds to subsidize student fees,
- The dominance of managerial and entrepreneurial approaches to and within higher education resulting in the fact that higher education institutions are run like income-generating businesses,
- The privatization of higher education services like catering and cleaning,
- The increasing development of labour market responsive curriculum reforms intended to appeal to employers and students as "customers and clients".

Social benefits are thus viewed through the prism of responsiveness to the market.

As Singh (2001:12) argues, what is lost in the process is the facilitation of social justice through enhanced access to higher education, the role of higher education in equalising life chances, irrespective of social origin. Even more worrisome is the lack of the pursuit of knowledge in a variety of fields critical to human development broadly understood and, as she puts it, the possibility for higher education to function as a "critic conscience of society". Market driven initiatives have limited access for women, minority ethnic groups and the rural poor.[7] This clearly shows a disjuncture between efficiency and social transformation imperatives.

But academic autonomy and freedom also pertains to what can and cannot be taught. Andre du Toit (2000:111) points out that, traditionally, the insistence that only the universities themselves could determine the academic content of courses meant that academic freedom required internal accountability in terms of peer review and strict disciplinary criteria. He argues that external accountability to faceless bureaucrats is foreign to academics and truly inhibits academic freedom.

As part of the response to the market the Department of Education required the creation of interdisciplinary or multi-disciplinary programmes that could respond to demands in the market (students have to be trained for "a job"). The creation of market-driven programmes challenges the idea of the intrinsic value of education, especially in the humanities and the liberal arts in particular. Yet, at the same time, the idea of programmatization should have benefitted a Gender and Women's Studies curriculum that is interdisciplinary by nature. But because the transformation initiative was replaced by the market initiative embedded in greater globalization, a field of study that could have been the core of the study of social justice becomes marginalized.

Mama (2003) has pointed out that as universities become less accountable to the local public and more accountable to technocratic, market-driven notions of efficiency and financial diversification, the gender equality agenda becomes increasingly threatened. Where gender mainstreaming has become the logic of the National Machinery for Women the link between feminist academics and women in government becomes attenuated through the machinery. Gender interventions became the preserve of the Gender Equity Unit in the Department of Education, a structure that concerns itself with primary and secondary education.

In this scenario, gender is not integrated into policy documents, and there is no consideration of the multiple overlappping inclusions and exclusions that occur when the intersecting identities of race, class and gender are taken together. Access to higher education has been shaped by racial policies of apartheid and class position more so than by gender. Once women are in the institutions they still face power relations – African women are the most underrepresented group and all women are underrepresented in managerial positions (Hassim and Gouws 1999:98).

Conclusion

The fragmentation of the Women's National Coalition since 1994 and the resulting loss of visible gender activism has delinked GWS from its activist base, leaving recourse to women in government that has not really been supportive of GWS programmes. A new form of activism is needed to link the academy with its broader societal base. Since the imperative for the corporatization of the universities is global, it is surprising that there is no global feminist academic movement to mobilize against the market-driven forces that now encapsulate teaching programmes. Women's organizations have come together on a global level to ensure solidarity among women around issues such as violence against women and sex trafficking and greater marginalization of the poor (see e.g. Stienstra 2000). But there is no comparable global organization for academics working in GWS.

In the African context, the AGI has taken up this challenge by connecting the institute with the wider continent. The GWS list-serve where women across the continent can talk to each other and support each other's work and institutions have made a great difference to the isolation in which women work across the continent. The online journal *Feminist Africa* also contributes to give a voice to research done on the continent. Yet despite these efforts, the AGI has to fight the challenge of limited institutional support and deliberate subversion from management on a continuous basis. The global needs to be connected to the local which means that GSW programmes need to get women in government on board to put pressure on the Department of Education to force higher education institutions to support GWS programmes as forces of transformation.

The irony of the lack of institutional support was exposed when the Cape Higher Education Consortium (CHEC)[8] used GWS in the Western Cape as a model of how regional integration can be achieved. CHEC had, however, no resources to put forward for the regional initiatives while these would require a considerable use of resources.

For all GWS programmes the link with the community is paramount but GWS needs to make the connection between the local and the global through activism when global imperatives becomes the greatest threat to its survival.

Notes

1   See S. Hassim, "Nationalism Displaced: Citizenship Discourses in the Transition" in *(Un)thinking Citizenship: Feminist Debates in Contemporary South Africa.* Ashgate Publishers 2004.

2   See e.g. Funani (1992), Fouche (1993), Funani (1993), Gouws (1993), Hendricks and Lewis (1994), Hassim and Walker (1992) and Gouws (1996)

3   See Carroll (2000:141).

4   See Salo (2000:6).

5   Gender Studies have become the more acceptable title for courses or programmes dealing with women's inequality. Whereas the notion of Women's Studies is rooted in the second wave western feminism in the West with its essentializing tendencies (ignoring the difference between women), gender studies incorporate the differences between women but also between men and women and pay attention to the relationships between men and women. This is important in the African context where African men have also been disempowered by racism and colonial practices.

6   Examples of these changes are the institutionalization of gender equity officers and sexual harassment policies and grievance procedures, see e.g. Salo (2000:8-10).

7   The same arguments apply to tertiary institutions in the rest of Africa, see Zeleza (2003, 2004).

8   This consortium consists of the deputy vice-chancellors of the five higher education institutions in the Western Cape.

References

Berlant, L., 1997, 'Feminism and the Institutions of Intimacy' in E. A. Kaplan and G. Levine *The Politics of Research*, New Brunswick: Rutgers University Press.

Caroll, B., 2000, 'Reflections on "2000 Subverversions" Women's Studies and the "21st Century"', *NWSA Journal*, Vol. 13, No.1.

Du Toit, A., 2000, 'From Autonomy to Accountability: Academic Freedom under Threat in South Africa?' *Social Dynamics* Vol. 26, No. 1.

Figaji, B., 2003, 'Over-regulation and Institutional Autonomy can the Two Co-Exist?' Paper delivered at the Conference for Excellence in Tertiary Education, Somerset West 14-15 October.

Fraser, N., 1997, 'Equality, Difference and Democracy: Recent Feminist Debates in the United States' in J. Dean, ed., *Feminism and the New Democracy,* London: Sage.

Funani, L., 1992, 'Nigerian Conference Revisited', *Agenda,* Vol. 15.

Funani, L., 1993 'The Great Divide', *Agenda,* Vol. 17.

'Gender Equity in Education', 1997, Report of the Gender Equity Task Team, Department of Education, South Africa.,

Goetz, A. M., 1997, 'Introduction: Getting Institutions Right for Women in Development' in A M Goetz, ed., *Getting Institutions Right for Women in Development,* London: Zed Books.

Gouws, A., 1993, 'The Angry Divide', *Agenda,* Vol. 19.

Gouws, A., 1996, 'Feminist Epistemology and Representation: the Impact of Post-Modernism and Post-Colonialism', *Transformation,* Vol. 30.

Hassim, S. and A. Gouws, 1999, 'Gender, Citizenship and Diversity' in M Cross, N. Cloete, E. Beckham, A. Harper, J. Indiresan and C. Musil, eds., *Diversity and Unity – The Role of Higher Education in Building Democracy,* Cape Town: Maskew Miller Longman.

Hassim, S. and C. Walker, 1992, 'Women's Studies and the Women's Movement', *Transformation,* Vol. 18/19.

Hassim, S. and C. Walker, 1993, 'Women's Studies and the Women's Movement in South Africa – Defining a Relationship', *Women's Studies International Forum,* Vol. 16, No 5.

Hendricks, C. and D. Lewis, 1994, 'Voices from the Margins', *Agenda,* Vol. 20.

Luke, C. and J. Gore, eds., 1992, *Feminims and Critical Pedagogy,* New York: Routledge.

Mama, A., 1996, 'Women's Studies and Studies of Women in Africa During the 1990s' *CODESRIA* Working Paper Series 5/96.

Mama, A., 2003, 'Restore, Reform but do not Transform: The Gender Politics of Higher Education in Africa', *Journal of Higher Education in Africa,* 1:1.

Manicom, L., 2001, 'Questioning the Terms of Local Translations: Globalising "Gender" in – or as – Governance?', *Agenda,* Vol. 48.

Muller, J., 1997, 'Citizenship and Curriculum' in N. Cloete, J. Muller, M.W. Makgoba and D. Ekong, eds., *Knowledge, Identity and Curriculum Transformation in Africa,* Cape Town: Maskew Miller Longman.

Salo, E., 2000, 'Making our Voices Heard: The Politics of Writing and Publication in African Higher Education' in E. Salo and H. Moffet, eds., *Associate Publications,* AGI.

Shefer, T., 2003, 'Women and Gender Studies at the University of the Western Cape' *African Gender Institute Newsletter,* Vol. 12.

Singh, M., 2001, 'Reinserting the "Public Good" into Higher Education Transformation' in CHE Kagisano Discussion Series.

Stienstra, D., 2000, 'Making Global Connections Among Women, 1970-99' in R. Cohen and S. M. Rai, eds., *Global Social Movements*, London: Athlone Press.

Tamale, S. and J. Oloka-Onyango, 2000, '"Bitches" at the Academy: Gender and Academic Freedom in Africa' in E. Sall, ed., *Women in Academia*, Dakar: CODESRIA.

Walker, M., 1997, 'Women in the Academy: Ambiguity and Complexity in a South African University', *Gender and Education*, Vol. 9, No 3.

Zeleza, P. T., 2003, 'Academic Freedom in the Neo-Liberal Order: Governments, Globalization, Governance, and Gender', *Journal of Higher Education in Africa*, Vol 1, No 1.

Zeleza, P. T., 2004, 'Neo-Liberalism and Academic Freedom' in P.T. Zeleza and A. Olukoshi, eds., *African Universities in the Twenty-first Century*, Dakar: CODESRIA.

4

Locating Gender Studies in the Pan-African Ideal: A Reflection on Progress and Possibilities in Uganda

Josephine Ahikire

Introduction

To what extent is the African intellectual agenda taking gender analysis seriously? And conversely, to what degree has gender studies sufficiently enhanced African discourse? When the book *Engendering African Social Sciences* was published, there was enormous optimism that African feminist scholars were beginning to talk beyond their circles, and to re-centre the feminist challenge within mainstream social science in Africa. Equally important, there was hope that key African intellectual spaces like CODESRIA were beginning to take gender seriously, which in turn would legitimate gender analysis in the social sciences. It is now useful to review progress towards that goal. Where are we with respect to these aims? Who are or should be the actors involved in attaining it?

Gender studies comes into the intellectual space as a critique of dominant frameworks of knowledge that presented and reproduced the androcentric or male view of the world. As Imam argues, much of the social sciences has been and is (although still refusing to admit it) a rudimentary form of men's studies' (1997:6):

> Here I am referring to the numerous studies, misleadingly titled 'the working class in Africa' or democracy in Africa and the like. More accurately they ought to be titled' the male working class in Africa' or man and democracy in Africa. The problem is that these studies of men's relations to the state or to agriculture, etc., masquerade as encapsulating the whole society.

This chapter is about assessing gender studies initiatives and the extent to which they have transformed the African Academy. Using the case of Uganda, the paper will attempt to map out the progress and possibilities in terms of how far the field has legitimated the study of gender, especially in the social sciences. But stopping at this position would paint a one-sided picture. There is an additional matter, that will be considered, about the nature of the intellectual space, both in terms of the academic institutions and the people within them—the intellectuals and the extent to which they are receptive to gender as an organising principle in social analysis.

While gender studies has by large become a legitimate discipline, it is recognised that biases in mainstream social science still exist. It may be argued that the different disciplines within the social sciences may vary in terms of substance and degree of the gender gap, but it is noted that the Social Sciences in general are yet to take on gender as a core concern. At a minimum, a number of scholars in Uganda will add a paragraph or two, in order to be accountable to donors in cases where the latter make it a conditionality. This has bred a kind of discourse that is predicated on a few rhymes about women's suffering with little analysis. The logical consequence of this is that the field of gender has been made to sound so simplistic that it is a widely held assumption that anybody can talk and write about gender, with or without any amount of serious reflection.

The chapter addresses two major questions. I begin with the issue of nationalism and the role of culture—how does gender studies engage with what we call 'African culture'? This relates to the whole issue of the need to constantly justify the legitimacy of a gender approach to social reality (Sow 1997), particularly defending it from accusations of western imposition of anti-family values to Africa while supposedly diverting African peoples from 'struggles of fundamental importance' (Sow 1997:41). Secondly there is the challenge of the academic versus the political and the whole question of managing success.

The Feminist and the Pan-African Ideal

My understanding of the Pan-African ideal, in terms of social science, concerns the pursuit of frameworks of knowledge for adequate understanding of Africa's past and present social, political, economic and cultural realities, which understanding forms the basis for social transformation. Without question Pan Africanism is predicated on the history of exploitation, oppression, marginalisation as well as struggle of African peoples. This means that all spaces of inequality and conflict in society such as in class, race, gender, ethnicity religion, region and age, have to be addressed. Of all these social cleavages around which social science in Africa has centred, gender seems to be the most contentious in terms of legitimacy for its study and articulation. This is what, for instance, Jayawardena alludes to in arguing that the concept feminism has been the cause of much confusion in 3rd world countries, variously alleged by traditionalists, political conservatists and even certain leftists, as a product of 'decadent' Western capitalism. Feminism is purportedly based on a foreign culture of women of the local bourgeoisie; and that it alienates or diverts women from their culture, religion and family responsibilities.

In a very unique way, gender tends to engage people at their own personal self. This is why, for instance, matters of sexuality and sexual rights of African women tend to provoke a fundamental sense of challenge and/or terror even from male academics (Hutchful 1997:193). In majority of cases scientific debate ceases as soon as reflection on the question of women and gender relations in the social sciences is underway (Sow 1997:33). Both men as well as some women academics tend to limit imagination by placing their person right in the midst of the narrative. This is not a debate about neutrality and objectivity in science but rather to highlight the very unique terrain of gender where the personal is placed differently from other disciplines.

People who advance gender equality are often blamed by ardent Pan Africanists of copying western culture and thereby discarding African values as traditionally barbaric and savage. I would like to argue here, that both sides must necessarily plead guilty- of upholding and reproducing decontextualised views about Africa. Those who blame African culture for being eternally anti-women lack the sensitivity of the fact that what we call African now is largely the distortion of African culture and realities due to the colonial invasion. Those who uphold traditional African culture have committed an additional sin. They are not willing to look and go back, for that matter to those aspects of African culture that pointed towards egalitarianism. There is limited imagination (Pereira 2002). They are negating historical reality by holding to the distorted cultural practice as 'the African Culture' to be protected from external influence. I use two cases arising out of electoral politics in Uganda to raise some questions about what we understand to be African Culture.

Case 1: Election Violence in Domestic Space

During presidential elections in 1996, election violence at household level was reported in the local press. Here I present just a caption of what was reported. In one case, a man was arrested for allegedly killing his wife for celebrating president Museveni's election victory (*The New Vision* May 15, 1996). When the reporter contacted the police, the Deputy Public Relations officer was reported to have said that when they conducted investigations the neighbours said that 'quarrelling was a normal issue between the deceased and her husband'. In the another related incident, Pross Nakyanzi of Masaka District, had one of her eyes damaged and her leg broken after she was beaten by her husband Joseph Bukenya for celebrating Museveni's victory. By the time of reporting Bukenya had not been arrested. Police was investigating the case (*The New Vision,* May 15, 1996). In another case, a man allegedly arrived from upcountry where he had gone to cast his ballot in favour of Paul Ssemogerere (the vanquished) only to find his wife jubilating over the victory of her presidential candidate, Yoweri Museveni. A neighbour who preferred anonymity said that real trouble started when on asking for food and water to bathe, the husband was allegedly told by the wife that with her candidates win, their roles in the home had changed, with her becoming the man.

Case 2: Women Kneeling for Voters in Local Government Elections

Decentralisation in Uganda has ensured that people select their leaders through periodic elections. One of the gendered ways in which these contests are played out is that women candidates are required to project themselves in specific ways as special political actors – to conform to the definition of the 'ideal woman'. In the central region for example, women are required to kneel for the voters. In the 2001 local election campaigns I observed that before they addressed rallies women were are required to kneel down and greet the voters.[1] Traditionally, in Kiganda culture, women and girls are supposed to show respect to men and elders by kneeling down, whether to greet or otherwise. This social practice was extended to the public space in a very powerful way, particularly with the onset of decentralisation. Before a woman candidate addressed a gathering, she had to kneel and greet the voters in a 'respectable' manner. There was one woman candidate who however lost the vote because she allegedly overdid the ritual. According to her contestant, she knelt everywhere, on the roadside and wherever she came across men and potential voters – sometimes kneeling for small boys who were not of voting age yet.

The two cases project women as a specific political constituency whose citizenship is circumscribed by social definitions of womanhood and wifehood. Specifically, in the case of kneeling for voters, women who did this were recalling traditional respect and subservience towards men. Transferring the practice into modern politics was at the same time articulating a new subordination that puts women 'in their place'. Thus the articulation of tradition with modern forms creates a new kind of subordination and secondary status for women. The significance of this articulation has to be characterised and historicised rather than merely being labelled African culture. The issue of election violence in private space says something about the public/private dichotomy, the interconnectedness and how gender relations are thereby intertwined within it, as well as the cultural definitions of wifehood.

Many gender analyses in Africa and elsewhere would immediately and without hesitation understand the above as cases and proof of African culture and tradition and how it denigrades women. Pan-African perspectives would probably have excluded considerations about women kneeling for votes as an issue worthy of academic scrutiny. And possibly election violence would be interpreted in terms of state interference into the family. Hence while uncritical gender analysis would concentrate on the internal, projecting Africanness as essentially repressive and inferior, the Pan-African perspective would on the other extreme end, exalt and homogenise Africaness and externalise the gender dynamics at play. This is normally done by arguing that some women in pre-colonial traditional societies wielded power as in the case of some members of the royal clans and the fact that production systems at the time did not project major gender inequalities and were based on complementarity rather that exploitation and oppression of one gender. The same analyses are advanced in questions of bride price (Muhumuza 2002). What purpose should the history for instance of African pre-colonial societies serve? Should it be to delegitimate concerns about gender relations and equity or rather give them more impetus?

Furthermore, gender studies sometimes tends to be turned into a subject of ridicule and laughter. It is also subjected to scrutiny, suspicion, supervision as well as biased evaluation. At a conference convened by CODESRIA in 1995, to specifically address the question of engendering African Social Sciences, Mkandawire, then Executive Secretary, is quoted to have confessed thus:

> When I opened this conference a few days ago, I confidently, or rather foolhardily stated: "I am not convinced that there is a corpus of methodologies, approaches or empirical studies based on gender analysis waiting to be appropriated by a newly converted social sciences community. Much work needs to be done." After listening to the discussions in the last four days and reading some of the papers presented here I am convinced that my remarks were as good a case of the total triumph of ignorance over intellectual humility and open mindedness as there was ever. I would therefore like to rephrase my remarks as follows: "I am now convinced there is corpus of methodologies, approaches and empirical studies based on gender analysis waiting to be appropriated by a newly converted social science community. I do however maintain much work needs to be done" (Imam 1997:1).

Our interest in the confession by such a distinguished African scholar, is at two levels. One is that gender studies no longer has to face stiff resistance. In many universities on the continent, including Makerere, Gender studies exists either at the level of a department or subject offered within the general social sciences both at undergraduate and post-graduate level, a phenomenon that dates back to the early 1990s. In contrast to the last three decades or so where social science discourse was blind to the gender variable, there is some degree of legitimacy as a result of these initiatives. The second relates to the closing remark of the confession to the effect that 'much work needs to be done'.

Which work needs to be done? Whose responsibility is it?

It could be argued that the comment by Mkandawire, to the effect that much work needs to be done in as far as gender studies is concerned, is still based within masculinist notions of knowledge. Any field of knowledge continuously calls for work to be done, and specifically singling out gender studies is not only an attempt to marginalise the field but also a process of 'othering' it, albeit in a way that sounds positive. However, we need to acknowledge that as a relatively young discipline, Gender Studies needs to go an extra mile in terms of not only filling the gap in knowledge about relationships between men and women, but also to have a conscious struggle in terms of fundamentally restructuring processes in the production of knowledge. Here the question is: Who has the responsibility to identify and actualize this daunting task?

Many a scholar would have one straight answer to this question, assuming that the above responsibility falls squarely on those popularly referred to as gender scholars. For instance, political scientists will more often than not challenge gender studies to develop an adequate feminist theory of the state, absolving themselves of any analytical responsibility (Parpart & Staudt 1990; Hassim 1998). Is there, for instance, a possibility of challenging political science to develop an adequately gender-inclusive theory of the state—to capture all realities of society, including that of the relationships between men and women? How do we define Pan-Africanism for instance? Is it a concept that has the potential to accommodate the complexity of African realities? Or, is it a homogenising discourse that blurs internal dynamics such as of gender?

It is important to acknowledge the strides that have already been made. The argument now is not whether or not gender studies is necessary as a discipline. What confronts us today is the 'how' of gender studies. Are we satisfied with a situation where gender studies is accepted in principle and yet social science proceeds as if nothing has changed, i.e. as if the existence of gender studies does not require any rethinking of mainstream social sciences? As according to Pereira, the situation where gender studies runs parallel to the malestream of scholarship in which gender blindness is accepted as the norm, 'raises the broader question of how successfully feminist thought has permeated non-feminist 'progressive' scholarship in Africa' (2002:15).

The challenge of gender studies is that it cuts across disciplines and is hence multidisciplinary in nature. But what does this multidisciplinarity mean? Is it supposed to only refer to a new breed of scholars that may sometimes translate into jacks of all trades and masters of none? It seems to me that gender studies will, as of necessity draw strength from both multidisciplinarity and interdisciplinarity—meaning that other disciplines in the social science and humanities have to be part of the process of legitimating gender as a fundamental category of analysis. Relating this to the fundamental goal of Pan-Africanism, it would therefore mean that feminist analyses have to seek to produce knowledge that can speak to critical African realities just as mainstream scholarship should speak to these very realities with the gender category on board.

The demand on social scientists other than specific gender scholars to take on gender studies within the core of their relevant disciplines may raise a basic issue about autonomy versus integration. Kwesiga argues that the integration/autonomy debate is between separation versus ghettoisation. Referring to Women's Studies Kwesiga summarises the debate as follows:

> If Women's Studies is fully institutionalised,…it runs the risk of being isolated and therefore becoming marginalised and ineffective and not being taken seriously. On the other hand, integrationist… approach is aimed at counteracting dangers of autonomy for a relatively new and perhaps not wholly accepted discipline. In this case the fear is for Women Studies to become invisible, and easily muzzled up. There is the possibility that only a few courses or concepts will be appended to the mainstream discipline, thus losing track of the initial objective- to transform the whole discourse of knowledge and knowledge production (Kwesiga 1998:4).

There is an additional fear around integration—the danger of depoliticising gender studies. The hesitation with regard to even contemplating the idea of integration is that it can be manipulated to play down what would otherwise be a conflict-laden terrain (Ahikire 1994). There is a fear that gender studies, might be turned into a neutral discourse, where scholars adopt a non-confrontational posture to fit within the academia requirements. This is what Schmidt (1993) refers to as the political price of professional and institutional acceptability. Since gender studies is motivated by a political aim of highlighting and challenging oppression, it cannot afford to cast the net so wide as to trap even those who are not politically motivated.

The integration versus autonomy debate remains largely unresolved and Kwesiga metaphorically illustrates it with the phrase—'to be or not be' (1998:4). We would like to see the entire social science community actively engaged in this debate, because we all have the analytic responsibility to develop a sophisticated analysis of society.

The Challenge of Managing Success and the Thin line Between Gender Academics and Activism in the African Context

The Department of Women and gender studies at Makerere University is often referred to as the academic arm of the women's movement in Uganda. This raises the question of whether members of the department belong to the world of academia or activism. The matter is not as simple as it looks. The thin line between academic feminism and activism becomes more complex when we consider the lived situation of professed gender scholars. They are often invited to a multiplicity of tasks – research projects, conferences, institutional meetings, workshops and seminars. They are expected (by general consensus) to make a position on any contentious issue in the media, on new government laws and policies or other key fora concerning women. With the onset of the concept of gender mainstreaming whose logic is predicated on the fact that gender is a 'cross-cutting issue', professed gender scholars are simply overwhelmed by the demands on their person.

My interpretation of this is to, first of all, count it a success that gender is even on the agenda. It is no longer as invisible as it was two decades ago, for instance. Particularly the few female (feminist) scholars who have managed to cut through minimum formal academic qualifications are on high demand. On average, a female academic has more opportunities for exposure (both nationally and internationally) than a male academic of the same qualification (especially within the generation of young African intellectuals). Given the current situation of gender politics, such women will also be required to assume administrative and decision making positions in the University. Some level of space and acceptability for women and gender has been created and a number of women are seeing themselves in positions of Deans, Directors, Heads of departments and membership to important committees in the university—and we need them there. But there is a vacuum created at another level—of building the discipline and more importantly, the feminist challenge. This is how I bring in the notion of managing success. The high demand on the few qualified women scholars ends up working against the broader objective as they become overstretched and possibly less effective in advancing the field of gender studies in a fundamental way. In analysing the status of the department of Women and gender studies at Makerere University, Kasente notes that:

> There is so much to do and there are so few people to do it that more time is spent on getting things done rather than on allowing space for reflection, strategic planning monitoring. It is also very difficult to challenge the status quo (2002:98).

Indeed one does not have to be a woman to advance the field of gender studies, just as one observer argued that: 'You don't have to be a peasant to undertake peasant studies' (Manyire in DWGS 2002). Which means that we could envisage a situation where both women and men scholars engage with the gender dynamic. But Hutchful (1997) reminds us in relation to the gender blind landscape of history as a field that women scholars would have to take the lead in excavating what Gerda Lerner (1973) referred as the female aspect to all history, 'sometimes working under lonely (and occasionally hostile) environment' (1997:198). Here Hutchful latently underlines the element of struggle for legitimacy that the field of gender studies still faces despite the fact that it is formally accepted in the academy. This means that the cohort of feminist women scholars has to necessarily reach a critical mass in order to engage with the multi-pronged mandate of gender studies in the African Academy. The minimum of this then points to enhancing numbers of women academics which, as indicated by Kwesiga's (2002) gender analysis of higher education access in Africa, are constrained by both institutional and broader cultural factors.

The second aspect about managing success is to do with the apparent direct link between gender scholarship and transformation of gender relations. While for instance an intellectual in Political Science or Sociology can afford to be purely academic, gender scholars are more often expected to demonstrate the link with the situation of women. In gender studies, the role of the intelligentsia is quite often envisioned in quite direct terms vis a vis the change in women's lives. While it is exciting to be engaged with a field that projects direct societal utility in terms of transformation, it is equally disarming when such expectations conflate roles and positions. In Uganda, for instance, the accusation leveled on gender studies is elitism – it has not done anything to liberate the grassroot woman, the rural woman, the poor woman[2]. These are specific questions targeted at gender studies, never or rarely (with similar magnitude) to other disciplines in the Social Sciences.

In a candid self-reflexive stance as a member of the department of Women and Gender Studies at Makerere University, Kasente (2002) for instance, observes that much as the department is based at the University, it was principally initiated by the women's movement, as part of the strategy to transform women's lives, many of whom live in rural areas. To Kasente, this initial vision of generating knowledge that would be practically applied to transform gender relations has been muzzled up by the very academic and patriarchal set up of the department.

Yet on the other hand, through the latent urge of fitting into the 'mane' of the academic arm of the women's movement, there is already an emphasis within gender studies in Uganda, on policy influence through (unwittingly) projecting women as the worst sufferers situations such as of poverty, armed conflict and in pandemics such as of HIV/Aids. These approaches which Harding (1987) would otherwise refer to as victimologies hence tend to dominate gender analyses at least in the Ugandan context. The tendency view women as eternal victims could be understood in political terms since gender studies is principally driven by the motive to highlight the plight of women. Typically people only take action once the issues at stake have reached alarming levels. Phrases such as 'women constitute half of the population, perform two thirds of the world's work, receive only a tenth of the world's income and own less than 1 per cent of the world's property', are evidence of this phenomena. This is also the language that donors, policy-makers tend to understand. This logic has been further spiced up by the instrumentalist argument that unless women are considered, full development would remain a futile exercise (World Bank 1993), implying that it is only efficient to include women in the development process rather that a basic concern about justice and human rights. There is an urgent need to realise that critical analysis also holds the door for effective political practice because simplistic notions and stereotypes tend to deliver equally simplistic notions of political practice hence undermining the very ultimate goal.

These are very critical questions. To what extent can a university department take on the mandate of providing knowledge that can be *practically* applied to address complex social relations? Does this very definition set it up for failure? What is the broader implication for gender studies then? For instance, Uganda as a country fits the full picture of what Ihonvbere (1994) refers to as Africa's predicament- of poverty, war, corruption—name it. The intersection of these realities with gender has for instance brought forth a realisation about the increasing feminisation of poverty in that women tend to be the poorest of the poor in specific contexts. However, Gender studies should not only focus on influencing top-down change in terms of policy for addressing 'women's problems'. It should also build critical resources for bottom up [African] women's agency taking into account the multiple spaces of struggle—what, in the words of Mama (2002) requires 'a high level of analytic and strategic capacity' combining locally acquired experience and knowledge with international acumen (2002:7). This is not an idea about gender scholars directly 'helping' ordinary women, but rather engaging the discipline to cause transformation in wider society. And in my view, that transformation would necessarily involve the broader African intellectual agenda rather than just the professed gender scholars and institutions.

Concluding Remarks

This is a reflection on a number of issues on the state of gender studies in the African Academy, which may have relevance for situations elsewhere. The main argument made here is that although gender studies is present in the form of a department and subject, it is still on the margins of scholarship on Africa. In other words, strategic presence of the gender perspective is yet to be achieved. Such a realisation has informed initiatives such as the journal *Feminist Africa* by the African Gender Institute (University of Cape Town), which is aimed at aggregating and/or concretising the feminist challenge on the African continent. The journal aims at providing a platform for informative and provocative gender work attuned to African agendas. There is need for such and similar initiatives at local levels, with the aim of recentering intellectual politics in order to take gender seriously. As I have argued, this is a goal that may have women/feminist scholars as key actors but we need to advance a political project that bestows guilt on the entire intellectual community—what Sow (1997) understands as entrenching the gender perspective within the domain of social thought as a whole.

Notes

1 Even at a national level, one woman parliamentarian was pictured in the press 'kneeling in advance' for voters. She was supposedly telling voters that she would be going to ask for their vote during the next parliamentary election (see *New Vision*, October 3, 2000) In a related incident, the wife of a parliamentary candidate went down on her knees and asked voters to vote for her husband 'throwing the rally into frenzy'. 'I have known my husband for 14 years, he is a good man and he does not even go out with other people's wives,' reported *The Monitor*, June 19, 2001.

2 More often these views are predicated on the conflation of poverty and gender oppression, such that middle class women whether in the academia or public politics or civil society are automatically conceived as bearing the more or less philanthropic responsibility of liberating the poor rural women.

References

Ahikire, J., 1994, 'Bringing Women Back', *Quest: Philosophical Discussions*, Vol. VIII No. 2, December.

Foucault, M., 1980, *Power/Knowledge: Selected Interviews and Other Writings 1972*, C. C. Gordon, ed., New York: Pantheon Books.

Harding, S., ed., 1987, 'Introduction: Is there a Feminist Method?' *Feminism and Methodology*, Bloomington: Indiana University Press.

Hassim, S., 1998, 'Politicising the Subject: Feminist Challenges to Political Science in South Africa,' *Politikon* Vol. 25 No. 2.

Hutchful, E., 1997, 'Marxist Responses to the Challenge of gender Analysis in Africa', in A. Imam, A. Mama & F. Sow, eds., *Engendering African Social Sciences*, Dakar: CODESRIA.

Ihonvbere, J. O., 1994, 'Pan Africanism: Agenda for African Unity in the 1990s', Keynote Address, All African Student's Conference, Ontario: May 27.

Imam, A., 1997, 'Engendering African Social Sciences: an Introductory Essay' in Imam et al., *Engendering African Social Sciences*, Dakar: CODESRIA.

Jacoby, M., 2000, The Politics of Women's Studies, http://chronocle.com

Jayawardena, K., 1986, *Feminism and Nationalism in the Third World*, London: Zed Books.

Kasente, D., 2002, 'Institutionalising Gender Equality in African Universities: Women and Gender Studies at Makerere University', *Feminist Africa*, Issue 1, Cape Town: African Gender Institute.

Kwesiga, J. C., 2002, *Women's Access to Higher Education in Africa: Uganda's Experience*, Kampala: Fountain Publishers.

Kwesiga, J. C., 1998, 'Theory and Practice for Gender Equity in Africa: The Critical Future Role of the academic Arm of the Women's Movement', Paper presented as a keynote address at a conference on Gendering the Millennium, University of Dundee, Scotland, 11–13 September.

Mahbub Ul Haq, 1995, *Reflections on Human Development*, Oxford: OUP.

Mama, A., 2002, 'Gains and Challenges: Linking Theory and Practice', Key Note Address, Women's World Congress, Kampala: Makerere University, July 21–26.

Mamdani, M., 1996, *Citizen and Subject,* Kampala: Fountain Publishers.

Muhumuza, W., 2002, 'Feathering the Eagles Nest: The Interplay of Elite and Regime Interests in Uganda's Women Empowerment Process', Paper Presented at the Women's World Congress, Makerere University, Kampala, July 22–26.

Murindwa, Rutanga, 1994, 'People's Anti-Colonial Struggles in Kigezi under the Nyabingi Movement, 1910–1930', M. Mamdani & J. Oloka-Onyango, eds., *Uganda: Studies in Living Conditions, Popular Movements and Constitutionalism,* Vienna: Jep Book Series (2).

Obbo, C., 1980, *Women in Uganda: Their Struggle for Independence*, London: Zed Press Ltd.

Oloka-Onyango, J., 1998, Governance and State structures in Contemporary Uganda, Working Paper No. 50, Kampala: Centre for Basic Research.

Pereira, C., 2003, 'Between Knowing and Imagining: What Space for Feminism in Scholarship on Africa? *Feminist Africa*, Issue 1, Cape Town: African Gender Institute.

Schmidt, U.C., 1993, 'Problems of Theory and method in Feminist History' *Women's Studies in the 1990s: Doing things Differently?* D. Groot & M. Maynard, London: Macmillan Press Ltd.

Sow, F., 1997, 'The Social Sciences in Africa and Gender Analysis' in A. Imam, A. Mama & F. Sow, eds., *Engendering African Social Sciences*, Dakar: CODESRIA.

5

From Aba to Ugborodo: Gender Identity and Alternative Discourse of Social Protest Among Women in the Oil Delta of Nigeria[1]

Charles Ukeje

A man must run for his dear life any morning he wakes up and sees a fowl pursuing him, because he does not know if the fowl grew teeth overnight! – African proverb.

The oil-rich Niger Delta became a hotbed of bitter rivalries and violent armed conflicts more intensely from the outset of the 1990s. Many of these conflicts degenerated into mass-based political mobilisations, hostage taking, and the disruption of oil production activities. Usually at the instigation of multinational oil companies, successive regimes have retaliated with military subjugation, harassment, intimidation, incarceration, imprisonment, and sometimes, the extrajudicial murder of notable militant elements as was the case with the hanging of Ken Saro-Wiwa and eight other Ogoni minority rights activists in November 1995. The cycles of community protests and state repression have, in turn, triggered a vicious regime of violence and insecurity in many oil communities in the Niger Delta of Nigeria. Community grievances have mostly revolved around issues of widespread unemployment, ecological degradation, lack or absence of social amenities and infrastructures, and irresponsible and unsustainable oil field practices by virtually all oil companies despite their claims to the contrary.

A recent study[2] based on empirical data gathered from six communities reveals that the major grievances of oil communities relate to ecological degradation, especially as it affects two subsistence economic activities, farming and fishing; and the lack of employment opportunities for indigenes as oil companies are accused of showing preference for non-indigenes of Niger Delta in their recruitment policies. Others grievances include the lack of basic social infrastructure and economic development opportunities at the grassroots; non-compensation for land use and degradation, corporate insensitivity on the part of multinational oil companies, divide and rule tactics employed by oil companies in oil-producing communities, sexual harassment of local women by oil workers, as well as epidemics related to oil exploration. Thus, rather than mere expressions of blind violence, it is obvious that the wave of violent protests by oil communities are symptomatic of the 'decision of hitherto voiceless, subordinate and underprivileged minority groups to take up the gauntlet and challenge state structures and institutions controlled by majority groups who have been grossly unjust over time in the distribution of national resources' (Ojo 2002: 8).

Even more remarkable in the annals of protests and repressions in the Niger Delta were the events of the months of July and August 2002, when a wave of solo protests by women led, in quick succession, to the occupation of major oil platforms operated by a major US multinational oil company, ChevronTexaco, and a mass protest in front of the main entrance to the administrative headquarters of the Shell Petroleum Development Company (SPDC) for the western division located in Warri, Delta State. The first one by Itsekiri women of Ugborodo began on July 8 when a handful of women peacefully occupied the sprawling Escravos Tank Farm operated by ChevronTexaco for about two weeks.[3] Soon afterwards, Ijaw women from Gbaramatu and Egbema Kingdoms organised similar actions resulting in the forcible occupation of four flow stations located at Abiteye, Maraba/ Otunana, Dibi and Olero Creeks. The latter lasted eleven days, and was concluded after the executives of the company negotiated with, and signed a Memorandum of Understanding (MOU) with the protesting women. The third protest which occurred in August differed slightly from the earlier two. Although it did not involve the physical occupation of oil installations, it started too peacefully when women gathered at the entrance to the SPDC complex and started singing, and dancing to protest songs, and preventing personnel and vehicular movements by barricading the main gates. The protest later led to violence when regular policemen and their notorious anti-riot wing popularly called 'kill-and-go' were invited to disperse the women using teargas and batons, leaving several injured and hospitalised.

Unlike the first two that involved rural women from similar ethnic backgrounds, the third protest drew heavily from the ranks of urban women drawn from the three major ethnic groups prominent in Delta State- namely the Ijaws, Itsekiris, Urhobos. Lastly, unlike the first two, the third event did not result in any peaceful negotiations with, or concession to the women; rather, as noted earlier, the protesters were dislodged.

My contention is that much can be learnt from the manner with which Itsekiri and Ijaw women successfully prosecuted their non-violent protests and occupations; just as the shortcomings that blighted a similar initiative by women drawn from the three ethnic groups who, in any case, are traditionally at loggerheads must also be properly reviewed for the important, although unsuccessful lessons they suggest. The section that follows contextualises the three protests against the background of the political economy of violent conflicts in the Niger Delta region – a political economy which, for a long time, has brought the Nigerian State and international oil capital into an alliance of incestuous relationships against the host oil communities. Thereafter, the paper focuses on various aspects and dimensions of the revolts by Itsekiri, Ijaw and Urhobo women either separately or together, against the background of the rich historical and contemporary antecedents of gender-specific social actions. Such would include but are not limited to the famous Aba and Egba Women's demonstrations against colonial legislation perceived as arbitrary and regressive, especially on taxation; the series of protests by women against the venality of military dictatorship in the 1990s; as well as those by women in the Oil Delta against oil companies and/or the Nigerian State with effect from the mid-1980s.

Briefly, by 'Aba to Ugborodo', the paper draws attention to the critical interface between the historical and recent logics of almost half a century of autonomous women's project in Nigeria. As shall become obvious shortly, the grievances of the women (and the manner with which they were articulated and implemented) during these specific historical moments between Aba and Ugborodo are not contextually or significantly different. The paper shows how the recent grassroots protests by women in the Niger Delta are in many ways a throwback to two dimensions of anti-colonial struggle. The first aspect was concerned with negating the crisis of capitalist accumulation, and the second, with challenging the contradictions that allow the crisis facing the Nigerian project to fester. The final section examines the alternative futures for women against the backdrop of possible and broader pan-Niger Delta rebellion by restive oil communities.

Oil and the Template of Violent Conflicts in the Niger Delta

The discourse on the formation and transformation of gender identity within the oil communities of the Niger Delta must be presaged by an acknowledgement of the wider template on which community protests flourished. Without doubt, almost three-and-a-half decades of uninterrupted crude oil production in Nigeria has benefited only a tiny fraction of the predominantly male elites to the neglect (and often detriment) of the majority of inhabitants of oil-producing communities in the Niger Delta. This is not surprising, bearing in mind that the history (and politics) of hydrocarbon oil has also been aptly described as the history, and politics, of imperialism, *par excellence*. Nascent oil capital made its earliest inroad into the emerging Nigerian formation in the 1930s when the imperatives of securing strategic oil minerals for the Imperial Navy led to frantic geological expeditions in the vast colonial outposts of Britain. By 1938, Shell D'arcy had confirmed the presence of oil in the southern Nigeria, although no one was sure at that time of the commercial value of this discovery. The outbreak of World War II, in 1939, slowed down the drive for crude oil, but only for the short period that the war lasted. By 1958, commercial deposits of crude oil were found in Oloibiri village in present day Rivers State, and in succession afterwards in other towns and villages throughout the riverine Niger Delta. Expectedly, the circumstances of its entry into Nigeria as well as its long, incestuous romance with the colonial government ensured that Shell continued to enjoy early-bird advantages in the oil industry. In turn, this unrestrained access to, and romance with successive post-colonial governments ensured that the company (and other multinational oil companies) could conveniently secure political insurance to engage in business without question and restraint in modern Nigeria.

The widespread expectations that commercial production of crude oil would accelerate national transformation were realised, but not without far-reaching economic, political and social consequences. In the first instance, the capital-intensive oil sector replaced the labour-intensive agricultural sector that traditionally had accounted for the bulk of domestic earning and foreign exchange, and in the process disenfranchised communities, oil-producing and non-oil producing alike. This process, in concrete terms, has severely affected – and in many cases, destroyed – subsistence economic opportunities on which many communities relied for close to a century of contact with European capitalism. In the specific case of the Niger Delta oil communities, the previous reliance on fishing, farming and other related income-generating activities is under severe threat from the side effects of oil exploration and production activities. Even non-oil producing regions experienced the dire consequences of increased attention to crude oil production as it intensified their immiseration and pushed many peasants towards violent revolts. Berry (1984: 5) has given a concrete example in the context of cocoa farming in Western Nigeria when the advent of oil pushed rural farmers away from intensive agriculture without really altering the underlying strategies of mobility and accumulation. It is this contradiction, according to Berry, that heralded a trend towards peasant solidarity and militant opposition to the existing political and economic order witnessed in the Agbekoya farmer's revolts.

The political consequence of the advent of crude oil was starkly manifested in the spontaneity with which the emphasis shifted politically from the Regional (later State) Governments to the Federal Government, a situation that raised the stakes of contests for access into, and control of the political and administrative infrastructures of the centre, and turned it to a zero-sum, do-or-die affair. The first sneak preview to the 'fight-to-finish' character of power and authority triggered the unsuccessful Biafran secession which plunged the country into three years of destructive civil war. With the benefit of hindsight, it is implausible to ignore the geopolitical and military calculations of the warring factions in relations to the control of the fabled oil deposits in the Niger Delta. Since then, the unspoken mind sets among political entrepreneurs across the federating ethnic units has been that whoever controls the oil-rich Niger Delta controls the proverbial honey pot. In the final analysis, rather than create a basis for balanced growth and development, oil has blurred the cognitive vision of the national elite to come to terms with the profundity of the crises facing the nation-state project in Nigeria. This development is a major tragedy given the manner in which clientilism bankrupts the country and shortchanges the ability to guarantee stability outside the framework of official repression (Ukeje et. al. 2002b).

To expand and effectively secure oil-based accumulation, successive governments have employed a repertoire of militaristic options: intimidation, incarceration, repression, and extra-judicial killings in order to quell uprisings and disturbances among oil communities. The interminable list of state sponsorship of repression against protesting oil communities began in 1990 against Umuechem villagers when the SPDC invited soldiers and anti-riot policemen to intervene. In the wake of this curious invitation, troops behaved much like occupation armies sworn to drawing 'the last drop of the enemy's blood'. They committed acts of arson, looted and damaged property, injured, raped women and young girls, and murdered harmless inhabitants, including children and old people. Although it is not the worst affected, the brutality inflicted on the Ogoni community under the Abacha regime has become another sad milestone signifying the extent that Nigerian State is willing and able to go in order to impose such a tenuous form of order and stability necessary for the undisrupted extraction of crude oil (Osaghae 1995). Indeed, as recently as 1999, the Washington-based Human Rights Watch (HRW) blamed oil companies for their pretentious claims of not being privy to, or in a position to avert, what was happening around them. After all, they are the direct beneficiaries of such crude attempts to suppress militant actions in their areas of operation.

It is important to summarise two important strands in the mobilisation of oil communities that intensified in the 1990s (Ukeje 2001; 2002a). One is the mounting awareness among the oil communities that their struggles cannot be isolated from the larger global discourse similar to those embarked upon by indigenous and minority ethnic populations against the intrusive impacts of international capital and globalisation. This consciousness, it is important to note, has provided the justification for popular violent protests aimed at redressing prevailing socio-economic, environmental and political injustices. The second strand derives from the fact that communities are moving away from previously isolated, informal and reactive forms of social protest to more structured, formalised and institutionalised interventions, exemplified by the proliferation of self-help movements and organisations throughout the Delta. There is no doubt, for instance, that Itsekiri and Ijaw women who recently embarked on protests benefited from these local, national and global resources, experiences, knowledge, consciousness and information about other experiences elsewhere. Turner (2001)[4] has demonstrated the utility of such civil society-based transnational alliances and networking, and how such can be of immerse benefits to oil communities confronting giant multinationals by pointing to a recent encounter between the Ogbodo community and Shell over a pipeline explosion that resulted in 18-day long oil spillage. According to Turner, Shell's 'extremely inadequate response left the community with almost no drinking water, and nothing for cooking food, washing dishes, clothes or their bodies'. By the time the company offered compensation of 100, 000 US Dollars to pacify the 150,000 strong community, the chiefs' counter claim was to ask Shell for copies of the full agreements with the last five communities into which Shell had spilled crude oil which are located in Western Europe and North America. The Ogbodo chiefs intended to seek comparable long-term reparations.

One of the strongest accounts of the genealogy of contemporary conflicts in the Niger Delta blamed the dialectics of globalisation and local resistance: the profit motive versus the survival of the people, as principally responsible for the contradictions of underdevelopment and conflicts in the Niger Delta (Obi 1997, 2001). The truth, undoubtedly, is what persistently irks oil communities is the reluctance by oil companies to openly accept culpability and responsibility for environmental degradation, and to take responsibility for alleviating the plight of the host communities. The companies often claim that they are not in the business of *Santa Claus* or of interfering with the principal duties, responsibilities, and constituencies of government. They ignore the fact that their corporate activities and inactions, if nothing else, compromise the well-being of host communities; and that only by engaging in socially responsible corporate behaviour can they enjoy cordial community relations necessary for rewarding business. This noncommittal corporate attitude is shared by most of the multinational oil companies operating in the Niger Delta as exemplified by the insistence in 1993 by the SPDC that

> The most important contribution that the company can make to the social and material progress of Nigeria is performing efficiently its direct line of business. It is neither feasible nor proper for the company to preempt the responsibilities of the federal or state governments in providing and maintaining social amenities and services (Cited in Ojo 2002: 39).

It is precisely this attitude of corporate aloofness and insensitivity on the part of oil companies that has intensified social frustration, anomie and violent conflict in host oil communities across the Niger Delta of Nigeria.

Gender Identity and the Discourse of Social Protest by Women in the Niger Delta

Two critical and interrelated facets have been poorly articulated, or sometimes, outright omitted in existing discourses on the response of communities to the crisis within the oil region of the Niger Delta. The first is how such conflicts affect women, while the second relates to the specific ways and manners in which women themselves struggle for an improved environment to carry out their productive (and reproductive) activities. In the later instance, conventional wisdom has significantly undervalued women's contributions by pursuing two sets of interrelated, but misleading assumptions. The first suggests that women are patently non-political citizens, assuming that their preoccupation is primarily with domestic, household issues, or the 'politics of the belly'. From this perspective, it is claimed on behalf of women that the terrains of local and national politics are too turbulent for women to participate effectively, even though that is the same site where authoritative value, wealth and power are negotiated and distributed. Such notions of inaccessibility are misinformed, giving the reality of the blurring dichotomy between private and public spaces. A deeper structural explanation for this pervasive assumption must be located within the dominant regime of patriarchy manifested in the superstructures of social, economic, institutional and traditional taboos, myths, and stereotypes constructed to blunt popular consciousness and awareness among women. Fall-outs become obvious in terms of the legion of visible and invisible barriers that are erected to frustrate and prevent women from autonomous political expression and association outside of the framework and structures constructed and imposed by men. In any case, processes of socialisation and differentiation from childhood through adulthood have served to entrench and perpetuate intricate networks of subservience and subordination. Consoling, of course, is that significant incremental advances are now ensuring that those boundaries and barriers are collapsing or losing their social utility and relevance. But there is still considerable scope for improvement. It is instructively obvious also, that in the broad sense such assumptions serve to engage womanhood in the template of victim-hood rather than that of a distinct gender group with autonomous agencies for negotiating social processes and other priorities (Ibeanu 2001).

Historically, the Niger Delta (in fact, southern Nigeria in general) was one of the nine major sites of African resistance to colonial rule. The most significant of the strategies adopted in those early times included crop hold-ups, tax evasions and boycotts, industrial actions, worker demonstrations, establishment of independent African churches as well as cultural/ welfare organisations, deliberately breaking the monopoly of European businesses, sporadic revolts and protests, and sustained armed struggles. (Ekwe-Ekwe 2001). Even though autonomous politically significant social protests by women were rare and far apart during those times, they certainly existed. One example was the Aba riots or women's war of 1929 precipitated by the anticipated taxation of women integral to the implementation of the Indirect Rule project of British colonialism in Nigeria (Afigbo 1966; JAH 1930: 542–43). The impracticality of the Native Revenue Ordinance (NRO) that mandated the imposition of taxation was such that it was preceded by a detailed assessment of people's wealth for the purpose of taxation, as well as a census of population, livestock, as well as economic trees. For a long time, however, the incorrect assumption was that taxation alone triggered the wave of women's protests that began from Aba. A closer investigation reveals that beyond taxation were a litany of other complaints, such as discontent with persecution, extortion, corruption and practices of Native Court members, the autocracy and high-handedness of appointed Warrant Chiefs, illegal and oppressive sanitary fines, continuance and enforcement of unpaid labour on civil construction, unfair or excessive imprisonment, and the abysmal low prices of farm produces (especially palm oil and palm kernel) as well as exorbitant prices on imported goods (especially tobacco and spirits) – both of which threatened or eroded the purchasing power of most families (Afigbo 1972; Arifalo 2001). It is interesting that a year earlier, in 1928, men in different parts of southeastern Nigeria had, without raising a finger, grudgingly succumbed to what was widely accepted as too repressive a taxation regime. In the final analysis, the women's protest became a rude awakening that not only jolted colonial administrators but also forced a reevaluation of this controversial piece of legislation.

The respected historian, Obaro Ikime, has rightly pointed out that the Aba protests were even more significant and complex than has often been portrayed in history textbooks, especially as the upheavals were 'protests against the sum total of grievances associated with contemporary British administrative practices and the allied inroads of western civilization' (Ikime 1980:444). The demonstrations began on 18 November 1929, and lasted almost three months until January the following year. Within a short period they spread to several areas: four divisions in the Province of Owerri, two out of the three divisions in Calabar Province, and to Afikpo division in Ogoja Province. A closer look at the spread of the protests reveals the less obvious reality that the demonstrations occurred most intensely along important trade and market routes dominated, if not altogether controlled, by itinerant women traders. As rightly pointed out by Ajayi and Espie (1965: 203, 394), this prevalence of markets and long distance trading encouraged interaction among women from different backgrounds outside of the prying eyes of and control by men. This is particularly interesting when it is borne in mind that in most traditional African societies, markets are important beyond serving as sites for buying and selling. They also serve as focal points for frequent social, political and cultural contacts, as most social engagements and arrangements are organised around market days.

Another celebrated case of a women's revolt occurred between 1941-1947 during which Egba matriarchs staged a drawn-out project of civil disobedience, demonstration and insurrection against colonial exploitation, taxation, market closures and commodity hold-ups. This culminated, ultimately, in the kidnapping of colonial officials and their local agents, as well as the dethronement of the traditional ruler, the Alake. The protests that broke out and spread widely caught the colonial administration in the southeast and southwest of Nigeria (and also the men) unawares, demonstrating that with determination women could embark on autonomous social actions outside the framework determined by their male counterparts.

What we know about the motives behind the revolt by the women is still very sketchy. In many fascinating respects, however, the protests cannot be ignored as they have become remarkable milestones in the long struggles by oil communities in the Niger Delta for access to subsidised socio-economic opportunities, environmental justice, political equality[5] as well as respect for democratic, human and minority rights. What is certain, based on my own internal knowledge of the Niger Delta as a result of intensive fieldwork, media accounts, and interviews with some of the women's leaders, is that all three occurred without the knowledge of male opinion-makers and traditional leaders as the women claimed to have declined taking them into confidence for fear of sabotage.[6] Another leader claimed that the women 'decided to take the driver's seat to make the Federal Government and the oil companies more sensitive to the yearnings and aspirations of our people'. The women also argued that in the past

> Our youths used to do this for us but the government and the oil companies would label them terrorists, mobilise soldiers to trail and kill them. But this time around, harmless women are in charge; let us hear their next story. Maybe, they would say we are armed invaders. We would send our children to school, when they complete their studies, they cannot get work, yet outsiders come here and they get jobs with relative ease. We are suffering... [7]

Overall, the protests and peaceful occupation of oil installations point unmistakably to autonomous, gender-specific action as against the conventional community (or youth) protests so prevalent in the oil Delta. Indeed, as one of the leaders of the Ijaw protesters, Madam Wariya, claimed, the women decided not to inform anyone, not even their leaders for fear of 'sabotage'. In addition to the markedly solo efforts of the women, their protests were marked by the non-violent but resolute manner in which they were conducted. Indeed, apart from symbolically carrying household utensils such as cooking pots, plates, pestles, frying pans, long spoons, and chanting protest songs, their only other 'weapon' seemed to be the moral undertone of their defiance. As one of the women's leader bluntly claimed: 'the Federal Government and the oil companies… like to oppress us. Since we are already suffering, we did not mind if we died on the flow stations'.[8]

The Itsekiri women of Ugborodo demanded, among other things, employment opportunities for their husbands and children, provision of basic social amenities such as drinking water, electricity, health care and education facilities, compensations for environmentally irresponsible oil-field practices, and assistance towards creating small-scale income-generating enterprises for women. Apart from making the usual demands, their Ijaw counterparts also insisted on the payment of N500 million compensation in return for long years of neglect of their communities, the construction of two ultra-modern palaces for the Gbaramatu and Egbema Kingdoms, the construction of foreshore walls and housing projects in about nine host communities to improve the environmental and living conditions of the people, land reclamation, and electrification.[9] The protesters also reportedly demanded the renaming of two of the facilities, Abiteye and Otunana flow stations, to reflect their Ijaw origin.[10] Some of these demands dovetail neatly with the 18-point demands adopted by a consultative meeting of Niger Delta women held in far-away Banjul, the capital of The Gambia, from 7-12 August 2000, to review the situation in the Delta, especially as it affected women.[11] According to the meeting, government and oil companies must commit themselves to legal and peaceful means in addressing the myriad plights of oil communities and women; abrogate all laws inimical to the development of the Niger Delta; put in place a comprehensive blueprint for genuine development in the region; end the militarisation of the Niger Delta; compensate victims of past military occupation and repression; compensate victims of oil spillages and fire disasters; and introduce micro-credit schemes for the development of small-scale enterprises for women.

The defiance of the women protesters forced the company to invoke a *force majeure* clause in its contracts with exporters on Sunday, 21 July. In monetary terms such disruptions must have caused the NNPC/ChevronTexaco Joint Venture partnership heavy losses, but it also served to accelerate the search for prompt and peaceful negotiations and resolution.[12] As negotiations commenced with the management of ChevronTexaco at Abiteye flow station, the Ijaw women protesters vehemently refused to vacate the oil platforms until each of the 10 communities were paid 2 million Naira (about 11, 000 U.S. Dollars) 'as compensation for the women who abandoned their various trades to occupy the flow stations'. The protesters also reportedly asked for a N20 million micro-credit loans scheme for each of the ten communities to enable the women to embark on small and medium scale enterprises after the siege, to be administered by a non-governmental organisation conversant with the operation of such an economic empowerment scheme. They also demanded more permanent jobs for indigenes.[13]

The demands of the women were no doubt 'bread-and-butter' in nature. Ordinarily such grievances are only known to eventually translate into public protest when they are mediated by what Kurzman (1996: 154) referred to as 'cognitive liberation'- that is, when an oppressed people break out of the pessimistic and quiescent patterns of thought and begin to do something about 'their situation'. In another sense, there is wisdom in the opinion that whereas social conflicts may be triggered by the denial of tangible resources, they are complicated by structurally embedded questions of identity. Indeed, as Fischer (1990: 95) pointed out, the centrality of identity is fundamental to the etiology of conflicts; especially in so far that it 'influences a great deal of social interaction at the group, intergroup and international levels'. This explains why the management and resolution of violent social conflicts tend at times to become intractable for the simple reason that fundamental identity questions often prove difficult to address. Rothchild reached a similar conclusion when he observed that social interest groups make two types of demands: negotiable demands, which tend to be 'elastic and modest in resource cost and to be accepting of the legitimacy of the political order in which they are asserted'; and non-negotiable demands, which concern their 'cultural identity status, participation, political and physical survival or other intangibles...' (Rothchild 1997: 209-213). In his opinion, 'when issues of identity and participation, or of basic personal privilege are at stake, and when the actions of one group infringe on the privacy or identity of others', the demands may be transformed into non-negotiable claims on the part of both state and state-linked civil associations. (See Rothchild, in Zartman 1997: 197-241).

What seemed like a sudden implosion of gender identity among women in the Niger Delta falls within the above genre. Perhaps, then, there is wisdom in the recent opinion expressed by Sideris (2001) in a different context that social conflicts and repression shape the identities of man and woman in significantly different ways that are not captured in the discourse on social conflicts. 'Identity' here is conceived in terms of 'contingency, agency and fluidity' – each of which questions the received wisdom about the role of women in social protest and violence. Like other identities, gender identities are socially constructed and influenced by opportunities and constraints that invariably are mediated by 'material conditions, local discourses and ideologies'. Such specific identities are also constructed from the way social forces relate with women, revealing not only that being a woman does not equate to non-belligerence but also that women are affected by violent conflicts in ways significantly different from their male counterparts. As we have been reminded, those who claim that mothering is a requirement for political naivety ignore also that it can also be a fundamental source of resilience that can galvanise social action with far reaching political implications. (Sideris 2001: 50). What comes out strongly from this theoretical exposition is the need to come to terms with and understand how women internalise, interpret and respond to the contradictions of oil-based accumulation, as well as their predisposition towards self-reliant efforts aimed at resisting subordination, exploitation, and marginalisation of the kinds so prevalent in the oil region of Nigeria.

What is then presented in the form of spontaneous (or sporadic) identity mobilisation by Niger Delta women can best be understood in the context of a prolonged disillusionment with the dominant male identity that has become inefficient, defective, maligned, compromised and unreliable in drawing attention to and seeking a reversal to the misfortunes of the oil communities. The question that should then be asked more forcefully is: in what ways have the contradictions and conflicts arising from oil production created, altered, and transformed the identity of women as distinct from those of men (and the larger community) in the oil region of Nigeria?

There is nothing novel about the occupation of oil installations by the women, as such options have become somewhat of a metaphor for the expression of grievances and powerlessness on the part of aggrieved oil communities. Perhaps much more than men, oil exploration activities have been shown to have adverse effects on women in the Niger Delta. This is not only so because they are socially more sedentary, or because they are constrained by labour-related migrations, but more importantly due to the fact that their involvement in fishing and farming forms a significant proportion of household income in those communities. Drawing on the experiences of women across the six research locations, a recent report 'Oil and Violence in the Niger Delta'[14] identified some real challenges facing women as a result of the negative impact of oil production. According to the report, the expansion and intensification of oil-related activities have significantly diminished women's access to pollution-free farmlands and fishing waters. With access to gainful socio-economic opportunities and activities often blocked, many women reportedly take up informal prostitution as a strategy for livelihood or survival (i.e. engaging in casual sex with oil workers who are ready to part with some of their high salaries). This may not be unconnected with the alarming rates of sexual promiscuity, girl-child pregnancies and single parenting, and sexually transmitted diseases among young women.

At the surface, of course, are bread-and-butter issues such as the lack of employment opportunities for their husbands and children, inaccessibility to small-scale income generating activities, basic health care facilities, educational institutions, and many others of socio-economic, environmental and political natures and/or ramifications. For instance, there is neither electricity nor portable drinking water in Ode-Ugborodo and six others where ChevronTexaco has been in operation for about thirty years. The only one of the Ugborodo communities with electricity is Ogidigben, and that is because the offices of the oil company are located there.[15] The women are frustrated by what they perceive as the reckless exploitation and criminal neglect of their communities by government and oil companies whom so far have merely paid lip-service to investing heavily in human and infrastructural developments aimed at alleviating the plight of oil communities.

Underneath these obvious grievances, however, are others that are subtly related but of deeper, far-reaching meaning. These are the notions of boundary and identity - two equally potent sources of violent conflicts in many developing societies. One fascinating but often ignored lesson from the Ugborodo women's revolt is instructive as it sufficiently demonstrates the centrality of these notions in the articulation of protest and conflicts. For the local women protesters, the multi-million dollars Escravos terminal represents the worst facet of capitalist exploitation among inhabitants of a weak social formation lacking the resources and wherewithal to negotiate favourable terms of engagement with international capital. This representation has a historical antecedent: the site of the oil terminal itself used to be the final 'loading' point for slaves destined for the Americas. Indeed, the name 'Escravos' has no parallel in the socio-linguistic and cultural frameworks of the local inhabitants for it means a slave depot or market in Portuguese. This point must be borne in mind as the local women who carried out the protest and siege on the terminal hardly mentioned 'Escravos', but preferred 'Ugborodo'- their community's ancestral Benin name. Of course, if Escravos represented the worst of slave capitalism in the early colonial epoch, it evokes even worse psychologically depressing meanings today as an infrastructure of exploitation, marginalisation and exclusion occasioned by the incestuous alliance between oil multinationals and the Nigerian State.[16]

It is important to recall that the architecture that sustained the rapacious extraction capabilities of international capital in Nigeria transformed at critical historical junctures through concrete changes in global regimes of production and consumption. In the case of the Niger Delta, the transitions in production relations occurred along three successive historical trajectories demarcated by the eras of slavery, oil palm and crude oil productions. This periodisation must also be qualified by recalling emphatically that nothing changed in the appetite for crass accumulation, sometimes through brute force, by national and foreign business elites in their quest for self-aggrandizement, class reproduction and survival. What the literature tends to overlook, again, is that very little substantive changes occurred in the nature, character, and behaviour of local forces; either in terms of mobilising social identities or in using such identities to challenge, negate or disengage from the contradictions of accumulation. We only need to place the legion of complaints against the monopolistic Royal Niger Company (RNC) by Nembe Brass people of Akassa prior to the attack on the company's factory almost a century ago, in 1895, side by side with those presently pursued by oil communities against multinational oil to appreciate the powerful elements of continuity in the dimensions and characteristics of communities's revolts against international capital in the present-day Delta region. (Jones 1963; Alagoa 1964).

The Nembe Brass people had persistently and bitterly complained against the closure and control of the lucrative oil market in the hinterland. It was a situation that triggered economic hardship for the coastal middlemen. Several entreaties and emissaries were made to the company as well as to the colonial administration, including to Consul MacDonald when he returned to establish the government of the Niger Coast Protectorate in 1891. Unfortunately, all these fell on deaf ears until an attack on the RNC depot on January 29, 1895. Three factors finally impelled and provoked Nembe chiefs to war. In the first instance, the RNC embarked on series of unprovoked (but provocative) attacks on Nembe people of Akassa whether they were carrying trade goods or merely foodstuff. In the process, people were killed and wounded, while the abandoned canoes and their contents were confiscated. Second, the RNC also warned other Ijaw communities not to pay any debts owed to Nembe men. Lastly, there was evidence that certain company servants taunted the people and treated them brutally, telling them that they would be forced to eat dust. Alagoa also reported an allegation against a Captain Christian, who ordered a woman to be stripped naked and covered with tar. (Alagoa 1964: 94). In the face of these provocations, the Brass people never hid their disdain for the RNC, openly swearing they would rather die that 'eat dust' as personnel of the company had openly taunted. In many ways, the situation at that time bore close similarities to events in the contemporary Niger Delta. Even to suggest that contemporary rebellions lack historical roots reveals an erroneous comprehension of history, especially of societies characterised by 'severely limited opportunities for indigenous participation in political, economic and cultural affairs'.

This is so in much of post-colonial Africa, making public spaces to transform into sites of marginalisation, exclusion, and plural violence (Mbembe 2001). In the prevailing post Cold War global order, as Ake argued, the intrusive impacts of globalisation have created a phenomenal orientational upheaval, anxiety and identity crisis. Rather than help secure the continent, therefore, such phenomena have intensified insecurity within the continent. (Ake 1995: 19-42). The seminal works of writers such as Scott, and Wolf awakens us to the reality that a peasant population like those in the Niger Delta can no longer be viewed as an 'object of history' (Skocpol 1982: 351-375). Whereas Scott linked peasant revolutions to the cultural and social-organisational autonomy of peasants to resist the intrusive impacts of hegemony ruling elite, Wolf noted that ultimately, the decisive factor in making a peasant rebellion possible lies in the relationship of the peasantry to the field of power which surrounds it. Accordingly, a peasant rebellion is most unlikely to start from 'a situation of complete impotence'. Arendt also reminded us in a broader theoretical context, that 'violence appears as an alternate to institutionalized political influence - the voice of the voiceless, the ulti-mate, and often effective insistence of the deprived in being taken into account' (Mitchell 1996: 156-7).

There are no doubts that past levels of protest increase current protest activi-ties, just as there are established links between official repression and escalation of community protests. It is here that the value of culture defined as lived traditions binding people as a result of shared memories of the past and collective destiny for the future becomes an essential instrument for politicised identity mobilisation in general, and the salience of the protests by women in the Niger Delta, in particular. After all, 'a culture includes the "map of meaning", which makes things intelligible to its members' (Kofman and Williams 1989: 1-23). Galtung developed this linkage between culture and violence further in his thesis on 'cultural violence' defined as 'those aspects of culture, the symbolic sphere of our existence…that can be used to justify or legitimize direct and structural violence' (p. 39). The exploitation of basic needs, according to him, is the root source of the prevalent and archetypal violent structure through which consciousness formation and mobilisation are impeded. Exploitation comes in four different patterns: penetration, that is, im-planting a top dog over the underdog; segmentation, that is, giving the underdog only a partial view of what obtains; marginalization, keeping the underdog outside; and finally, fragmentation, that is, keeping the underdogs away from each other (1999: 42). Earlier, Galtung captured the conditions of structural violence in which the poor are denied decent and dignified lives because their basic physical and mental capacities are constrained by hunger, poverty, inequality, and exclusion. (Galtung 1969; Uvin 2000). Incidentally, these aspects of exploitation are so deep and widespread even as they transform the gender domains of women in Nigeria's oil region.

As the protests that greeted the colonial policies of taxation as well as those against international mercantile capitalism have shown, a history of women's resistance to perceived injustices in not new. There are smaller, isolated revolts by Niger Delta women that are, cumulatively, important, but will not detain us here. Two major uprisings solely by women that occurred in the 1980s are however pertinent. First, there was the 1984 Ogharefe women's uprising which took place in the Ethiope local government council. Second was one embarked upon by Ekpan women in the Okpe council area in 1986. Both communities are predomi-nantly from Urhobo ethnic groups, but their protests against a US oil corpora-tion, Pan-Ocean, were impelled by separate circumstances in two different con-texts related to the fact that oil-based capitalism 'not only breaks up women's social order but also created or strengthened the conditions for resistance' (Turner and Oshare 1994: 123-60). Yet, according to them, the 1984 uprising succeeded largely because, arising out of their frustration with their financial compensation for pollution and alienation from farmland, the women were able to mobilise *en-*

masse at the corporation's production site, and in a rare display of collective nudity as a weapon of protest 'threw off their clothes and with this curse won their demands' (Ibid., p.123). The second uprising reportedly failed because it was embroiled with wider class and ethnicity-mediated concerns and interests. According to the same authors, the template for both initiatives by women was made possible by existing gender solidarity, consciousness and identity. The analysis of the women's uprisings, in summary, yields three salient facts. First is that they were clashes resulting from class formation spurred by oil-based capitalist development. Second is that the gender character of the uprisings followed from changes in gender relations that took place in the process of oil-based capitalist development. Last is that the degree of success enjoyed by women in their struggles reflects both the extent to which peasant relations persisted or were eroded by proletarianisation, and the degree to which men acted in solidarity with women. Influenced by Boserup's (1970: 126) insightful theoretical construct on how the expansion of capitalism disempowered women in peripheral social formations, Turner and Oshare, argued that

> …in Nigeria not only did capitalism break up women's social order but it also created or strengthened the conditions for resistance. The uprisings are products of capitalist development just as much as is women's marginalisation.

The late 1980s and 1990s witnessed even more gender-based protests by women across many oil communities in the Delta region, especially against the background of a biting socio-economic crisis (Elson 1989; Ihonvbere 1993; Obi 1997). It is instructive to recall the critical roles played by Ogoni women and groups in the course of the struggles embarked upon by their community during much of the first half of the 1990s. In 1995, women seized the Odidi oil well owned by Shell in protest against the destruction of economic crops as a result of an oil spill over 10 days. In September 1998, a large assemblage of Egi women marched on the Obite gas plant, the largest in West Africa, owned by the French multinational oil company, ELF. As the women approached the site, a detachment of anti-riot mobile police barricaded the entrance to the company ensuring that all the women could do was to sing and dance as a means of making their message heard. In the end, their demand for the relocation of one particular senior security personnel of the company was heeded.

Conclusion

Despite the restoration of civilian rule after a long and tiring period of autocratic military rule, the widespread crisis of authority arising from people's loss of faith in the prevailing order has not changed positively in any fundamental way. Recently, Human Rights Watch warned that the end of military rule in Nigeria has brought little benefit to the people living in the oil producing communities of the

Niger Delta. In fact, the level of discontent among the inhabitants remains very high, leading to frequent protests against oil companies and government (HRW 2002). Rather than lessening, violent protests and conflict have intensified in various parts of the country since the inauguration of the Fourth Republic under the Olusegun Obasanjo Presidency.

Beginning from May 29, 1999 when the inauguration ceremonies were in full swing in the Federal Capital Territory, Abuja, various ethnic factions in Warri were up in arms against one another- as usual, over the question of ownership of the oil-rich city. In another case, the administration demonstrated how it planned to react to the surge of violent conflicts in the Oil Delta when it ordered troops to raze the village of Odi, close to Yenogoa, the capital of Bayelsa State, as a reprisal for the killing of seven soldiers by bandits terrorizing the village and its neighbours (Ukeje 2001a). Such insensitivities and lack of concrete policy responses on the part of government confirm the view that acts of protest tend to escalate into violent conflicts because official responses are more likely to be diversionary and repressive than reformist (Gurr 1995: 215).

Despite the bleak prospects for peace and stability in the Niger Delta, it is impossible to resist the temptation that more than any other time in Nigeria's post-independence history, the present civilian administration of President Obasanjo has a good chance of alleviating the myriad plights of the inhabitants of oil communities. But that will require demonstrating sincere and genuine political will beyond the usual rhetoric. The new government would seem to have taken one step in the right direction when it acknowledge in a *Note Verbale* reference 127/2000 to the 28th session of the African Commission on Human and Peoples Rights held in Cotonou, Benin, that gross violations of human rights were committed by past regimes and that atrocities are still being committed in the Niger Delta.[17] There is no question that the government must translate such an acknowledgement into concrete restitutions to oil communities who continue to suffer the debilitating effects of crude oil exploitation and state repression. Unfortunately, there is a serious shortfall in terms of translating public rhetoric into concrete blueprints for development as witnessed, for instance, by the way government authorised military reprisals against the entire Odi village near Yenogoa in Ijaw-dominated Bayelsa State, for the criminal murder of some policemen by bandits. Also, there are genuine complaints that the much-taunted institutional framework for the integrated development of the oil basin, the Niger Delta Development Commission (NDDC), may suffer the same fate as its predecessors – the Niger Delta Development Board (NDDB) and the Oil Minerals Producing and Development Commission (OMPADEC). It would seem that this new creation is another 'jobs for the boys' as there are complaints that the NDDC can only further institutionalise the culture of patronage and clientilism with little, if anything, to show for the huge sums of money allocated to it.

By way of conclusion, there is a growing undercurrent of opinion that women may be able to forge a pan-Niger Delta alliance across the six oil-producing states in Nigeria, an expectation that has so far failed to materialise among the various ethnic and sub-ethnic groups in that region.[18] Already, the Lagos-based *Vanguard* newspaper recently reported ongoing consultations among various women leaders in oil communities across the Delta to stage a week-long co-coordinated protest on all oil installations in the six major oil producing states. The main objective of this pan-Niger Delta alliance, according to the paper, will be to paralyse oil exploration activities in the Niger Delta and by so doing, force government and oil companies to act promptly and decisively to alleviate the plight of oil communities. While on the surface this is appealing, it is unlikely to come to fruition in the near future based on past attempts and the deep ethnic fault-lines that existing among the various social and ethnic groups in the region.[19] Many doubts have been raised regarding the staying power of new social movements of the nature that are emerging in the oil region. Beyond this is the question mark on the long term utility, durability and effectiveness of women's socio-political interventions beyond the moral and symbolic notions they articulate. This question arises out of the widespread scepticism that women's interventions are too temporary and eventually lose steam as they reveal their powerlessness in the face of real challenges and reprisals (Amin 1993: 87). This note of caution does not diminish taking wise counsel from the idiom of the man and the pursuing fowl.

Notes

1. An earlier version of this paper was presented at the fourth plenary session of the 10th CODESRIA General Assembly held in Kampala, Uganda, from 8–12 December 2002. I wish to thank Drs. Amina Mama, Charmaine Pereira, Joy Ezeilo, for their comments, and Professor Adetanwa Odebiyi of the Department of Sociology, Obafemi Awolowo University, Ile-Ife, Nigeria, for reacting to earlier drafts.

2. Two oil communities each were selected from three oil-producing States – Akwa Ibom, Bayelsa and Delta. Cf. Charles Ukeje, Adetanwa Odebiyi, Amadu Sesay and Olabisi Aina, 'Oil and Violent Conflicts in the Niger Delta', CEDCOMS Monograph Series No. 1, 2002.

3. The enormity of the logistic troubles that the women went through to carry out the operation can only be appreciated when it is realised that the Escravos facility is entirely located on an island surrounded by creeks, swamps, and the Atlantic Ocean to the south. Indeed, employees of ChevronTexaco posted to the site arrive and leave by helicopter or fast boats.

4. Teresa Turner, 'The Land is Dead: Women's Rights as Human Rights: The case of the Ogbodo Shell Petroleum Spill in Rivers State, Nigeria', June–July 2001.

5. The issue of political domination and exclusion of women, even at the grassroots, traditional level, was alluded to by a woman respondent from Elebele, Bayelsa State, in the report published by the Centre for Development and Conflict Man-

agement Studies, CEDCOMS. According to the respondent, 'Our society does not give any role to women. Women are mostly to care for children at home, and cannot be present where men hold meetings or take political decisions. A woman here, whatever her age is treated as a minor. Even a mother cannot talk where her own son is part of, or presiding over a meeting'. (p. 25).

6. 'Ijaw Vs Chevron: Women to the Rescue', *ThisDay*, August 2, 2002.

7. 'Resource Control: Tension as Niger Delta Women Plan Another Mass Protest', *Vanguard*, August 3, 2002.

8. Statement credited to the traditional Prime Minister of the Gbaramatu Kingdom, Chief Wellington Okrika.

9. To forestall a hostage situation, ChevronTexaco preemptively evacuated personnel from Ewan Production platform, located eight kilometers offshore Ondo State, following invasion by Ilajes in the area. The company claimed that the protesters were not from their areas of production. See 'Chevron Evacuates Staff From Oil Field Besieged By Ilaje Women', *ThisDay* (Lagos), August 17, 2002.

10. Claims to ownership of land, especially with proven deposits of crude oil has been a major bone of contention among oil communities, especially as 'legitimate' owners can then claim compensation and occasionally obtain favours from oil companies. See Frynas George Jedrez, 'A Socio-Legal Approach to Natural Resource Conflicts: Environmental Impact of Oil Operations on Village Communities in Nigeria'. Paper presented at the 'African Environments: Past and Present' Conference sponsored by the *Journal of Southern African Studies* and St. Anthony's College, University of Oxford, 5–8 July 1999; For list of demands, see 'Ijaw Women Demand N500m Compensation From Chevron', *This Day*, July 19, 2002; 'The Picketing of Chevron', *The News* (Lagos) August 5, 2002; 'Women Occupy Chevron/Texaco Facilities in the Niger Delta', *Drilbits and Tailings*, volume 7, number 6, July 31, 2002.

11. The meeting was held under the auspices of International Alert, a renowned environmental watchdog active in the oil sector.

12. There are conflicting figures about the exact monetary costs of the closure of the Escravos loading facility per day. According to *Drilbits and Tailings*, it could amount to a calculated daily revenue loss of US$7.8 million. See, 'Women Occupy Chevron/Texaco Facilities in the Niger Delta', *Drilbits and Tailings*, volume 7, number 6, July 31, 2002.

13. 'As Chevron Moves to Resume Production in Escravos…' *ThisDay*, Lagos, July 25, 2002.

14. Focus Group Discussion Extract, Field Survey, 2000 (Cf. Charles Ukeje, Adetanwa Odebiyi, Amadu Sesay and Olabisi Aina, 'Oil and Violent Conflicts in the Niger Delta', CEDCOMS. Monograph Series No. 1, 2002.

15. For details, see 'Women Protesters Sack Chevron's Export Terminal', in *The Punch*, Lagos, July 10, 2002, p. 9.

16. I would like to thank Dr. Charmaine Pereira, researcher at the Centre for Research and Documentation (CRD), Kano, Nigeria, for introducing me to this very important, but definitely ignored, historical connection and reality.

17. See *MOSOP Press Release*, June 20, 2002. For full text of the ruling of the African Court of Human and People's Rights, visit http://www.cesr.org/ESCR/africancommission.html.

18. See 'N-Delta Women's Protest Were Against Vicious Cycle of Injustice – Clark', *Vanguard*, Lagos, August 18, 2002. It is important to note that Government has fuelled the controversy over the exact number of States comprising the Niger Delta. While the core Niger Delta States are Delta, Bayelsa and Rivers States, the official gazette establishing the Niger Delta Development Commission (NDDC) added six more: Abia, Akwa Ibom, Cross River, Edo, Imo and Edo States. By so doing, the Niger Delta, in official parlance, has become coterminous with oil-producing states. See Federal Republic of Nigeria, *Official Gazette* on 'A Bill for an Act to Establish the Niger-Delta Development Commission, 1999'. N. 46, V. 86, 12 July, 1999, Lagos: The Federal Government Press.

19. 'We've Been Pushed to the Wall – Mabiaku', *Vanguard*, Lagos, August 17, 2002.

References

Ade- Ajayi, J.F., and Ian Espie, 1965, *A Thousand Years of West African History*, Lagos: Thomas Nelson and Sons Limited.

Afigbo, A.E., 1966, 'Revolution and Reaction in Eastern Nigeria, 1900-1929', *Journal of the Historical Society of Nigeria*, 3: 3, December.

Afigbo, A.E., 1972, *The Warrant Chiefs: Indirect Rule in Southern Nigeria, 1891-1929*, London: Longman.

Alagoa, E.J., 1964, *The Small Brave City-State: A History of Nembe Brass in the Niger Delta*, Ibadan: University Press.

Alder, Christine, 1999, 'Violence, Gender and Social Change', in Manfred B. Steger and Nancy S. Lind, eds., *Violence and its Alternatives: An Interdisciplinary Reader*, New York: St Martin's Press, pp113-128.

Ake, Claude, 1995, 'The New World Order: A View from Africa', in Hans-Henrik Holm and Georg Sorenssen, eds., *Whose World Order? Uneven Globalization and the End of the Cold War*, Boulder: Westview Press, pp19-42.

Amin, Samir, 1993, 'Social Movements at the Periphery', in Poona Wignaraja, ed., *New Social Movements in the South: Empowering the People*, New Jersey and London: Zed Books, pp. 76-100.

Arifalo, S.O., 2001, *The Egbe Omo Oduduwa: A Study in Ethnic and Cultural Nationalism*, Akure, Stebak Books and Publishers.

Berry, Sara, 1984, 'Oil and the Disappearing Peasantry: Accumulation, Differentiation and Underdevelopment in Western Nigeria', *African Economic History*, 13:1-22.

Boserup, Esther, 1970, *The Role of Women in Economic Development*, New York: St. Martin's Press.

Davies, K.G., 1960, *The Royal African Company*, London: Longman Press.

Elson, Diane, 1993, 'How Is Structural Adjustment Affecting Women?, *Development*, 1, pp. 67-74.

Ekwe-Ekwe, Herbert, 1993, *Africa 2001: The State, Human Rights and the People*. Reading, International Institute for Black Research.

Fatton, Robert Jnr., 1992, *Predatory Rule: State and Civil Society in Africa*, Boulder: Lynne Rienner.

Galtung, Johan, 1999, 'Cultural Violence', in Manfred B. Steger and Nancy S. Lind (eds.), *Violence and its Alternatives: An Interdisciplinary Reader*, New York: St. Martin's Press, pp. 39-56.

Giddens, Anthony, 1996, *Sociology*, Cambridge: Polity Press.

Gurr, Ted Robert, 1995, 'Communal Conflicts and Global Security', *Current History*, 94, 592, May, pp. 212-17.

Human Rights Watch, 2002, 'The Niger Delta: No Democratic Dividend', Vol. 14, No. 7 (A), October.

Ibeanu, Okechukwu, 2001, 'Healing and Changing: The Changing Identity of Women in the aftermath of the Ogoni Crisis in Nigeria', in Sheila Meintjes, Anu Pillay and Meredeth Turshen, eds., *The Aftermath: Women in Post Conflict Transformation*, London: Zed Books.

Ihonvbere, Julius O., 1993, 'Economic Crisis, Structural Adjustment and Social Crises in Nigeria', *World Development*, 21, 1, pp. 141–53.

Ikime, Obaro, ed., 1980, *Groundwork of Nigerian History*, Ibadan: Heinemann Educational Books (Nigeria) Limited.

Jones, G.I., 1963, *The Trading States of the Oil River: A Study of Political Development in Eastern Nigeria*, London: Oxford University Press.

Journal of African Society, 1930, 'A Women's Riot in Nigeria', Editorial Notes. XXIX: CXVII, October, pp. 542–43.

Lynne, Hanna Judith, 1990, 'Dance, Protest and Women's "Wars": Cases from Nigeria and the United States', in Guida West and Rhoda Louis Blumberg, eds., *Women and Social Protest*, New York and Oxford: OUP.

Kofman, Eleonore and William, Colin H., 1989, 'Culture, Community and Conflict', in Colin H. William and Eleonore Kofman (eds.), *Community Conflict, Partition and Nationalism*, London and New York: Routledge.

Kurzman, Charles, 1996, 'Structural Opportunity and Perceived Opportunity in Social Movement Theory: The Iranian Revolution of 1979', *American Sociological Review*, 61, 1, February, pp153-170.

Maier, Karl, 2000, This House Has Fallen: Nigeria in Crisis. London: Penguin Books.

Mba, Nini Emma, 1982, *Nigerian Women Mobilized: Women's Political Activity in Southern Nigeria, 1900-1965*, Institute of International Studies, Berkeley: University of California.

Mbembe, Achille, 2001, *On the Postcolony*, Berkeley: University of California Press.

Obi, Cyril I., 1997a, 'Globalization and Local Resistance: The Case of Ogoni Versus Shell', New Political Economy, 2: 1.

Obi, Cyril I., 1997b, *Structural adjustment, Oil and Popular Struggles: The Deepening Crisis of State legitimacy in Nigeria*, Dakar: CODESRIA Monograph Series.

Obi, Cyril I., 2001, 'Global, State and Local Intersections: Power, Authority and Conflict in the Niger Delta Oil Communities', in Thomas Callaghy, Ronald Kassimir, and Robert Latham, eds., *Intervention and Transnationalism in Africa: Global-Local Networks of Power*, Cambridge: Cambridge University Press.

Ojo, J.B., 2002, *The Niger Delta: Managing Resources and Conflicts.* Research Report No. 49. Ibadan: Development Policy Centre.

Skocpol, Theda, 1982, 'What Makes Peasants Revolutionary?', *Comparative Politics*, 14: 3, 351-75 (Review Article).

Sideris, Tina, 2001, 'Problems of Identity, Solidarity and Reconciliation', in Sheila Meintjes, Anu Pillay and Meredeth Turshen (eds.), *The Aftermath: Women in Post Conflict Transformation*, London: Zed Books, 46-62.

Turner, Terisa E. and Oshare, M.O., 1994, 'Women's Uprising against the Nigerian Oil industry in the 1980s', in Terisa E. Turner (with Bryan J. Ferguson), eds., *Arise Ye Mighty People: Gender, Class, Race in Popular Struggle*, New Jersey: African World Press, 123-60.

Ukeje, Charles, 2001, 'Oil Communities and Political Violence: The Case of Ethnic Ijaw in Nigeria's Delta Region', *Journal of Terrorism and Political Violence*, 13: 4, Winter.

Ukeje, Charles, 2002, 'Youth, Violence and the Collapse of Public Order in the Niger Delta of Nigeria', *Africa Development*, XXVI, 1-2: 1-27.

Ukeje, Charles, Adetanwa Odebiyi, Amadu Sesay and Olabisi Aina, eds., 2002, *Oil and Violent Conflicts in the Niger Delta*, CEDCOMS Monograph Series No. 1, Obafemi Awolowo University Press, November.

Uvin, Peter, 1998, *Aiding Violence: The Development Enterprise in Rwanda*, Connecticut: Kumarian Press.

Watt, M. and P. Lubeck, 1983, 'The Oil Boom and the Popular Classes', in William Zartman, ed., *The Political Economy of Nigeria*, New York: Praeger, pp.105-45.

6

Gender and Culture in Indigenous Films in Nigeria

Ayodele Ogundipe

Introduction

The world of films in any human culture is a world of magic, creativity and imagination. It could be the heaven of inspired storytelling, flight of fancy, morality, beauty and emotions. It could also be the depth values, knowledge and wisdom, in short, the best in us. On the other hand, it could be the hell of violence, gore, sexual depravity and emotional and mental grossness, in other words, the beast in us.

Filmmaking is the outcome of the application of modern developments in the field of technology (celluloid and electronics), theatre arts and mass communications to the production of entertainment. It is a world of visual education, pleasure and relaxation. It has come to become a staple in the cultural menu of the developed world.

In Nigeria, black Africa's most populous nation and developing society, the story is far different but interesting. Celluloid film's short life had its beginnings in the 1970s when Nigeria boasted close to 100 cinema houses. Now they are down to a handful. These film theatres were owned and controlled then by Indian and Lebanese proprietors who brought to Nigeria mostly grade B Indian and Lebanese movies. Occasionally they showed good films, but these cinema houses were most appreciated for their news of the world. They dominated and decided film fares absolutely until the Indegenisation Decree of 1972 made it unprofitable to import foreign films. It became very difficult to obtain import licenses to import foreign films.

Little by little, indigenous filmmakers began treading the tortuous waters. Hubert Ogunde, the veteran Yoruba dance drama performer, brought the performance of his traveling dance drama troupe to the celluloid screen. It was novel, magical and heavily patronised even outside Yoruba speaking states. In 1976, the late Francis Ladele brought Wole Soyinka's 'Kongi's Harvest' to the screen. Ola Balogun and others like Adeyemi Afolayan, Moses Adeyemo a.k.a. Baba Sala came on board. The years of military misrule made life more difficult, and harsh with increased unemployment and high living costs. As crime increased, streets became unsafe and few wanted to be out at night watching movies in cinema houses. As it became more difficult and expensive to bring in 35mm films, theatre audiences dwindled.

The economic collapse of the oil-boom 1970s saw the end of celluloid films in Nigeria and the 1990s saw the rise of the home videos. Shooting a celluloid film was unaffordable and video makers lacked the knowledge of celluloid film technology and the necessary resources. However, there remained a huge appetite for film drama and the home video makers cashed in to fill that gap. Electronics and video equipment sellers finding that their customers did not like to buy blank cassettes started producing video films based on local subjects, stories that Nigerians could relate to, could see themselves in. For as little as N10,000 (naira) movies were shot within one or two weeks on Nigerian locations. Most plots were simple minded as well as sensational and sentimental. The plots were forgettable, the story line thin, the acting poor, the directing absent and the lighting and camera work pedestrian. The masses nonetheless, lapped them up because they dealt with witchcraft, cultists, armed robbers, search for love and poor take-offs of western gangster films.

One of the first home video films *Living in Bondage* (1993) created quite a stir. It first came out in Ibo, followed by *Evil Passion, Taboo, Fatal Desire, Nneka the Pretty Serpent, Circle of Doom, Forbidden* and *Glamour Girls Parts I* and *II* in rated success. None of the above home videos is any longer in production. While they lasted, they sold an average of 350–400 copies per day at each marketer's store!

Since 1993, many more home video films have been released. In fact, there has been an avalanche of home videos. According to the Nigerian Film and Video Censors Board, the following numbers of films were produced between 1994–2001: Abuja (1997–2001), 916 films; Onitsha (1999–2001), 455 films; Abuja (1994–2001), 2,010 films. This makes a total of 4,297 films within a period of 8 years. Of the 3,380 films rated by the Censors' board, 1,191 were in Yoruba while 1,183 films were in English. From information from 5 film production companies in Lagos, it was ascertained that 10 best selling Yoruba films were:

Ti Oluwa N'ile Parts 1, 2 and *3* (The Earth is the Lord's)
Saworoide (Brass Bells)
Kosegbe (Immovable)
Agogo Eewo (Taboo Gong)

Thunderbolt (Magun)
Asiri Nla (Big Secret)
Oko (Missile)
Asewo to re Mecca (Prostitute who went to Mecca)
Maradona Eewo, 1 and *2* (Taboo 1 & 2)

The five best selling films sold from around 25,000 to 65,000 copies.

The ten best selling English films were:
Power of Love, 1 and 2
Ukwa
Okada Man
Stupid
Atinga
He Goat (1 and 2)
Sharon Stone (1 and 2)
The Orphan
Church in Crises
Christ in Me

The following twelve best-selling films were selected for our discussion of gender and culture in Nigerian Home Video films:

English	Yoruba
Power of Love	*Thunderbolt* (Magun)
Stupid	*Kosegbe*
Ukwa	*Ti Olowa N'ile*
Atinga	*Saworoide*
Okada Man	*Agogo Eewo*

Women's Issues

Agony of a Mother
Ungrateful

Synopsis of Selected Video Films

In order to convey something of the content and character of the films under discussion, the following short synopses are presented.

(a) Films in English

Power of Love Part 1

Christopher, the lead player falls in love with Juliet, the girl who finances him to get a visa to the USA where he makes good. He returns home to marry her, but Juliet has been crippled in an accident and was not very receptive because of her disability and because she heard a lie that Chris has a white wife. Feeling rejected, Chris turns to an old flame Sandra and they marry, but Sandra's reputation ruins the marriage. Miraculous healing sets Juliet on her feet again and finding her lover married, she attempts suicide by jumping off the top of a building but is again miraculously saved. Sandra comes after Chris with a gun and there ensues a shoot-out with the police who kill her. Chris and Juliet are now free to marry at last.

Power of Love Part 2

Sandra's mother swears revenge. Sandra's sisters plan an elaborate and generally unbelievable revenge on Chris and Juliet. Conniving with Mary, former girl friend of Chris, fake compromising items are sent to Chris to make him think Juliet has been unfaithful. Sandra's mother uses Juliet's intimate garment in a magical ritual to curse her with bareness. With Juliet's infertility, pressure of work and suspicion of infidelity by her husband, the marriage falls apart. Cynthia befriends Juliet and with each visit to her house slowly poisons her drinks. Disillusioned with women and his marriage, Chris falls into the arms of conniving Mary, the former New York girl friend who pretends to be pregnant in order to break his marriage. Things fall apart for the plotters when Chris overhears the plot to ruin his marriage and kill Juliet. Cynthia meets her Waterloo when Juliet switches their drinks and Cynthia dies of her own poison.

Stupid

Two low-lifers more stupid than immoral get themselves involved with a number of incompetent but greedy crooks and lose their lives in the encounter. The story opens with a five-man gang double crossing themselves over a large sum of money ill-gotten from an unrevealed source. A member of the gang disguised as a white-garment pastor cons two of the thieves into praying and while they pray he shoots and kills them. He takes the money and joins the remaining two criminals in a waiting car but they had plotted against him. During the celebratory drink, his glass is poisoned and his corpse is thrown callously out of the car by his co-criminals, a Chief and a woman. Knowing what each can do, they watch each other like hawks. After sharing the money Chief goes a spree of debauching with his married lover whose dwarf husband returns inadvertently on them causing Chief to scale down from the second storey in his underwear. The security men let him out for a fee. The next day they call at his office for gratification and he cleverly thinks of using them to double-cross his female partner. She, in the meantime had secured a crooked deal with a white expatriate who was willing to pay two million naira for a piece of land on which to dump toxic industrial waste from overseas. The two brothers were to pose as policemen and rid the expatriate of his money with which he was going to pay the female partner. The two brothers succeed in relieving the expatriate of his money, but they do not deliver it to the Chief, meaning to keep the money for themselves. This leads to both the Chief and the woman chasing after the two brothers leading to further mayhem and in the end, everyone dies leaving the suitcase containing two million naira, standing forlornly surrounded by corpses.

Atinga

Atinga is a pointless tale about the rich exploiting the poor at every turn. The rich have every advantage it seems. Atinga, an indolent village bumpkin who kept by his girl friend in the village, eventually loses her to a city slicker, Chief Aguijeigbe, a millionaire cosmetics tycoon. Swearing deadly vengeance, Atinga goes in pursuit of the Chief armed with magical charm from the village medicine man. The charms were to make the Chief so docile that he could be thoroughly humiliated before being finally killed. The charm does not work because Atinger is too scatterbrained to follow instructions. He is told not to eat before and while applying the charm but his girlfriend Amaka, now wife to Chief Aguijeibe, persuades him to taste her food to please her, which he did. When he then attempts to command the Chief with the charm to do demeaning things he is given a severe a beating by the outraged Chief, and Atinga ends up as a servant in the Chief's house. Amaka for old times' sake persuades Chief to open a supermarket for Atinga. Here again Atinga is too daft to be able to cope with the demands of running a supermarket and therefore appeals to the Chief to bring his friend, Damian, fellow daftee from the village to assist in the shop. Meanwhile Amaka is sent away to the US for childbirth. In her absence, Chief's roving eyes fall on Nkechi, who widowed by Damian's brother, is expected to marry Damian. Money from Chief however persuades Nkechi's mother to go along with the new arrangement and both friends Atinga and Damian not only lose their women to Chief but also find themselves lowly servants to Chief. They plot unrevealed revenge which one is sure will be stupid and unsuccessful knowing how daft they both are.

Ukwa

This is the story of the chequered life of a ne'er–do-well with a good heart. Unrepentantly jobless and impecunious, he lives off his charming family, a wife, 3 children and a frustrated father in the village. He is a problem at home with his roguish ways until big brother Aguiyi takes him to Lagos with him to make something useful out of him. Ukwa in Lagos is a disaster. He seduces his sister-in-law's sister and dresses down the sister-in-law. He exposes Aguiyi's prophet-futurologist by revealing him as the lecherous and fake character he is. Hoodlums who assault him and relieve him of his property egg on his sudden return to the village. An ejected tenant and his young hoodlum associates kill Aguiyi, the elder brother. The prophet is lynched and Ukwa's attempt to seduce his newly widowed sister in law ends up in his getting the beating of his life. He goes back to the village.

Okada Man

This is a rambling comedy about various aspects of Nigerian life with a running commentary and reactions by Nicholas, a.k.a. Nicho Loudmouthed, unrepentant non-conformist rogue, liar, thief and seducer. He is a Nigerian Peter Pan, a forty-year-old who does not grow up. Various areas of Nigerian life and culture feature. Nicho's iconoclastic humour pervades family life, domestic servitude, Okadamanhip (Motor cycle taxi), police, human sacrifice, ethnic conflicts, tenement dwelling and witchcraft.

(b) Films in Yoruba

Magun

Magun is a brief tale with an Othelloish plot. Irrationally jealous Yinka falls in love and marries Ngozi at the cost of her own status and position in her Igbo culture. Fuelled by baseless rumours of extra-marital affairs lapped up by Yinka, a Yoruba man, problems develop in the marriage. The subsequent distrust leads Yinka to engage the services of a trado-medical practitioner who injects Ngozi with Magun, a magical drug which among other ill-effects may result in an adulteress, unknown to herself causing her lover to die.

Kosegbe

A dedicated professional officer takes over the Immigration and Customs services in a city after the previous senior officer is relieved of his duty due to rampant corruption. The efforts of the new officer at cleaning the Aegean stables of Immigration and Customs are severely undermined by a cartel of disgruntled dismissed officers, smuggling barons and corrupt police officers. Bound together by the love for ill-gotten wealth, they use a loose society woman to photograph Kosegbe while being seduced and plant fake drugs on his son. In spite of these setbacks, he is unrelenting and engages the smugglers in a shoot out. Despite being wounded, he worsts his enemies by tape-recording their confessions of bribery, blackmail and corruption.

Saworoide

Saworide is a story of a traditional rural community, Jogbo, with a deeply rooted pact with its ancestors that the ruler of the community, the Onijogbo, must rule to serve the community and not the community to serve the ruler. The ruler must take an oath and must be ritually incised to keep his pledge; failure to do this means he will be removed by the ancestors. Lapite, a rapacious Oba, takes the throne by having all threatening opposition killed or exiled. He declined to take the oath or be incised. He buys the Chiefs to his side and together; they milk the town of its natural resources and put their ill-gotten gains in foreign banks. When the suffering and deprivation become too much, the youths revolted only to be crushed by Lagata, an army officer at the behest of Lapite. But Lagata having tasted power, does not want to relinquish it and he kills Lapite and usurps the throne. Nemesis catches up with Lagata when he dons the brass crown without the protective incision and the brass crown strangulates him as the royal drum with brass bells is beaten for him.

Agogo Eewo

Corrupt traditional Chiefs of Jogbo, after the deaths of Lapite and Lagata the military dictator, conspire to put their man on the throne so as to continue business as usual with corruption. They pick on Adebosipo, a retired police officer. Adebosipo on becoming king, chooses to depart from evil and corruption and to actually fight for the peace and progress of his people. Here begins a battle royal between the Oba and his Chiefs. With advice from Ifa the deity of wisdom and divination, he restores the old oath taking ritual whereby Chiefs swear to uphold the morality and values of the community. Erring and guilty Chiefs must confess past misdeeds and be cleansed before taking the oath. Failure to comply means summary death. Two recalcitrant Chiefs, the Balogun and Seriki who have been causing murder and mayhem, refuse to capitulate and therefore die on the spot.

Ti Oluwa N'Ile 1, 2 and 3

An uneven tale of the fatal sale of traditional ancestral land by two greedy citizens who engage the services of a traditional Chief, the Otun, to help them carry out the deal for a handsome payback. The oracle reveals that the land belongs to deities and therefore not suited for the siting of a petrol station. When the two perpetuators die suddenly one after the other, the Otun realises he is next in line and seeks the oracle's intervention. The oracle says that as long as he can prevent the second conspirator's corpse from being buried, he would be safe. Parts 2 and

3 are the stories of his Herculean task to stay alive. The second conspirator's body is buried after a long delay. Another application to the oracle gives him a short lease of life during which he runs away in a boat, the boat is wrecked, he is captured as an armed robber, and rescued from the police by a rich lady who eventually marries him. Otun, the traditional Chief, goes home to find both his wife and title taken and his clothes shared among family members who presume him to be dead. After his futile fight to reclaim his title, he runs out of time and the ghosts of his two friends reclaim him after all.

Films relating to Women's Issues

Male dominance is apparent in all twelve films examined in this study, although more heavily so in *Saworoide, Agogo Eewo, and Oluwa N'ile* set in traditional rural settings. But even in urban situations like in *Power of Love* and comical *Ukwa, Stupid, Atinga* and others the men have upper hand and take all the decisions. Sites of patriarchy include domestic work, paid work, male violence, sexuality and cultural institutions like the levirate and widowhood. *(Power of Love, Sowaroide, Ukwa, Agony of a Mother)*. Widowhood is given full treatment in *Agony of a Mother* where Aswani suffers, true to culture, accusations of having a hand in her husband's death, insensitivity from kinsmen and mother in-law, neglect by family, impoverishment, loss of status and humiliation. On the other hand, the loss of spouse by a man does not warrant any punitive or derogatory action. Vesico-Virginia Fistula (VVF), a serious woman's issue afflicting young girls who are forced into early marriages and therefore premature birthing in northern Nigeria, is treated unrealistically and sentimentally as a grown up affair in *Ungrateful* as a knight in shining armour comes out of the blues to rescue this tertiary institution student with VVF from a fate not worse than death, pays her enormous hospital bills for restorative surgery and marries her in the end in spite of her dilly-dallying.

Synopsis: Agony of a Mother

Aswani, a deeply religious woman is happily married with two children, a boy, Joseph and a girl, Edith. Her travails begin when unknown assailants murder her husband. At the news she runs to her husband's wealthy younger brother who refuses to assist her because her husband refused to sell his land to his business partner to use to dump toxic waste. Outwardly he pretends to be sympathetic by giving her a cheque, which bounces. She is blamed for her husband's death but vehemently she declares her innocence. Ostracised and abandoned, the children suffer, the brother-in-law is callous and merciless and a friend who tried to assist her provokes the fury of his wife who assaults Aswani. As Aswani seeks refuge in her religious faith, her brother-in-law intensifies his applications of charms provided by a sorcerer. Didi is killed by a hit and run driver driving Aswani to greater desperation. When Joseph is attacked several times by unknown assailants, he leaves for Lagos. The sorcerer pursues him with long-distance charms and fails due to his mother religious intervention. Frustrated by the sorcerer's failed attempts to take Joseph's life Chief sends his murder squad to have him killed. In the meantime, Joseph is doing very well in Lagos, works in a company and is married to the boss's daughter. When Chief learns of Joseph's success, he could not stand it any more and decides to go and kill Aswani in the village. Unfortunately, Chief's wife discovers Chief's pot of magical concoctions in the wardrobe, brings the pot outside and sets it on fire, an act which immediately sets the Chief on fire. This makes him take off all his clothes, lose his mind and begin to confess all his crimes throughout the village.

Ungrateful

This is a poor treatment of a tale of VVF (Vesico-Vagina-Fistula). Jennifer suffers VVF from a mishandled gynaecological surgery. She is deserted by her boyfriend and ostracised to take her lectures from outside the class. A stranger arranges and pays for her surgery to the chagrin of his family. Jennifer is mended; Emeka her benefactor proposes, but she still has feelings for her ex-boyfriend, who knowing that she is mended wants to marry her. Dramatically on her wedding day, she changes her mind, and marries her benefactor.

Gender and Culture in Indigenous Films

Although considerable literature is available on gender, discussion of the topic gender is still contentious, conflicting and somewhat confusing. There are many perspectives and approaches to the subject. Clatterbaugh's eight perspectives on gender which include the moral, pro-feminist, men's rights, mythopoesis, socialist, homosexual-male, African American, and evangelistical-Christian, are too involved and masculinist for the purpose of this paper (Clatterbaugh 1992). Rather, gender will be simply defined as any approved way of being an adult male or female and while acknowledging the existence of an essentialist perception that gender is biological. This paper would rather take the view that gender is conditional and constructionist by the application of the mythopoesis and social constructionist approaches to our analysis of gender and culture in indigenous films in Nigeria. The mythopoesis approach expressed here involves the examination of folklore such as traditions of stories, myths, and rituals in a non-neo-Jungian sense of deep, unconscious patterns or archetypes or male mythopoesis as found in current discourses on masculinities (Bly 1990, 1991). Our social constructionist view is one that looks at gender through the male roles of supplier, safe keeper and spouse; and female roles of mother, nest builder and nurturer as forged by role socialisation by institutions and practices grounded in traditional societies.

Culture in this paper will be taken to mean the identifying totality of the way of life of a people as enshrined in their material and non- material aspects of life.

It includes their material production such as architecture, food, and belongings, creative and recreational objects such as houses, cuisine, clothing, books and music. The nonmaterial aspects include their cognitive culture, their way of being, thinking and perceiving. Beliefs, songs, dance, music, ideology, laws and customs are also subsumed under culture.

Society Portrayed in Indigenous Films

Nigeria is an amalgamation of numerous societies and cultures with over two hundred and fifty languages. Mercifully, this paper will be examining Nigerian culture from the perspective of indigenous filmmakers who are either Yoruba or Igbo and whose themes are therefore situated or given a perspective from either the Igbo or Yoruba cultures. All the films in this paper examine a slice of life in Nigerian culture.

The society portrayed in indigenous films is clearly Nigerian, the setting being rural or urban Igbo or Yoruba society. Rural life in the village is simple, poor, and agricultural with subsistence farming and lack of many amenities and utilities. Three of our twelve films are situated in a rural setting. *Ti Oluwa N'ile*, *Saworoide*, and *Agogo Eewo* all play out in the traditional rural setting. The background is not pre-colonial but nonetheless it is distant from western style central modern governance. The themes are about various aspects of life where the locals are rural dwellers. The presence and influence of traditional kingship structure of Oba and traditional Chiefs and the royal court are much in evidence in the Yoruba films; and the traditions of elders in council palpable in the Igbo films. On traditional matters such as land, beliefs, heritage, traditional social institutions still carry much weight. The village school with its poor facilities and ever so influential village headmaster are depicted in *Magun*. The larger family, not the nuclear family, is depicted in *Ukwa* where the family is headed by grandfather, the final arbiter of family conflicts. *Agony of a Mother* captures the impoverished setting of the village as well as the tyranny of tradition and belief regarding widowhood and women's rights. Nonetheless, in spite of the material deprivation, a sense of greater humanity and cohesiveness shines through the rural rather than the urban settings.

Alienation, corruption, slum dwelling and general hustling to make ends meet, often overshadow town or urban settings. *Kosegbe* examines corrupt social institutions and services like Customs and Immigration and the Police departments. Urban problems like greed and criminality are satirised in *Stupid*. *Okada Man* is a running commentary on corrupt city life, social ills, ethnic conflicts, police brutality, tenement dwelling and alienation in urban centers. *Power of Love* is set among the near affluent that talk big money and peddle fake foreign culture in dress and mannerism. There is prevalence of immorality, fraud, violence, gun totting, use of poison to settle scores and an amazing belief in witchcraft and sorcery. *Un-*

grateful hints at tertiary education and the upwardly mobile dwelling in urban centres. But all in all, the urban settings depicted in the films are only as urban as cities can be in developing countries. So many social indicators of development are lacking: good roads, absence of power outage, and potable water amongst other things.

Gender in Family and Marriage Relationships

Family life is historically and culturally specific. All twelve films depict family and marriage relationships. Love and marriage are authentic within Igbo and Yoruba traditions. Where they are not, they ring hollow and unbelievable. In *Power of Love*, Juliet and Chris's western style love and married life are a mystery to their parents but the problem of childlessness generates traditional intervention from Chris's father who advocates his son taking an additional wife (polygamy) even in the face of the fact that he the father is monogamous and does not contemplate marrying another wife. Cultural perceptions of the male as supplier, safe keeper and head spouse are brought up but not treated satisfactorily. They are introduced irrelevantly or just to move the plot forward. It is not clear what Chris does eventually and how successful he is at it. If he is a good provider, it is not clear why Juliet works so hard and is sexually harassed at work unless to gratuitously bring in issues of domestic violence, sexual harassment and infertility which are not fully treated. Chief Aijuigbe in *Atinga* as a good supplier is wealthy and therefore a monarch of all he surveys. He is the societal ideal of the successful, mature, responsible and respectable citizen. Like Aguiyi in *Ukwa*, the source of wealth does not seem to matter. Being wealthy by hook or by crook is the modern morality in Nigeria. It is not supported by traditional values. The rolling stone, hapless protagonists like Ukwa in the film of the same name, Nicho in *Okada Man*, Atinga, the two brothers in *Stupid* are caricatures or spoofs of the immature, irresponsible, never-do-well personages who cannot be providers and protectors. They are embarrassments, social failures, and useful as slapstick commentators. Yet they are very perceptive in their analysis of the ills of the society in spite of the fact that they are portrayed as crude and unintelligent.

The family as a social unit is strongly depicted in all the stories. Issues such as domestic life, male infertility (*Power of Love*), and wife inheritance (*Ti Oluwa ni ile* and *Ukwa*) all feature. The family as a social unit is strongly depicted in all the stories. The women are conceived as nurturers, care-givers. In their domestic role, they provide the food and serve it respectfully to their husbands, a chore which is despised by men as Ukwa is insulted when his sister-in-law asks him to go and buy her tomatoes and onions from the market. Not even the queens in the traditional stories are exempted form domestic chores. *Submission* is interesting because it deals with an out-of-character domineering and insubordinate wife, but the veiled implication is that she misleads her children and comes to a bad end herself because she is not submissive.

The woman as an agent of socialisation is also stressed. Mothers have a great impact on their child. It is the grandfather and the mother who teaches their children the norms of the society through folk tales, stories, and riddles (*Saworoide, Agogo Eewo*), and grandfather also teaches by storytelling (*Ukwa*). Lapite's wife advises her daughter to face her studies and beware of palace intrigues. Ukwa's Peter-Pannish ways are also indirectly blamed on the permissiveness of his mother and not on the father's weakness in controlling his son. The traditional stories more consciously depict the family as an agent of socialisation. Families are closer and establish the rule of authority. The eldest male, grandfather, father, husband, dominates everyone else; and if he is a king, even more so because traditional ideology supports it. The patriarch allocates tasks, settles disputes and takes other important decisions affecting the family. So, grandfather decides that Aguiyi take his brother Ukwa to Lagos never mind that Ukwa a grown man who does not want to go. In the absence of the grandfather, in Lagos, the older brother becomes the patriarch and also can force Ukwa to go to the prophet with him and even attend church against his will. The family provides for sexual regulation, so Otun's wife and Aguiyi's wife go to their husband's brothers in order to keep their status within the family. The family also provides for socialisation, economic cooperation and emotional security.

Gender Roles in Production and Power Structures

That women work either in the private or public, formal or informal sectors, is clearly depicted in all of the films here presented. In the films in English, for example *Power of Love Parts 1 and 2,* Juliet, one of the protagonists works, first in her father's business and after marriage to Chris works in the formal sector in a bank where the problems of juggling the demands and home contribute to the ruin of her marriage. She suffers long working hours, insults and sexual harassments from her boss and lack of understanding from her jealous and suspicious husband. Cynthia and Mary are also examples of educated women who hold their own in city life. Women in the city or village could also work as prostitute as in *Submission* or courtesans as in *Kosegbe*. Women in low-income jobs live in tenement buildings, where everyone shares a courtyard. In the Yoruba films, we find Ngozi, a devoted schoolteacher in a village school where sexual harassment from the headmaster is reduced to innocence by her flirtation. With its more traditional setting, women in *Saworoide, Agogo Eewo and Ti Oluwa N'ile* engage in more private and practical work. They process and cook food, they sell vegetables and food items at the market. They sell clothes from house even to the palace as the woman who attempts to seduce Oba Adebosipo. The titled women Chiefs, the Iyalode and Iyaloja trade and are paid gratification along with the other Chiefs.

We see a successful businesswoman in *Ti Oluwa N'ile* but we do not know what particular business she is in, but she is well connected and influential. *Agony of a mother* presents the rural widow in subsistence farming and poverty. Poverty makes her subservient and humiliated. She has no voice.

In the social power structure, women are not very evident. Not as bank workers, prostitutes, members of the police force, market women, farmers, processors and producers of food are they empowered. Nor do they have a voice. It is only in *Submission* that the matriarch attempts to manipulate everyone and she is depicted as an unsympathetic figure. Only as traditional Chiefs do the Iyalode and Iyaloja and Akewe belong in the traditional power structure as members of the royal court in their own right. They are involved in the making of policy and sharing of resources, which is what power is all about. In return they are respected and recognised and can step outside the normal social constraints of women.

Beliefs

Belief is arguably the single most important issue in indigenous films in Nigeria. It is a huge bone of contention in the determination of quality in indigenous films in Nigeria. Belief is a cognitive system or a system of perception shared by members of a group. It provides understanding, explanations, and meaning to the eternal 'whys' of life. It gives a cohesive view of the world and serves to integrate the various parts of the culture. Its major elements are cosmology, values, myth and ritual.

Cosmology

All indigenous home video films in Nigeria reflect a culturally given belief system and it is this belief system that makes the films peculiarly Nigerian. The belief system of a culture forms a mirror by which people visualise the nature of the world and of the powers that govern it, man's reality and the process of creation as reflections of a single reality. Belief can be divided into different areas such as religion, ideology, science and magic. All of them have elements of cosmology, values, myth and ritual. These elements explain the nature of the world, its history, man's place in it and they express values and guide behaviour. To further clarify the use of the following terms: religion consists of beliefs dealing with the supernatural; ideology, with a non-supernatural explanation of the nature of society, magic with man's ability to control aspects of the supernatural and science, with empirical understanding of reality. We shall examine these various aspects of belief in the films at hand.

Three films, *Saworoide. Agogo Eewo and Ti Oluwa N'ile* situated in Yoruba culture explore and integrate various aspects of Yoruba belief very aesthetically, educatively and successfully. *Saworoide* and its sequel *Agogo Eewo* demonstrate great fidelity to traditional Yoruba culture. The plot is based on a Yoruba community with deep roots in the past, in the origin of history and religion. There is a cosmology, a world-view inculcating a theory of the universe, its different parts and the beings that populate it. There is heaven and earth; a spiritual world of ancestors, spirit beings, deities, ghosts and an earthly world of people. These two worlds are interconnected. Thus in Jogbo, there is the pact between heaven and earth. The will of God, Olodumare, and of the deity Orunmila is communicated through Ifa the channel of divination by his priests, the Amawo. The spirit world is constantly watching and guarding and guiding the earthly world through the medium of the Ifa oracle. All is well when earth follows faithfully, but there is disaster when it does not. There is reparation when earth confesses, it is cleansed, and then restored. *Ti Oluwa N'ile* depicts ancestral land as the land belonging to deities (*ile orisa*) separated (sacred) to spirits departed, ancestors and deities. This land should be considered sacred, holy, but greedy citizens decide to sell it off to make room for a petrol station. Those who engaged in this activity lose their lives one after the other.

In every cosmology there is an evaluation of the elements composing the universe, that is a set beliefs and feelings regarding what is good and what is bad, what is desirable and what is undesirable. These beliefs known as values help to mould behaviour and thought. Values in the kingdom of Jogbo are handed down from the cosmology. In the pact between the ancestors and the community, service is the value preached. It said 'if you love life you do not aspire to be the king of Jogbo. Onijogbo serves the people, not the people serving Onijogbo. Onijogbo cannot seek affluence like modern day kings because of deep secrets. If the king wants to be affluent, he should not be incised or swear oaths'. In other words, the peace and prosperity of Jogbo should be of primary importance to any Onijogbo who should be selfless, moral, a role model to his people. Spiritual endeavours or growth should be more positively valued than material things.

Saworoide and Agogo Eewo are replete with values, communicated in maxims, folksongs, riddles, incantations, allegory, myth, legends folktales. In the two films there is a Yoruba chorus who like the Greek chorus comment chorally on the action, the prologue and the epilogue. The verse or songs are full of values. Of Jogbo, he chants

> Jogbo, bitter as bitter kola
> Dangerous as the Oro Cult
> With two eyes you can cope at the riverside
> With two eyes can survive Kaduna
> But you need two eyes to survive in Jogbo
> With two months you get by in Lagos
> But you need 18 months to survive in Jogbo

With two hands you can handle Ekiti
With two hands you can handle Egba
But you need 24 hands to manipulate Jogbo
Jogbo, bitter as bitter Kola.

(From *Agogo Eewo*).

Jogbo, here is an allegory of Nigeria: Nigeria, difficult to handle, to please, to
serve: as all Nigerians, if not the world, know.

Earth and Heaven killed a rat,
Quarreled over seniority,
But earth took the rat away.
Heaven protested, retreating to the skies,
So, rain refused to fall,
Plants sprouted and dried up,
Maidens suffered stunted growth,
Take note of my song,
It is a proverbial song,
You form your various parties,
Promising to reform Jugbo,
But your parties embezzle funds,
You become partial,
You indulge yourselves and forget the masses,
Let's be watchful,
We shall be vigilant.

(From *Agogo Eewo*).

Myth and Legend

People do not learn their cosmology and values passively. They absorb a theory
of reality and values in active daily life. They learn them in part from the stories
and legends that explain the world and its history. Anthropologists call these
stories myths. Heroes embody the culture's virtues and villains embody its vices,
and the stories are filled with fabulous events. Myths and legends provide the
specifics about the origin of the world, where man came from and how society
got to be the way it is. So in *Agogo Eewo*, the Narrator and chorus tells us about
ancestral Jogbo kings, to illustrate how things should be or not be.

The reign of Abiodun was noted for hard work
Abiodun's reign was a period of prosperity

Aole's reign was full of trouble
Arogangan's reign was a time of pestilence
The king passed on, leaving behind the pestilence
Abiodun, please come back for another term.
(From *Agogo Eewo*)

Rituals

And finally, we come to rituals. It is a term so badly misunderstood and some-times used out of context in films that the Censors' Board has a field day mis-ranking any and everything it considers 'rituals'.

Belief systems are more than values, folktale and cosmology. There are also a system of rituals and symbols to which the believer responds profoundly. As Geertz (1965) puts it, a person does not hold such beliefs but instead is held by the beliefs. Ritual symbolically recreates incidents and value of the belief system often in a dramatic form. Thus the deity consultant (Amawo) consults the oracle the deity of divination, Ifa in a ritual. He acts, but he acts in a special, predeter-mined stylised way. He says incantations, words laden with spiritual power to the spirits in the spirit world to make them react. He makes use of objects, the *opele* (Ifa Beads) on the divination board . These objects embody his concept of the universe and replicate the tenets of these beliefs. Ifa consultations are found in *Saworoide*, *Agogo Eewo* and *Ti Oluwa N'ile* representing serious aspects of belief, cosmology and values. For example in an incantation before oath taking:

Those who get such by the use of force
Don't last a year
those who acquire instant wealth like soldiers
Don't last a day
The patient ones are still alive
Enjoying a life of bliss
A day of retribution is a hand
If a youngster violates taboo and gets away
Eventually he will face the law of retribution.

Magic, Witchcraft, and Sorcery

Magic, witchcraft, and sorcery are related but somewhat different types of belief systems. Classifying them separately is somewhat arbitrary because they consti-tute part of a common cosmology. Like religion, magic, witchcraft and sorcery are concerned with the supernatural. They convey methods of compelling the supernatural rather than imploring it. If religion is the emotional and philosophi-cal aspect of the supernatural world, magic is the engineering. The magician seeks practical results. He knows the formula or ritual that will force the desired outcome. Supplicants use the services of a practitioner of magic to solve specific problems in return for a fee. The goal is concrete, specific and usually devoid of moral or ethical meaning. So in *Ukwa,* Aguiyi goes to the false prophet-futurologist who is actually an unbelieving magician. This man for a fee gives his clients a magic stick for protection and prosperity. When the 'prophet' is lynched, the magic wand fails to work to save Aguiyi from his vengeful former tenant.

Sorcery on the other hand is where powers we used to cause illness or bring bad fortune. Sorcery incorporates the knowledge of formulas, medicines spells. Thus in *Thunderbolt* M*agun*, jealous Yinka laces his wife Ngozi with *magun*, a sorcery concoction which among other ill effect may result in the adulteress, unknown to herself, causing her lover to die in various ways.

from constant coughing (magun elegbe)
somersaulting (magun olokiti)
being in a state of extreme languor (olorere)
crowing like a cock before dying (alakuko)
(Abraham 1958:259)

In *Submission,* Lebechi goes for a sorcerer's vial to eliminate Azuka's husband but she does not meet the condition that the contents of the vial may not be spilled. In a fright from being caught in the process of wanting to poison the meal at the table, she slips, drops the vial, and becomes insane from contact with the contents of the vial. *Okada man* is instructed not to eat before using his portion in his magical duel with Ade but he eats and the portion does not work. In *Power of Love*, Sandra's mother with a view to killing her slowly uses Juliet's personal effects to cast a spell of barrenness on her. Ade is a male witch in *Okada Man* who has inherent psychic powers that permit him to do evil. Unlike the sorcerer who has props and concoctions, the witch uses nothing besides willing his evil and saying some powerful words. Feared, despised and rejected, Ade can be intent on harming others who despise and reject him. So calling on his mothers, the witches, he becomes the neighbourhood terror.

Conclusion

Of the twelve best selling indigenous films, three Yoruba films *Sawooide, Agogo Eewo* and *Ti Oluwa N'ile* are quite good. The last two are really good because they are carefully crafted, beautifully filmed, true to the culture they represent and are educative and entertaining. So giving *Agogo Eewo* a rating of 18 NTBB meaning Not to be Broadcast by the Nigerian Film and Video Censors Board on the grounds of rituals and violence and seduction is grossly ignorant on the part of the Censors. And there is a raging contest going on even as I write [2002]. *Ti Oluwa N'ile* could do with some editing of its slow sections. It really does not deserve to be in three parts. The story line is too thin. But nevertheless is a good try. *Kosegbe* is a good little morality tale. *Magun* start well but loses focus and does not treat its subject well. Is there really Magun? The ending is muddled.

As regards the English films, they are rather shallow, with thin plots and poor directing. They bear out the observation that most of these films are made for quick money by people who are basically traders and who lack knowledge, skill and training in film-making. *Ukwa* and *Okada Man* are the two that have prospects as comedic genres. They are really the stuff of stand-up comics and it is instructive that the main character in the two is the same comedic actor. *Stupid* is really stupid, pointless and not funny, but it is a very popular film. *Agony of a Mother*'s treatment of widowhood is ruined by the insertion of magical charms. It could have stood out on its own.

It is a wonderful thing that in the age of overwhelming globalisation from American culture through the media, most Nigerians want to watch films in which they see themselves and to which they can relate. There is a market for Nigerian films from here to Cameroon or Senegal. But the knock offs and the glutting of the market with poorly produced films must stop.

Gender and culture are not well treated in most films indigenously produced. Admittedly, the films do not set out to be anthropological or sociological. They set out to inform, educate, and entertain. They fail for the most part to do any of these three. They fail to provide a balanced view of Nigerian society on which they are based. The society as a homogenous integrative whole is totally unbalanced. The plots are pointless and disjointed. It is very difficult to appreciate gender roles in the films because they are not true to what obtains, and where they begin well, they are not fully developed. So, they are unbelievable and unrealistic. Serious themes are shoddily presented. Religiosity is at once ridiculed but at the same time implied to work and be effective. Magic, witchcraft and sorcery are thrown in gratuitously in over 90 percent of the films even when they do not move the plot forward or add anything to the film. Comedic levels or spoofs are crude, noisy and boisterous. All in all, most of the films become a parody of the society. Sensationalism is the order of the day, lurid topics, witchcraft, rituals out of context, cultism, murder and mayhem make it seem as if Nigerians are a superstitious, murderous, criminal lot.

It is perhaps encouraging that producers, directors, actors and marketers have recently agreed to the Resolutions of the 43rd Art Stampede by the Committee for Relevant Arts (CORA). These Resolutions urge the following:

- That Nigerian movie practitioners need to be caring in their approach to their trade.
- That they should iron out their differences, constant conflicts and bickering.

- That there should be a film practitioners' council to prevent the activities of quacks and characters who have *invaded the industries*
- That they should desist from making negative statements about the sector
- Practitioners should take advantage of the services of training facilities available such as Nigerian Film Institute etc.
- Those in the industry should ensure that the contents of films are sufficiently sensitive to avoid themes and materials capable of projecting wrong impressions about the culture and people of Nigeria.
  (*Guardian*, Thursday, July 11, 2002).

References

Abraham, R., 1958, *Dictionary of Yoruba Language*.

Adegbola,Tunde, 2002a, 'Agogo Eewo: An Issue in Democratic Rights', *Guardian*, November 17, p.38.

Adegbola,Tunde, 2002b, 'Censor's Board: A Hen Perching On Rope', *Guardian*, November 17, p. 38.

Akpovi-Esade, Justin, 2002a, 'In Recess ...The Business Goes on', *Guardian*, April 19, p.30.

Akpovi-Esade, Justin, 2002b, 'No Shine in Moviedom yet', *Guardian*, May 30, p.58.

Akpovi-Esade, Justin, 2002c, 'Despite Rain, Art Stampede Bares out the Moviedom', *Guardian*, June 7, p. 34.

Akpovi-Esade, Justin, 2002d, 'Rapture unsettles Producers Censors Board', *Guardian*, September 5, p.52.

Akpovi-Esade, Justin, 2002e, 'Movies ...Battle on the Classification Turf', *Guardian*, October 11, p.26.

Akpovi-Esade, Justin, 2002e, 'More Gains of Recess in Moviedom', *Guardian*, November 7, p.52.

Akpovi-Esade, Justin and Afolabi Taiwo, 2002, 'Producers Tackle Colleague over Obscene Film',

Guardian, August 8, p.46.

Bly, Robert; and Iron, John, 1991, *A Book About Men*, Reading, Massachusetts, Addison Wesley.

Clatterbaugh, Kenneth, 1991, *Contemporary Perspectives on Masculinity: Men, Women and Politics in Modern Society*, Second Edition, Boulder, Colorado: Westview Press.

CORA, 2002, 'Communique of the 43rd Art Stampede Organised by Committee For Relevant Arts (CORA)', *Guardian*, July 11, p. 58.

Faris, Stephan, 2002, 'Hollywood: Who really needs it?', *Time Magazine*, May 20.

Gilmore, David, D., 1990, *Manhood in the Making: Cultural Concepts of Masculinity*, New Haven, Connecticut and London: Yale University Press.

Husseini, Shaibu, 2002a, 'Movie in the Razzmatazz Lane', *Guardian*, April 19, p. 30.

Husseini, Shaibu, 2002b, 'Recess Over, But Old Vibes Remain', *Guardian*, August 15, p. 58.

Husseini, Shaibu, 2002c, 'Ugomah: Movies, A Way of Life in Eddie Ugbomah's Movie World', *Guardian*, August 24, p.35, 44-45.

Nwanonyiri, Ngozi, 2002, '...What Artistes Resolved at the Stampede', *Guardian*, June 7, p.39.

Ogundipe, Ayodele, 1999, *Belief System*, Benin City, Ambik Press.

Onyeka, Ben Victor, 2002, 'Pete Edochie...Gospel of a Movie Lord', *Guardian on Sunday* August 11, p.36.

Sesay, Amadu and Adetanwa Odebiyi, eds., 1998, *Nigeria Women in Society and Development*, Ibadan: Dokun Publishers.

Sowole, Taju, 2002, 'Travails of a Viable Sector', *Guardian*, April 19, p.30.

Steinglass, Matt, 2002, 'When There's Too Much of a Not-Very-Good Thing', *New York Times*, May 26.

7

Conceptions of Gender in Colonial and Post-colonial Discourses: The Case of Mozambique

Signe Arnfred

Introduction

Seen in terms of conventional political science, and also as experienced by Mozambican men and women, the recent history of Mozambique has been very dramatic. There have been several changes of political regimes, and almost three decades of war, from the onset of the armed struggle in 1964 to the Rome peace agreement in 1992. There have been two remarkable political shifts during this period. First there was the transition in 1975 from Portuguese colonialism to political independence and Frelimo socialism after a successful war of liberation. Second, in the late 1980s the government moved from Frelimo socialism to neo-liberal economic policies and a structural adjustment programme (PRE – *Programa da Re-estruturação Económica*) under World Bank leadership. This time the name of the government did not change. Frelimo remained in power, but with a somewhat different political and economic agenda after its fifth Party Congress in 1989.

The point I want to make in this paper has to do with the contradiction between on the one hand the ways in which each of these different politics of government have seen themselves as radical breaks with the immediate past, and on the other hand the ways in which these different political regimes (in theory as well as in practice) have approached issues of gender. Examined through a gendered lens these apparently radically different political lines have much in common. Considered from this angle the political continuities seem much more dominant than the radical breaks.

From one point of view these decades of history include dramatic changes in government. The process has moved all the way from colonial dominance and economic exploitation, to socialist politics and (attempts at) a planned economy in a one-party state, to multi-party democracy and neo-liberal economic structures. From another point of view the dramatic changes are overshadowed by persistent continuities. With regard to the field of politics and policies on gender, the lines of thinking of each new period can be shown to build heavily on the previous one. This is the case in spite of the fact that for each of the decisive breaks, first Independence, and later the neo-liberal turn, part of the very profile of the change has been its gender policies. Frelimo Socialism boasted a high profile regarding women's emancipation, as in the famous words of Samora Machel: 'The liberation of women is a necessity for the revolution, a guarantee of its continuity and a condition for its success' (Machel 1973). Similarly the present period of donor-dominated development stresses the importance of gender mainstreaming in all political spheres.

This paper examines political documents – political speeches, official reports and so on – from these three major periods: First there was the transition in 1975 from Portuguese colonialism to political independence and Frelimo socialism after a successful war of liberation; second, Frelimo socialism; and third, the SAP/PRE period of donor-dominated development. I shall focus on lines of thinking and implicit assumptions, but also on actual policies on gender issues in the respective periods.[1]

Portuguese colonialism

Portuguese colonial documents and political speeches make for interesting reading for their ideological bluntness: 'To us Portuguese, colonization is essentially to lift the indigenous populations to our own level of civilization, by teaching them our religion, our language, our customs. (...) It is our mentality that we want to transmit to the people of the colonies, we are not intending to take away their riches' (Ministro das Colonías, in *Boletim Geral das Colónias*, 1940). Colonisation for the Portuguese, according to the Archbishop of Lourenço Marques, is about civilisation, Christianisation and *aportuguesamento* – Portugalisation – of the indigenous population (Cardeal-Arcebispo, Lourenço Marques 1960: 2).[2]

Gender issues are rarely mentioned in these political statements. In the colonial context, gender relations matching a Christian ideal are taken for granted as an aspect of the civilising, Christianising and Portugalising mission. The conception of gender embedded in the civilising mission only becomes explicit when it is challenged. One example is the difficulties Portuguese observers encountered in coming to terms with the matrilineal societies of northern Mozambique.

It is pathetic to see how the writers of colonial reports[3] struggle to make the position of women in the matrilineal North[4] fit the pre-conceived image of oppressed subordinated African women in need of liberation. According to da Silva Rego (1960) in the North it is the woman who dominates the family. The husband must leave his own village in order to marry. If the marriage does not work out he must leave, and the woman can re-marry (da Silva Rego 1960: 85). This of course is unacceptable by Christian standards, but women take pride in the system, and they fight against changes. This *matriarchy* (ie matriliny) might even look like women's emancipation, da Silva Rego says, hastening to explain that in actual fact this is far from the case. First because the *individual* dignity of the woman is not respected – women are subordinated to the clan. Second, true emancipation of the woman is for her to be part of a Christian family, with the man as the natural head of the family *(chefe natural da família)* and the woman at his side (da Silva Rego 1960: 86, 25).

Measured against Christian marriage – monogamy, indissolubility and the man as head of the family – everything is wrong with family relations under conditions of matriliny. Marriages are not particularly stable, and worst of all, the husband/ father has no entrenched position. Men's positions are derived through women (not the other way round) and men are important as uncles (mothers' brothers), not as fathers/progenitors. To the colonial administration, matriliny – or matriarchy (*matriarchado*) as it is called in contemporary texts – is unacceptable, presenting 'indisputable inconveniences' (Rita Ferreira et al 1964: 78) for a series of reasons. Apart from family life being less stable, and the father not head of the family, 'it is an acknowledged fact that patrilineal societies are better suited than the matrilineal ones for adaptation to rapid social and economic change' (Rita Ferreira et al 1964: 78). Matriliny conforms neither to the demands of Christianity, nor to the demands of development; and furthermore these societies are irritatingly resistant to change.

The difficult matrilineal societies in the north are described as primitive and backward. Women are embedded in demeaning traditional customs. They enjoy less access to schools and they are burdened by heavy workloads. Thus defined, women are now positioned in the usual subordinate situation, and Christianity and civilisation can come to their rescue with offers of dignity in Christian marriages, courses in sowing and hygiene (sowing was considered important as the semi-nudity of women was perceived as offensive), and men taking over agricultural work (Rita Ferreira et al 1964: 79).

There is an interesting relation between work and gender in this colonial discourse. As for men, inducing (or forcing) them to work is part of the civilising mission. The image of the lazy African is the point of departure; work as such has a civilising effect, and the repression of idleness is a goal in itself 'dignifying and uplifting the native through the work' (Governador Geral de Mozambique, in *Boletim Geral das Colónias,* 1948). This line of argument seems only valid for men, however. As for women, the opposite seems to be the case. For women a heavy workload is an indication of subordination, the civilising mission being to lift it off her shoulders, in order to enable her to devote herself to housework.

'Development goes in the direction of leaving the bulk of agricultural work to the man. Also in Africa the woman shall become the queen of the home: a *Rainha do lar*' (da Silva Rego 1960: 26). Civilisation thus also includes the well known division between public and private spheres, with the husband 'the natural head of the family' as worker and breadwinner, and the wife and mother as 'queen of the home'.

This is how things worked – or were supposed to work – at the level of ideology. In practical terms Portuguese colonialism was indeed based on women's productive work in family agriculture, feeding the family while the men were away on forced or contract labour. Colonial exploitation of Mozambican wage labour was conditioned by salaries being kept very low, as male workers' families were supported through women's work on the land. Also the forced cotton cultivation in the North depended heavily on women's labour. According to Allen Isaacman (1996) the physical burdens of the cotton regime – forced cultivation on family plots, usually one hectare for husband-and-wife, and half a hectare for single women – fell disproportionately on women's shoulders. 'Women were forced to help their husbands clear new fields and, in men's absence, to cut trees and remove heavy stumps and even plow – strenuous tasks that in the past had been performed almost exclusively by men' (Isaacman 1996: 53). At the same time, of course, women retained the principal responsibility for food production and household work. The colonial regime, thus, depended on women's double workload: In the official ideology they were (or ought to be) housewives; in actual fact they were major producers.

An additional problem with the '*Rainha do lar*' ideology is that it naturalised women's procreative capacity, and restricted their role as mothers to the private sphere. In this way, the ground was pulled from under the feet of women in northern Mozambique taking pride in their role as mothers, *not* in the private context of nuclear male-headed families, but in powerful positions as lineage elders. Power based on maternity and fertility is not recognised in the civilised Christian context, however, where fertility is trivialised as a function of nature, and maternity is reduced to the education of children in the seclusion of the patriarchal family.

Yet another aspect of women's lives, also not accepted in its own right in Christian/colonial thinking, is sexuality. The general attitude of the Portuguese colonial power was a strong condemnation of female initiation rites, because of their focus on development and education of female sexuality. [5] Female initiation rites were considered by the colonial administration as well as by the Catholic church as 'immoral and offensive to the human nature' (Medeiros 1995: 5). The attitude of the Protestant missions was no more permissive. In the writings of Henri-Alexandre Junod, a clergyman of the Swiss Mission,[6] customs relating to female sexuality were so 'vile and immoral' (Junod 1912/1974: 176) that he could only speak of them in an appendix for 'doctors and ethnographers' written in Latin. It was bad enough to think of explicit education of male sexuality; but to confront education of female sexuality would be beyond the pale.

Similarly, Terence Ranger reports from Masasi district in Southern Tanzania, populated by matrilineal Makhuwa, Maconde and Yao peoples immediately north of Mozambique, how 'the missionaries did not approve of the concept of womanhood in Masasi society' (Ranger 1972: 237). Ranger's discussion relates to Protestant missionary attitudes to female initiation rites, which were considered as 'much more obscene than the male ceremony'. 'It was difficult', writes Ranger, 'for the missionaries, perhaps especially for the white laywomen who had most to do with female initiation, to see the rites as Africans saw them. (....) There was a constant tension between the mission view of the role of women in Masasi, and the women's view of their own role' (Ranger 1972: 237, 247). On the 'civilised' background of the Victorian ideal of female passionlessness[7] and 'the Angel of the House' *(a Rainha do lar)* – as opposed to the demonised and demeaning image of the sexualised woman as prostitute and whore – it is not surprising that explicit celebration of female sexuality should be considered obscene and repugnant. According to this logic explicit female sexuality is indistinguishable from prostitution.

In the analysis of colonial attitudes to gender I have focused on the matrilineal societies in Northern Mozambique, because here the clashes between Christian 'civilisation' and African realities were most explicit. In actual fact, however, the situation was very similar in other parts of Mozambique. To the missionaries and colonisers' relief, thanks to patrilineal kinship systems, the man and father was the 'natural head of the family', and thanks to the bride-price *(lobolo)* marriages would tend to be more stable. Nevertheless, it is interesting to see that Rita Ferreira in 1964, pointing to the preponderant and prestigious position of women in 'traditional' society, also remarks that women's powerful positions in the south of Mozambique, instead of disappearing in fact had been *increasing* in recent years, due to the absence of many men for prolonged periods (six to eighteen months) on work contracts away from home (Rita Ferreira et al 1964: 76). But this is a limited power, Rita Ferreira adds, as the women continue to be more traditional and backward, less educated than the men. Thus the analysis ends up with the expected conclusion of subjugated women in need of civilisation and education.

Summing up the colonial attitude in terms of work, family, maternity and sexuality, the situation looks as follows:

Work: According to colonial ideology the men were lazy and the women overworked.[8] Men were urged, if not forced, to work more, with the legitimation that work in itself is a civilising activity. In the case of women, however, non-domestic work was an indication of oppression and subordination. At the level of ideology women should remain in the private sphere and devote themselves to housework as *Rainhas do lar*. At the level of practical policies, however, the colonial economy was based on women's productive work in agriculture, partly to feed their families, but also to secure agricultural output for export, as in the case of cotton.

Family: At the level of ideology the family in colonial politics should follow the Christian model, a goal for which the missionaries (Catholics and Protestants alike) were perpetually struggling. This ideal family did not correspond very neatly to family structures anywhere in Mozambique. The ideal family was monogamous, stable (divorces not tolerated) and with the man and father as family head. The missionaries speak of course of *equality* between man and wife, but it was a kind of equality for which the *natural* superiority of the man was a precondition: with woman as man's companion (and subordinate) but 'with equal dignity in front of God', as put by a Swiss Presbyterian historian in 1987 (Biber 1987: 64). At the level of families, however, colonial realities were different from colonial ideology: Families were broken up and dispersed by migratory work and by forced labour. Struggling to keep family networks intact was one of many forms of resistance to colonial oppression.

Maternity: Women's roles as mothers were located in the private sphere, as one aspect of their positions as *Rainhas do lar*. Since the Christian family structure is unwaveringly patriarchal, and since motherhood in addition to being privatised is also naturalised and trivialised, no (or very little) potential female power is embedded in the role of mother.

Sexuality: Female sexuality was considered a tool for procreation and nothing more. The civilised norm for women is passionlessness – 'Close your eyes and think of England' – allegedly the Victorian advice given to young women facing their sexual debut. To acknowledge the existence of female sexuality, to focus young women on their sexual potential, educating them in the area of sexual pleasure was considered vile, immoral and offensive to human nature.

Frelimo socialism

Unlike in colonial times, when gender was not a policy issue in itself, for Frelimo gender, or rather *women's emancipation*, becomes an goal in its own right. During the armed struggle against Portuguese colonial power, issues of gender equality had been put on the agenda by women themselves, demanding the creation a women's wing of the Frelimo guerilla army. In addition to the important female support to the guerilla struggle in terms of transport of weapons and other material, production and preparation of food etc., women claimed the right to become soldiers and to fight along with men (Casimiro 2001). The *Destacamento Feminino* was created in 1966, and a few years later (1973) was supplemented by the creation of a non-military women's organization, the *Organização da Mulher*

Moçambicana (OMM) in order to facilitate the mobilisation of peasant populations in support of the guerilla war. In one sense the OMM was a political organisation, created to support Frelimo; in another sense it was a politication of female gender networks which had always been there, creating a link from these networks to political power, i.e. Frelimo. As I was told by women in Cabo Delgado in 1983: 'During the war we held meetings, we mobilised women to transport war material, to grow food and to cook for the soldiers. Women volunteered, but sometimes husbands tried to prevent them from participating in the tasks of war. When that happened, we called in Frelimo. I remember a case of one man who was beating his wife. We tied his arms behind his back and took him to Frelimo. Frelimo told him that he should not fight his wife; it was better to fight the Portuguese together. The man became a soldier and the women continued her war work. During the war women were respected because we were organised' (Arnfred 1988: 6). Interviewing in the north of Mozambique in 1983–84, I realized that in daily talk 'OMM' was often synonymous with 'women'.

During the war it seems that women were still in command in the OMM, and even supported by Frelimo. After Independence in 1975 however, Frelimo took over. Matters as important as development of a policy for women's liberation could not be left to women – and certainly not to the largely uneducated peasant women who had struggled with Frelimo in the north of Mozambique. Centrally positioned in the Frelimo political line was the fight against 'traditional society' and the whole array of 'habits and customs', *usos e costumes,* around which the daily lives of most Mozambicans were constructed. The performance of customary ceremonies was not directly criminalised, but strong political campaigns were waged against them. These were the years of what has later been termed '*the abaixo politics*'. '*Abaixo* ' means 'down with', and slogans of 'down with *lobolo*', 'down with polygamy', 'down with initiation rites' were shouted at every political meeting. Frelimo's socio-historical analysis was put forward in the documents for the 2nd OMM conference in November 1976. This conference preceded the 3rd Frelimo congress in March 1977 by only a few months, and these two events together mark the transformation of the previous political front Frelimo into a socialist party. The fingerprints of a communist party's socio-historical analysis are very visible in the OMM 2nd conference documents. 'Traditional society' was seen as 'feudal' and it was analysed in terms of exploitation and oppression, not just by colonialism, but in equal measure by indigenous power structures. Any customary beliefs and practices were considered obscurantist, oppressive and an obstacle to progress and modernity. Central in all of this was the alleged oppression and humiliation of women.

Regarding the understanding of women's position in 'traditional society', Frelimo's analysis was not very different from the colonial one. Women were constructed as humiliated and oppressed. The analysis goes as follows: All

Mozambicans, men and women alike were exploited and oppressed by the colonial system, but in addition to this 'the Mozambican peasant woman is the victim of another form of oppression which is linked to the traditional-feudal ideology. This ideology sees the women as having only the role of serving the man – as object of pleasure, producer of children and worker without a salary. (...) This position of women is reinforced through institutions and ceremonies such as 'initiation rites', as well as the whole system of marriage, including *lobolo*, premature and forced marriages, and polygamy' (OMM 1976: 89).

Just as it was the case in colonial writings, however, a certain ambiguity may be discerned. In some writings produced by the colonial power, even if the image of the oppressed and overworked woman was maintained, it had been conceded that 'women in traditional settings enjoy a considerable preponderance and prestige' (Rita Ferreira et al 1964: 75). Similarly, in some OMM/Frelimo documents, even if also here the dominant line was the one about the oppression of women in 'feudal-traditional' society (this being one major legitimation for Frelimo's push for modernization), here and there a different understanding can be felt, indicating that women's positions *might* also be threatened, and *not* improved, by modernisation. This understanding, which from my point of view, is much more precise, remained however an undercurrent, only popping up here and there in OMM/Frelimo writings, as in the following passage from the OMM 2nd conference documents: 'In the countryside, where in reality it is the woman who make plans, who organize and who has since immemorial times been the main producer, we nevertheless see her relegated to the role of simple workforce in our cooperatives and communal villages' (OMM 1976: 58).

Anyhow, in the dominant OMM/Frelimo view the way to women's emancipation goes through her participation in the principal task – *tarefa principal* – of the revolution. As put by Samora Machel in his speech to the 2nd OMM conference in November 1976: 'The decisive factor for the emancipation of woman is her engagement in the principal task, the task which transforms society. At that time [i.e. during the liberation war] it was the struggle for liberation. What then constitutes the principal task in the present phase of the revolution? The principal task of the present phase of our process is the following: The construction of the material and ideological base for building a socialist society. Thus for the implementation of this strategy, which has as its objective the construction of socialism, the principal task is production and the principal form of action is class struggle' (Machel 1976: 23).

Whereas participation in the war of liberation in many cases *did* bring about changes in male/female gender relations, strengthening the position of women *vis-à-vis* men at a local levels, participation in production or, as it was later re-phrased, participation in 'the increase of production and productivity so as to fulfill the economic plan' (Rebelo 1981) did not hold similar promise, from women's point of view. In post-independence Frelimo politics women were instrumentalisd as a workforce for the state and nation building. In Rebelo's 1981 speech[9] to the OMM national council, the focus was on the state and the economic plan, not on women. Women were requested to work hard in production, which in fact they had always been doing, and doing increasingly during the colonial period, and in addition to this were not to forget their tasks as wives and mothers. Nevertheless, this kind of politics was launched as 'women's emancipation'.

In actual fact what happened was just that the double workload for women – production as well as domestic work – was maintained, only with a different emphasis compared to the colonial ideology. Where during colonialism the lead image had been the *Rainha do lar,* with women's productive role maintained and increased, the lead image now was the woman soldier and the woman producer – the image of the state farm tractor driver being very popular in Party contexts – however with the domestic roles as wife and mother maintained. In the socialist theory of women's emancipation, from which the Frelimo women's politics drew inspiration, the emancipatory effect of 'women as wage workers' was conditioned by state organised alleviation of domestic tasks in terms of creches, kindergartens etc. Such conditions were not in place in Mozambique.

The Frelimo ideology regarding gender equality was also characterised by a certain ambiguity, however of a different kind, more like double standards, similar (again) to the colonial double standards of the 'social priority of the man over his wife, but equal dignity in front of God' (Biber 1987: 64). In OMM/Frelimo contexts the position of the man as family head was taken for granted, and the gender equality aspect amounted to woman being seen as man's companion, not his subordinate. Unlike the colonial writers, however, the Frelimo leadership was not troubled by matriliny, presumably because they knew nothing about it. Most of the programme-writing party cadres (the educated intellectuals) came from the patrilineal South. Matriliny was only 'discovered' in Frelimo contexts in the course of the preparations for the extraordinary OMM conference in 1984.[10]

The man as family head/the woman as man's companion were standard ingredients in the so-called 'socialist family' strongly supported by Frelimo as well as by OMM. Just like the Christian family model, the so-called 'socialist family' should be monogamous, stable and indissoluble. Women's easy access to divorce in the (matrilineal) North was frowned upon by the Party (Arnfred 1988). In the concluding document from the OMM extraordinary conference in 1984, the OMM (as always) toed the Party line: 'The OMM Extraordinary Conference emphasised specifically the vital importance of the coherence, stability and harmony of the family, because this is the basic cell of our society, the foundation of the Mozambican Nation, and the basis for the consolidation of our State' (OMM 1984).

In a speech during his travels in Gaza province in 1982 Samora Machel acknowledged the similarity between Frelimo and Christian morals: 'We have the same ideas regarding the combat of alcoholism and prostitution, but we differ regarding the ways of interpreting phenomena in the world' (Machel 1981: 42). In this speech Samora Machel specifically paid homage to the Protestant missions in southern Mozambique. The Protestants, like the Frelimo militants, had their reasons to be opposed to the Catholic colonial regime, enforcing *aportuguesamento* and greatly impeding Protestant missionary work. Thus an alliance developed between the Protestant church and the Frelimo militants,[11] as expressed by Samora Machel in the Gaza speech: 'Here, in the province of Gaza, the Protestant church, which was a centre for the struggle against colonialism, cultivated some of these values' (Machel 1982: 40). The values to which Machel refers are those regarding the importance of monogamous and stable marriages based on love, and the rejection of 'idleness *(vagabundice)* alcoholism, prostitution and marginality' (Machel 1982: 40). 'The Protestants helped us a lot', Machel continued, 'they educated us in order to for us to know the value of a human being. Ever since the Portuguese effected the total domination of our country, the Protestants constructed churches, and there they taught us about our history, our value as human beings, our identity. They taught us that we were Mozambicans, Africans and not Portuguese. (…) For this, *obrigado protestantes* (thank you, Protestants)' (Machel 1982: 40). In this speech Machel also spoke of the values of individual and collective hygiene and cleanliness, of clean nails and well-combed hair, and of the dignity of the family. Here as elsewhere he came down hard on women having children with different men, i.e. children without fathers, 'children of the bush': 'Such children are born like goats, coming from the bush, without knowledge of their father' (Machel 1982: 39). To be human in Samora's eyes was to live in a patriarchal, monogamous family: 'We are human beings, we have family, we have parents, we have sons and daughters, we have husbands and wives, we form a cell of society. For this reason we condemn adultery, for this reason we condemn "children of the bush"' (Machel 1982: 40).

Even worse than 'children of the bush' were prostitutes, 'women who transform their bodies into shops. (...) A prostitute is a rotten person with a foul stench' (Machel 1982: 33). A particular kind of prostitute, according to Machel, consisted of 'girls of twelve to sixteen years' who hunted down adult men in political power. Interestingly, the President's blame was laid exclusively on the girls, and not on his fellow Party members, the powerful politicians letting themselves be seduced. In a later speech, at the Extraordinary OMM conference in 1984, Samora Machel continued this line of blaming the women: 'It is a shame to be a single mother. The phenomenon, the very concept, should be extinct' (Machel 1984. Quoted in Arnfred 1985: 18).

I am quoting the Frelimo (and Mozambique) President at length, because I find the similarities between Frelimo and Christian/Protestant morals sadly striking. In spite of all talk of 'women's emancipation' Frelimo's moral worldview was strictly androcentric and even patriarchal. In the speeches of Samora Machel this whole moral package was termed 'socialist ethics' (Machel 1982: 40). In actual fact, however, it was very similar to the 'Protestant ethic' outlined by Max Weber in his famous work (Weber 1920/1984).[12] Even Machel's critique of *vagabundice* belongs here. According to Weber, for Protestants, the 'waste of time is the first and in principle the deadliest of sins' (Weber 1920/1984: 167). Weber also notes how Protestantism even more fiercely than Catholicism bans sexuality: Catholicism decrees celibacy for priests, monks and nuns, but it does not interfere with sexual life in general, as long as it is practiced in matrimony. Under Protestant puritanism, however, 'sexual intercourse is permitted, even within marriage, only as the means chosen by God for the increase of His glory, according to the commandment: 'Be fruitful and multiply' (Weber 1920/1984: 168). The Frelimo approach has many similarities with the Protestant line. Female initiation rites were considered, if not explicitly as vile and immoral, then certainly as oppressive and humiliating, and they were centrally positioned among the *usos e costumes* considered social problems for women, and which should become extinct. The 1976 OMM 2nd conference documents, just as later the 1984 extraordinary OMM conference documents, refer to initiation rites, *lobolo,* polygamy etc as 'women's social problems'. Seen from my vantage point, however, these *usos e costumes* were not *women's* as much as they were *Frelimo's* problems. These so-called 'women's social problems' pointed to aspects of Mozambican social life that did *not* conform to Frelimo's strongly Christian /Protestant-inspired version of modernity and development – aspects which Frelimo struggled to change and to control.

Also in denouncing 'tradtional-feudal society', *lobolo,* polygamy and the rest of it, there is an interesting ambiguity in Frelimo's line. Samora Machel in the 1982 Gaza speech was, as usual, strongly against 'traditional-feudal society', but he was *also* against young people who want to marry without a specific ceremony and without consulting the parents: 'They think that this is Independence', the President snorted, 'they behave like animals, and they say that this is Independence!' (Machel 1982: 34). Furthermore these youngsters, when reproached by their parents, call them old-fashioned and outdated, *ultrapassados.* In this dispute the President was on the side of the parents, who were instructed to maintain their authority *vis-à-vis* the misbehaving offspring. Thus traditional marriage was bad, but no marriage at all was even worse, and the parents, much more rooted in 'tradition' that the younger generation, were given support. This ambiguity later developed into the idea of 'positive and negative aspects of tradition' The decision regarding *what* is positive and *what* is negative remained, however, with Frelimo. As it was put in the General Resolution resulting from the OMM extraordinary conference regarding initiation rites: 'The Extraordinary Conference recommends that the local bodies of OMM, in coordination with the institutions of Education and Health, should go deeper into the study of context and practice of initiation rites, in order carefully to concretizise which are their negative and which their positive aspects. These bodies should submit their considerations to the Party leadership in order for it to have appropriate foundation for issuing directions as to what should be combated and what should be maintained' (OMM 1984).

One aspect of women's lives, which was not considered a social problem and thus did not figure in the OMM/Frelimo list of 'women's social problems' was motherhood. Frelimo had policies on work, family and (female) sexuality, but regarding maternity OMM merely advised a 2-year period between births (which conformed more or less to prescriptions of 'tradition'),[13] and projects for *saude materno-infantil* – mother-child health /reproductive health were established. Like 'gender' in colonial days, to Frelimo 'motherhood' was uncontroversial. As long as women produced the necessary amount of children for the Nation, all was well. Mozambique is fairly sparsely populated, so the Frelimo government welcomed a population increase. Talk of family planning was in terms of *spacing* births, less of limiting families. Also in this aspect, thus, women were instrumentalised and subordinated in relation the Nation's needs.

Summing up, I have characterised Frelimo ideology as follows:

Work: The model is the Soviet-socialist inspired 'women in men's jobs': The woman soldier, the woman tractor driver. Tacitly however, it is presumed that women also take care of domestic tasks. In actual reality women work a lot, particularly in agricultural production, as they have always been doing.

Family: The 'socialist family' is put forward as the ideal. This family model however is indistinguishable from a Christian, particularly a Protestant, ideal.

Sexuality: Female sexuality is dealt with only in negative terms (as prostitution, blaming the woman). Campaigns are waged against female initiation rites.

Maternity is taken for granted.

I have focused critically on Frelimo ideology, because of its deplorable lack of understanding of the actual conditions of male/female relations in Mozambican daily life, and because of its unsavory (to my taste) mix of socialist/communist ideology with Protestant puritanism, both of these lines of thought being strongly androcentric and patriarchal, if not outright misogynist. Nevertheless, in actual political practice in the post-Independence years, much did happen that was also beneficial to for women. There were wide-ranging programmes of education and mobilisation and political participation at local levels, to name just some of many important changes in the early years of Independence. Before long, however, the Frelimo-Renamo war paralysed political and economic change, and the Mozambique that emerged from the war in many respects was very different from the Mozambique of the immediate post-Independence period.

Donor-dominated development

The Mozambique of Frelimo socialism was a very particular country with a very particular colonial past and an equally important history of struggle. The Mozambique of SAP and PRE is just another poor African country. From the late 1980s onwards Mozambique became integrated in the 'normal' development setup under the neo-liberal auspices of the IMF and the World Bank, with donor agencies pouring in and with masses of international NGOs. Maputo's bumpy streets were flooded with donor agencies' expensive cars, and the previously empty shops were filled with goods for those who could afford them.

These transformations also brought changes in the field of gender. With the first UN Women's conference in 1975 in Mexico City and a further series of UN conferences on women, population and human rights, a globalised approach to 'women' and 'gender ' in development contexts was created. In a strange kind of dialogue between struggling women and accommodating/coopting state and donor bureaucracies, a standardised language and approach to gender issues were developed. Gender policies in this era greatly depend on gender struggles from below. The ideas of 'women in development' and later 'gender and development', were invented by women's groups and introduced into development language through lobbying and advocacy. Most frequently the government and donor agencies - in a general climate of neo-liberal politics - do their best to coopt and integrate, if possible by undermining in practice the political implications of the gender language that they have felt obliged to apply.

The very language of *gender* is a case in point[14]. When the vocabulary of gender-and-development was introduced into the development debate in the 1980s, it was advocated by feminists, who wanted to criticise the dominant women-in-development (WID) approach for dealing only with *integration* of women into existing development policies, with no critical analysis of development as such, and with no criticism of the unequal power relationships between men and women. Nevertheless, in spite of the good intentions, which were to politicise the WID debate through gender-and-development (GAD) thinking, the opposite seems to have happened. Instead of speaking about *women*, which implied an awareness of women' specific and often marginalised positions, the term *gender* came into use as a neutral term, referring to both women and men.

Because of the overall standardisation of development approaches in neo-liberal economic contexts, the situation in Mozambique is not very different from development approaches to gender elsewhere. The specificity is provided, not by the donor-and-government approaches themselves, but by challenges to government and development machineries from lobby groups of women activists, women's NGOs and intellectual women. During the Frelimo era Mozambican civil society organisations were almost non-existent, and OMM had been the one and only women's organisation. With the political changes in the late 1980s – the introduction of PRE (*Programa de Re-estruturação Economica*), later re-named PRES (*Programa de Re-estruturação Economica e Social*) – NGOs emerged all over the place, including a series of local women's NGOs. An umbrella organization, *Forum Mulher*, was created, embracing national and international NGOs, government institutions working with women's issues, as well as women/gender-aware individuals from trade unions and political parties.[15] Over the years *Forum Mulher* has become a focus for debate on women's issues and quite an important lobby group, pushing women's issues where and when it is felt needed. After the 1995 Beijing Fourth World Conference on Women, *Forum Mulher* was active in the setting up of a so-called operative group *(Grupo Operativo)* led by the Minister for Co-ordination of Social Welfare, and incorporating representatives for fifteen different ministries, as well as in the drafting of a Post-Beijing National Plan of Action (da Silva and Andrade 2000: 81). The planning in this case took place at a very general level, but nevertheless it could be used as a tool for putting further pressure on the government.

The PROAGRI Programme

That pressure is needed is obvious. The development of a unified, donor financed and supervised plan for the ministry of Agriculture, the so-called PROAGRI: National Programme for Agrarian Development, may in this context serve as an example. The PROAGRI process started in the mid-1990s and since then a series of plans have been elaborated and a series of joint donor evaluations have taken place. From the side of the donors there has been a more or less steady insistence regarding consideration of gender factors in the PROAGRI planning process, and various gender focal points internally in the Ministry of Agriculture as well as in the Directories for Agriculture in the provincial governments have been established. Nevertheless the push for gender awareness in PROAGRI contexts continues to be an uphill struggle.

As expressed by Wenke Adam, who was involved at an early point in the PROAGRI process, all the talk about 'gender awareness' is in actual fact very simple:

> Actually it is nothing revolutionary, it is just simply to acknowledge the fact that in agriculture men and women generally perform different tasks, complementary and socially defined, and that when somebody plans to make an intervention in this sector, it will be a good idea to make an analysis regarding who does what and why, in order to be able to direct the support to the proper persons, in the most adequate form, for the best effect. (...) An important aspect, in this context not to be forgotten, is that in Mozambique, for historical reasons, the major part of the actual work with the crops in the field is done by women, as their regular and permanent work. The men will clear the bush, and they may participate in

the sowing and the harvesting, but for the rest of the time they will often be on the lookout for waged employment in order to be able to buy such non-agricultural products as the family needs. The men also deal with the cattle. If we consider the fact that the family sector produces around 95 percent of the country's basic agricultural products, it becomes abundantly clear that is the Mozambican women who feed Mozambique with grain, potatoes, groundnuts and vegetables. Any support to the family sector should thus be directed to this group... (Adam 1997: 9).

This indeed seems very simple and straightforward. That the main producers in family agriculture are women is a well known fact, and since in Mozambique the family sector in agriculture is by far the largest one[16] in terms of persons engaged in production, as well as in terms of produced goods, women obviously are centrally positioned. How then is this reflected in the plan?

It is not. The PROAGRI Master Document, containing the 1998–2003 plan, is a masterpiece in deliberate gender blindness. The family sector figures fairly prominently. It is acknowledged that this sector comprises some 3,000,000 families occupying a total farming area of 3,500,000 ha of land. It is also acknowledged that about 55 percent of the total farmed area is concentrated in the three northern provinces of Nampula, Cabo Delgado and Niassa. But gender aspects are not mentioned at all. In the text of the document neither men nor women are agents; the way it is put is as follows: 'the family sector grows commercial crops such as ....', 'the family sector engages in the cutting and sale of firewood...' (Ministry of Agriculture 1998: 29). To be noted here is first that the 'sector' as such is the subject, neither men nor women, and secondly that what is mentioned are *commercial* crops and firewood *for sale*. That women in the family sector produce food to feed the vast majority of the Mozambican population *outside* the market economy is apparently of no concern. Also not mentioned is the fact that the three northern provinces are populated by Makhuwa, Maconde and Yao peoples, all matrilineal.

That this fact is not mentioned comes, however, as no surprise. Especially as the general strategy of the whole PROAGRI endeavour is defined as 'the transformation of the subsistence agriculture into one that is more integrated in the functions of production, distribution and processing, in order to achieve the development of a subsistence agrarian sector which contributes with surpluses for the market and the development of an efficient and participatory entrepreneurial sector' (Ministry of Agriculture 1998: 37). The gender effects of this strategy are not investigated, and maybe for good reasons. Transformation of subsistence agriculture into more market-oriented production will, especially in the matrilineal areas where generally women control not only food production but also the distribution of food, imply the transfer of social power from women to men.[17] And as for the development of 'an efficient and participatory entrepreneur sector' – one may wonder if these 'entrepreneurs' in their majority will be women – or men?

Oddly reminiscent of the colonial as well as the Frelimo ambiguities, acknowledging women's 'preponderance and prestige' in traditional settings (Rita Ferreira et al 1964: 75), or admitting that in the countryside it is 'the woman who organize and who has since immemorial times been the main producer' (OMM 1976: 58), the PROAGRI plan contains such ambiguities, in however weak an undercurrent. No talk of women, no! But it is acknowledged that in the family sector 'producers are highly efficient in the utilization of the existing means and that they possess an enormous potential to increase the current levels of production' (Ministry of Agriculture 1998: 53). The way, however, in which this potential will be developed is through marketisation, which by all indications is most likely to favour men.

Thus the PROAGRI plan is full of gender, but it is all implicit, and the strategies advocated will be to the advantage of men. Perhaps this is the reason for the consistent gender blindness. The issue of gender (men/women) is mentioned only *once* in the 94-page document, in the following words: 'An evaluation of the PROAGRI in the light of the gender issue will be conducted in 1988' (Ministry of Agriculture 1998: 92). In my reading, this looks like a war against women. No wonder that the present coordinator of the Gender Unit in the Ministry of Agriculture is frustrated: 'We have difficulties in getting the leaders within the Ministry to take gender seriously. Some within the Ministry say that we are doing this work related to gender because it is the wish of the donors, and that we are doing it in order to ensure that we get the funds' (personal communication from a November 2002 review team).

In the Post-Beijing peroid Gender Units were created in several ministries, without however a clear mandate and outside the hierarchies of power. The 1998 review requested in the PROAGRI Master Document has this to say about the Ministry of Agriculture Gender Unit: 'It is placed in a situation where it has neither sufficient authority nor autonomy for doing what it ought to do. (...) At the moment the coordinator of the Gender Unit in the Ministry of Agriculture does not participate in the management group meetings, nor does she participate in the counseling group. In this way there are few possibilities of letting the women's views be heard in these fora, or for introducing and promoting gender perspectives in the Ministry's policies and plans' (quoted in Arthur 2000: 14).

The situation in the Ministry of Agriculture may be extreme, but it is not unique. In a critical evaluation of the Mozambican governments gender politics and programmes post-Beijing, from 1995-1999, commissioned by Forum Mulher, Maria José Arthur gives several similar examples. Summing up regarding the ministerial Gender Units she says: 'If these units are not given capacity to make interventions, power to take decisions and means to carry them out, they will remain no more than symbols of an intention which will never get beyond dead words on paper' (Arthur 2000: 14).

The new Family Law

At a very formal level all looks well. Male/female equality is guaranteed in the constitution, and the government, as in most African countries, has ratified the CEDAW convention. At the level of political practice, however, things work very differently. An example here is the long struggle for a new family law. Very early in the immediate post-independence period, a Family Law project was developed, in order to replace the Portuguese *Código Civil* of 1967, containing several clauses which contradicted the constitution. The Family Law project contained clauses regarding acceptance of 'de facto' unions in order legally to protect the majority of women who were married 'traditionally' and not according to any written law; the concept of a 'male family head' was eliminated, divorce was facilitated and polygamy was made illegal. Perhaps for these reasons the Family Law project did not result in a new law. In 1982 a directive was issued, by virtue of which parts of the Family Law project could be used as guiding principles for juridical decisions. But in 1992 this directive was annulled, with the implication that it was now again the patriarchal values of the Portuguese Codigo Civil which ruled family relations. As an aspect of the post-Beijing mobilisation women's groups have since 1997 been pushing for parliamentary action regarding the Family Law. The law has been on the parliament's agenda several times, but was been repeatedly and systematically postponed. At long last in April 2003, the new Family Law was finally discussed and passed in the Assembly of the Republic (AIM April 29, 2003). That this new law has not constituted a regression with regard to any of the radical suggestions brought forward in the first draft of 1980 is remarkable, the general political situation taken into consideration. As far as I can see the explanation for this is to be found in one particular fact: the perpetually active Maputo lobby groups of researchers and activists regarding women's issues, who have been feeding the Frelimo minister of Justice with facts and arguments, and also, of course, the minister's willingness to listen. As noted in local media: 'The parliamentary debate showed that this is one of the few issues where the government is to the left of the Frelimo parliamentary group. While every speech broadly welcomed the bill, they usually contained reservations' (AIM April 29, 2003). According to the new bill the husband will no longer automatically represent the family; either partner may do so; 'de facto' marriages will be recognised, which means that children of this type of union will have the same protection and recognition as children of any other form of marriage, and that the father, if the marriage breaks down, will be obliged to pay maintenance. Polygamous unions are not outlawed, but they are also not recognised, except at the time of the man's death, in order to safeguard the inheritance rights of his wives and children.

I shall leave the current situation here, with these examples, one rather negative (the PROAGRI case) and one surprisingly positive (the new Family Law) from the point of view of women's activist groups. Now for a brief summing up regarding the four aspects of work, family, maternity and sexuality.

As for *work*, women's work in the market sector is considered an indication of gender equality. This is not much different from the socialist vision of the woman wage worker and tractor driver: that is to say, women in men's work. What women have to do with apart from this kind of work, in terms of housework and care-taking, seems more invisible than ever.

Family: The family position is ambiguous, due to the recent passing of the new Family Law. In a Government programme proposal for 2000-2004, Frelimo flags its old preference for Christian family values, stating that 'the Frelimo government will (...) guarantee the continuation of the Fatherland and stability of the family, the basic cell of our society' (Frelimo Comité Central 1999, quoted in Arthur 2000: 11). Women's groups have been struggling for different visions of family life, more on women's terms. Now the women's groups' visions have been turned into law. Of course realities still do not change overnight, but obviously this is an important step in the right direction.

Sexuality: Female initiation rites, which were a burning issue in colonial times as well as during Frelimo socialism, are a non-issue nowadays. People are free to perform any ritual they wish, and initiation rites are now again openly taking place, particularly in the northern part of the country. Because of the HIV/AIDS pandemic, which is widespread also in Mozambique (the prevalence rate of HIV infected on a national level is currently 12 percent [Danida 2002]) sexuality is often being associated with risk and danger. The strong moral tone of previous politics has eased, but has been replaced by a discourse of risk and danger.

Motherhood is only an issue in practical terms, as for example in the contexts of health (where women's reproductive health is integrated in the Family Health Section), and of maintenance payments. *A Rainha do lar* has disappeared, but motherhood as a basis for female power receives no political recognition.

Conclusion

In spite of the overall conclusion that examined through a gendered lens the political continuities during the latest fifty years of turbulent Mozambican history have been more apparent than the radical changes, some changes *have* taken place. One of the more important ones is the appearance of civil society lobby groups for women's rights, gender equality and the promotion of women's perspectives. But these groups fight an uphill battle. First they must fight just to keep women's issues on the agenda, and secondly they must fight on the issue of *how* women's issues are integrated into the political process. But by their actions, they might, with time, be able to integrate some of the forms of female power which are still embedded in the social systems of the vast and populous matrilineal societies in the north of Mozambique into the mainstream of the nation's life.

Notes

1. The discussion is based on my knowledge of Mozambique from four years of life in Maputo and work as a sociologist in the OMM 1980–84, including several travels to the provinces; frequent visits to the country during 1985–97, and six months of fieldwork in Nampula province 1998–99.

2. Portugalisation in practice was among other things forced use of Portuguese as language of instruction in mission schools, to the great annoyance of the Protestant missionaries, who were not of Portuguese origin, and who preferred to teach in local languages. (On these and related issues, cf. the excellent paper by David Hedges, 1985).

3. The two reports under consideration here are A da Silva Rego 1960: *Alguns problemas socio-missionárias da Africa Negra*, and Antonio Rita Ferreira et al 1964: *Promoção Social em Moçambnique*. Both reports are published by *Junta de Investigações do Ultramar* in Lisbon.

4. Major ethnic groups, all matrilineal, in northern Mozambique are Makhuwa, Makonde and Yao. According to the data collected in *II Recenseamento Geral da População e Habitação* in 1997, almost 40 percent of the Mozambican population speak Emakhuwa or Elomwe (closely connected languages spoken by Makhuwa people), Shimakonde or Ciyao.

5. Female genital cutting or mutilation is not a part of initiation rituals in Mozambique. As opposed to cutting, the rituals, particularly in Northern Mozambique, focus on female sexual capacity building.

6. Only in the 1960s did the Swiss Mission (*Missão Suissa*) change its name to *Igreja Presbiteriana de Mocambique*. (Cruz e Silva e Loforte 1998: 43).

7. Cf Nancy Cott 1978: *Passionlessness: An Interpretation of Victorian Sexual Ideology, 1790–1850*.

8. Cf. Ann Whitehead 2000 for contemporary versions of similar ideological presumptions.

9. Jorge Rebelo at that point was Secretary for ideology of the Frelimo Central Committee.

10. Cf Arnfred 1988, 1990.

11. Cruz e Silva (2001) highlights the importance of the Swiss-Presbyteran mission in southern Mozambique for the formation, particularly from 1930 onwards, of an educated, politically conscious (i.e. nationalist and anti-colonial) elite.

12. Cf. Arnfred 1990.

13. 'Traditionally' in most of Mozambique, mothers are/were supposed to breastfeed children at least until they walk; in this period chastity is/was prescribed.

14. Cf. Arnfred 2001a.

15. Cf. Arthur 2002, in itself an important, critical contribution, commissioned by *Forum Mulher.*
16. According to the 1997 census (*II Recenseamento Geral da Popula> ão e Habitação 1997*) 79 percent of the Mozambican population are 'peasants', i.e. family farmers. Among these two-thirds are women.
17. Cf. Arnfred 2001b.

References

Adam, Wenke, 1997, 'Quo vadis, gender?', *NotMoç – Notícias de Moçambique,* no 99, Edição especial de 7 de Abril.

AIM – Agencia de Informação de Moçambique.

Arnfred, Signe, 1985, 'Rapport från kvinnokonferensen i Maputo', *Afrikabulletinen,* no 81.

Arnfred, Signe, 1988, 'Women in Mozambique: Gender Struggle and Gender Politics', *Review of African Political Economy,* no 41.Arnfred, Signe. 1990. 'Notes on Gender and Modernization. Examples from Mozambique', in A. Weis Bentzon, ed., *The Language of Development Studies,* New Social Science Monographs, Copenhagen.

Arnfred, Signe, 2001a, 'Questions of Power: Women's Movements, Feminist Theory and Development Aid', *SIDA studies* no 3, SIDA Stockholm.

Arnfred, Signe, 2001b, 'Ancestral Spirits, Land and Food: Gendered power and land tenure in Ribáuè, Nampula Province', in Rachel Waterhouse and Carin Vijfhuizen, eds., *Strategic Women, Gainful Men. Gender, Land and natural resources in different rural contexts in Mozambique,* Maputo.

Arthur, Maria José, 2000, *Políticas da Desigualdade?* Maputo.

Biber, Charles, 1987, *Cent ans au Mozambique, Reportage sur l'histoire de l'eglise presbyterienne du Mozambique,* Lausanne.

Boletim Geral das Colónias, 1940, Sessão Inaugural do Congresso Colonial, Discurso de S.Ex O Sr Ministro das Colónias.no 186:

Bolemin Geral das Colónias, 1948, Entrevista no 'Oriente' com o Governador Geral de Moçambique, reproducido em BGC., Junho.

O Cardeal-Arcebispo de Lourenço Marques, 1960, *As Missões Católicas Portuguesas em Moçambique. O Nosso Depoiment.*

Casimiro, Isabel, 2001, *Repensando as Relações entre Mulher e Homem no Tempo de Samora,* Centro de Estiudos Africanos, Unversidade Eduardo Mondlane.

Cott, Nancy, 1978, 'Passionlessness: An Interpretation of Victorian Sexual Ideology, 1790-1850', *Signs,* Winter.

Cruz e Silva, Teresa and Ana Loforte, 1998, 'Christianity, African Traditional Religions and Cultural Identity in Southern Mozambique', in James L. Coz, ed., *Rites of Passage in Contemporary Africa,* Cardiff Academic Press.p.43

Cruz e Silva, Teresa, 2001, *Protestant Churches and the Formation of Political Consciousness in Southern Mozambique (1930 – 1974),* Basel: P.Schlettwein Publishing.

Danida, 2002, *Review of Danida-suppported Activities in the Agricultural Sector Programme Support*, Copenhagen.

Hedges, David, 1985, 'Educação, missões e a ideologia política de assimilação, 1930–1960', *Cadernos de História* no 1, Boletim do Dept da História, UEM.

Instituto Nacional de Estatística, 2000, *Situação linguística de Moçambique. Dados do II recenceamento geral da população e habitação de 1997*, Maputo.

Instituto Nacional de Estatística, 2000, *II recenceamento geral da população e habitação de 1997, Resultados Definitivos*, Maputo.

Isaacman, Allen, 1996, *Cotton is the Mother of Poverty*, London: James Currey.

Junod, Henri-Alexandre, 1912/1974, *Usos e Costumes dos Bantos*, Imprensa Nacional, Lourenco Marques.

Machel, Samora,1973, 'Discurso na 1a confererencia da OMM', Maputo 1976.

Machel, Samora,1976, 'Discurso no acto de abertura da 2a conferéncia da OMM', in *Documentos da 2a Conferencia*, Maputo, 1977.

Machel, Samora, 1982, 'Discurso na Província de Gaza. Marco 1982', *Revista Tempo*, 600/ Abril.

Medeiros, Eduardo, 1995, *Os Senhores da Floresta*, Universidade de Coimbra.

Ministry of Agriculture,1998, *PROAGRI Master Document 1998–2003*, Maputo.

OMM, 1977, *Documentos da 2a Conferencia*, Maputo.

OMM, 1984, Resolução Geral da Conferéncia Extraordinária da OMM, in *Revista Tempo*, 737, Novembro.

da Silva Rego, A., 1960, *Alguns problemas socio-missionários da Africa Negra*, Junta de Investigaçoes do Ultramar. Lisboa.

da Silva, Terezinha e Ximena Andrade, 2000, *Beyond Equalities. Women in Mozambique*, WIDSAA, the Netherlands Government Directorate of International Co-operation (DGIS).

Ranger, Terence, 1972, 'Missionary Adaptation of African Religious Institutions: The Masasi Case', in Ranger, T.O. and I.N.Kimambo, eds., *The Historical Study of African Religion with Special Reference to East and Central Africa*, Heinemann.

Rebelo, Jorge, 1981, *Discurso no Conselho Coordenador Nacional da OMM*, mimeo, Maputo.

Rita Ferreira, A, et al., 1964, *Promoção social em Moçambique*, Junta de Investigaçoes do Ultramar no 74, Lisboa.

Weber, Max, 1920/1984, *Die protestantische Etik I*, Tübingen.

Whitehead, Ann, 2000, 'Continuities and Discontinuities in Political Constructions of the Working Man in Rural Sub-Saharan Africa: The "Lazy Man" in African Agriculture', *The European Journal of Development Research*, Vol 12, no 2.

8

Traversing Gender and Colonial Madness: Same-Sex Relationships, Customary Law and Change in Tanzania, 1890–1990[1]

Babere Kerata Chacha

Introduction

The main aim of this paper is to shed light upon woman-to-woman marriage, which I view here as a system that radically disrupt[ed] male domination and allowed women to traverse gender barriers in order to rectify reproductive, social and economic problems. The paper examines the institution within the framework of colonial and post-colonial judicial systems and in the context of African customary law. It is argued here that colonial authorities took several ineffective measures to abolish the practice and even the post-colonial state seems to have taken an even more ambivalent attitude towards the practice, especially as far as rights of the children are concerned. The matter as we shall see was even complicated when the authorities held that this marriage was not a form of customary marriage and even went ahead to order divorce decrees.

Woman-to-woman marriage is a predominantly African institution. This form of marriage is an unfamiliar subject to most people outside Africa and even Africans themselves. It is only vaguely understood by historians and social scientists. It remains relatively obscure, and in family studies discourse, the topic is pushed to the extreme margins by an historical fixation on western nuclear families as a universal ideal (Njambi & O'Brien 1998).

While this type of marriage occurred in different forms, debates have emerged on whether the marrying woman attains a transformed status or not. Also, the idea of same sex relationships has spurred discussion of the sexuality of women in such marriages. A few texts imply that there may be sexual involvement in these marriages, Herskovits (1937), for example, suggested that Dahomey woman-

woman marriages sometimes involved sexual relations between the women. Blackwood (1984) argues that lesbian behaviour cannot be ruled out while others consider the marriage a non-sexual institution. Evans-Pritchard (1951) observed that woman-to-woman marriage occurs among the Nuer where a female is barren. The barren woman will take a wife, hence becoming a cultural man, and also arranges for what Ramet calls a 'progenitor' for the wife so that 'she' becomes a father (Ramet 1990). Similar forms of marriage are mentioned by Gluckman (1970) among the Zulu of Natal and Uchendu for the Igbo of Southern Nigeria, Uchendu relates that his own mother married several wives (Uchendo 1965). Among the Lovedu, Krige invariably uses the term 'female husbands' to describe women who raise the bride-wealth. She *inter alia* suggests that a female husband can be a woman headman who marries another headman of a district (Krige 1974).

The practice of woman-to-woman marriage among the Nandi of Kenya, as it has been described by Oboler (1980), is another interesting case. According to this writer, a Nandi woman with no sons can use the cattle belonging to her 'house' to marry a wife of her own. Therefore, the Nandi woman who takes a wife is fundamentally recorded as a man, a situation that is quite unique with other cases of woman-to-woman marriage on the African continent. The woman ceases to have sexual intercourse with a man and even dresses like a man and so on.

Several authors have studied the Kuria and attempted to address the issue of woman-to-woman marriage. However, a lack of a properly historical approach to the subject has allowed speculation on the role of these marriages in Kuria society. Rwezaura, for example, claims it was a 'pre-capitalist tradition' in the region (Rwezaura 1985), while Bonavia and Baker who worked as officials in Musoma District in colonial Tanganyika call it an old custom. Bonavia held it was abolished by common consent in 1927 (cited in Alsaker 1995). However the practice arose long before the colonial period and increased in popularity towards the end of the twentieth century. Scholars of the Kuria like Rwezaura, (op cit.) and Tobisson (1986) have themselves tended to neglect the subject and more specifically the sexual praxis involved in this type of marriage. The authors have identified the marriage as woman-to-woman marriage i.e daughter-in-law marriage which is correct in describing a conventional marriage but wrong in this context.

The Abakuria on whom this study focuses are an agro-pastoral society straddling the Kenyan and Tanzanian border. They inhabit the vast districts of Musoma, Mara and Serengeti. Centuries of geographical isolation had permitted the indigenous growth of a culture and social organisation different in striking aspects from those of nearby communities and from the general cultural patterns of the East African people (Chacha 1998).

Woman-to-Woman Marriage and House Property System in Late Pre-colonial Tanzania

For most of the communities in pre-colonial Tanzania, ownership of important resources was communal. Even where families and individuals had rights to use a particular piece of land, their rights were not conceived of as absolute in the terms of current private property rights regimes. These resources were used according to collective communal rules. No single source controlled the resources and access to them was limited to an identifiable community with set rules on the way those resources are to be managed. Non-members of the community were excluded from accessing the resource. Collective arrangements usually made at the community level regulated access to and use of such resources.

Family life among most of the communities in Tanzania was (and still is) organised along patriarchal lines whereby the male is the head of the household. Succession to property was through the male lineage whose duty it was to ensure that all members of the family had access to the property. Studies carried out in eastern and southern Africa have revealed that the basis for the male inheriting property was the fact that men stayed within the family unlike women who, when married, left their domiciles of origin and joined their husbands' families. The desire to keep family wealth within the community dictated that it be held by the man. As we shall see these family structure and inheritance procedures tended to complicate the rights of barren and sonless women in Tanzania.

Procedurally, the relationship was formed in the same way as a conventional marriage, being usually preceded by the transfer of cattle from the 'house' of the female husband to the bride's father. The bride-wealth for this marriage was usually higher than the ordinary marriages, however, this fact differ from Ruel's' (1959:109) findings though this may have been due to difference in time of research. The main aim of woman to woman marriage was to serve a son for the 'house' to which the young woman was sociologically married. This 'house' would be represented by the old woman who could not bear a son for it in her marriage.

The Abakuria had a saying that *inyumba etana moona wi kirisia ne ntobu*, i.e., 'a sonless house is a poor house', and therefore, must have a wife married for it in order to raise seed and ensure its prosperity. Such marriage occurred at a time when it was obvious that a particular wife had failed to bear a son and she was of course past child-bearing age or if she had failed to get a male child in her marriage. The husband of the old lady normally gave the requisite marriage cattle or if he was deceased, this would be obtained from his estate.

It is important to mention here that, the girls who were married into woman to woman were not 'normal' girls but were either those who became pregnant before circumcision (*amakunena*) or those that conceived before formal marriage (*ubuiseke ubusigenche*). However, as we shall see, the girls married into the marriage kept a changing. After the married woman has been brought into the homestead, a male consort *(umutwari)* was normally appointed to enter her hut and raise seed for the house of the female husband (Rwezaura 1985:145). According to the Kuria custom the *umutwari* was not a husband and did not have any rights concerning the children born following his association with their mother, nor do the children themselves inherit from his property. *Umutwari* was ordinarily appointed from the lineage of the husband of the marrying woman or any other close relative. He was only allowed to enter to the house of the woman late in the evening and leave very early the following morning, he was not allowed by tradition to make any decision concerning the life of the woman. In some Kuria clans, the *(abatwari* pl) were never respected, they often came from poor background or unsuccessful families. However, they had a saying that justified their activities and satisfied their ego *'moteti atana mokagi, bonswi mboreo bakorara'* i.e. there isn't any foolish married man, all sleep on the right side of the bed.

The purpose of the woman to woman marriage was to ensure the posterity of a household represented by each wife. As in other societies, the ideology of procreation and personal immortality was strong among the Abakuria and each wife would not be happy until she has had own son. However, possession of a son by a Kuria wife was not merely a matter of life after death, it also concerned the economics of production, resource control and social security during old age (Tobisson 1986: 176–80). The Kuria economic system with the polygamous household provided sufficient incentive for the occurrence of the woman-to-woman marriage, the basic aim being to protect the resource of the particular house by procuring for it a son who inherited its property – Rwezaura argues that the Kuria law of succession was most unfavourable to sonless widows. As soon as her husband died, she became part of his estate and liable to be inherited by her late husband's relatives. However, if she was past child bearing the woman to woman marriage became a viable solution to her dilemma.

As noted by Huber, 'the availability of cattle which have been obtained either by a woman's own efforts, or as bride wealth of her daughter, is the indispensable condition and an immediate incentive for a sonless wife to "marry"' (Huber 1969:764). Also, a son stood in place of a protector for his old mother and if her husband was dead or if he was cohabiting with young co-wives. Having a son was so significant to a Kuria wife that had she failed to bear one in her second marriage, Kuria law permitted her to take one of her sons born in a previous marriage into her new marriage where he will be counted as belonging to her new house. According to Rwezaura, Kuria law also provided that when a wife failed to bear son in her second marriage she would be allowed to return to her first husband – which in effect meant to the protection of her sons. A Kuria wife therefore, counted on a son to provide her during the old age, to procure grandchildren who would ensure the prosperity of her house and a daughter who will help her in housework and so on. As already noted, resources and property were very significant part of a marriage so that therefore, woman to woman marriage could be discussed in the context of the 'house property system' (Rwezaura 1985: 20; Tobbison 1986:182). Where each maternal 'house' essentially and ideally functioned as an independent and self contained units as far needs and availability of marriage-cattle were concerned. Such a marriage was primarily a mean of coping with reproductive, social or economic problems caused by an 'imbalance' in human or material composition of a maternal 'house' as an operative part of a two-generation agnatic family. The 'house property system' finds expression in the way the Abakuria referred to the practice, in terms of the problems it was intended to solve. For instance, people would explain the woman to woman marriage by reference to the fact that 'a sonless house is a poor house'. Thus to 'marry' would be referred to as giving cattle on behalf of the poor house in order 'to prop the house up' – a similar phrase is used by the Kipsigis who claim that a sonless woman marry to 'strengthen the wooden pillars of the house' (Peristiany 1939: 81).

A woman who had not conceived within a year after her marriage and who feared that she was barren, did everything to make sure she got pregnant. At first measure; she would visit sacred places or magician or follow advice of local midwives' on dietary practices, which would increase her fertility. If these measures proved unsuccessful, other women would always pressure her in a popular euphoria, *'taichaba wiibore'* i.e. 'go aside and have a child', meaning that woman could as well have a baby outside her established marriage. This was often considered normal in Kuria society and in fact Tobisson (1986: 180) found out from one of her informants who she had asked about this, she answered 'who will ask which bulls had impregnated a cow?'

The woman marriage improved the 'married' women's image and personhood in many respects: for one, and obviously, the woman's social status changed completely, she no longer would be regarded as an outcast or barren but now she had 'resurrected her house'. According to a Kuria saying, *arooba irigoti* meaning the woman has 'joined a body with the head', or *'arichokia moe'*, she has 'brought forth her house'. Such a woman was empowered by the society to make many decisions regarding her 'house' was under her care and she would raise her own *irihicho* (a herd of cattle). She would be regarded as the senior-most woman in her village, and she would be approached in face of conflicts occurring among other women. Finally, when she got into old age, she would be honoured into being initiated into an elder-hood ceremony known as *isubo yu umukungu*. This was an elaborate ceremony that took about three days and it was normally sanctioned by the *inchaama* or Kuria council of elders. Therefore, this was the tone and practice of the woman-to-woman marriages in Bukuria, during the precolonial years, however, there were a few changes that occurred in the late nineteenth century and affected this marital relation.

In the 1890s the Abakuria, like other East African communities were faced with drought and famine which rendered farming and animal production precarious and harzadous occupations. (Chacha 1999:56) Equally, the legal implications of the woman to woman marriage changed significantly to the tunes of these changes. A decade of natural catastrophe opened when rinder-pest entered Western Kenya and Northern Tanganyika. Bukuria was struck by the epidemic in unprecedented proportions (Iliffe 1979:10). Kuria oral traditions commemorate these events clearly. It tells of cattle, sheep and goat skeletons strewn in great quantities. (Cf. Maroa 1989:4-16)

During this time, the position of poor woman and girls was especially precarious. Food became so scarce that people were forced convert and eat discarded ox hides and the goats skin's that they wore for clothing into a devastating meal. The destruction was so crippling that the children and grandchildren of survivors continued to recount the storm of the famine called *gitura maho* 'roasted skin' (Cf. Schmidt 1992:152). This famine was so harsh that women made certain kind of cry known as *ekerarati* as they saw their children and die one by one. Marriages were rarely conducted, owing to lack of livestock for bridewealth. Families experiencing famine during this period had no choice but to barter their women and children for food. (Wakefield 1870). While poor men suffered through the mortgage of their futures, female household members were literally pawned to the rich women of the Mbungu and Warutu in Northern Tanganyika (Chacha 1999:39).

Likewise, the Bukira clan which was least hit by the nineteenth century famines, received many women refuges whom they turned into wives. However, the number was too high that some women ended up getting into the woman to woman marriage. These pawned females would be redeemed at a later date with cattle or some other form of wealth. Otherwise, the future of the women or girls lay in the hands of the Bukira women bearing male children for them. As the Kuria were being hit by famine at the close of the Nineteenth century, to the Maasai (Kuria neighbours) the condition was worse since it coincided with the 'ilaikipiak war and the rinderpest epizootic' (Bernstein 1996:1–11). The result was complete disaster for a number of the Maasai. Contemporary observers estimate that they had lost 95 percent of their cattle (Cf. Sharpe 1983; Kholmann 1894). This made their pastoral life impossible for years and many Maasai women took refuge with agricultural neighbours in order to survive. Those came to Bukuria were known as *abatebia* , then came in caravans of between thirty to sixty women. They brought with them beads and other valuables.

According to oral narratives, these women never went back to Maasai land instead they were married into woman to woman in Bukira, men wouldn't normally take these women as wives since this would cause conflicts with Maasai. Kirsten writes about a wealthy widow known as Masoborroa Waitebe who moved from Bukira and settled in Nyabasi with her cattle and 'married' the Maasai woman but she later sent a message to the Maasai accusing them of being lazy, she was in turn raided and killed by the Maasai spies (Kjerland 1995:123).

The Abahirimasero clan of Bukira who inhabit the present-day Ikerege, are thought to have been the off-springs of this woman. Many similar incidences took place between the Kuria women and the Maasai especially during the period of drought and famine. To substantiate this claim, the colonial administrators were struck by the physical similarity between the Maasai and the Abakuria. Marx Weis for example, repeatedly points to how Maasai ornaments, dress and weapons were found among the Abakuria (Weiss 1910).

In fact, the degree to which the Abakuria warriors resembled the Maasai morans is clear from the photos Weiss took in 1904 while in Bukuria. Also, Baker claims that the Abangirabe (clan of the Kuria) pierced ears and facially resembled the Maasai. Therefore, and perhaps, it may have been through *inter alia* woman-to-woman marriage relationship with the Maasai that the Abakuria tended to physically resemble the Maasai and not through political assimilation as claimed by many Kuria scholars.

Colonial 'Madness' and the Rejection of Woman-to-Woman Marriage

Bukuria became part of the German colony following the Anglo-German agreement of 1890 according to which a border-line skirted the northern slopes of Mt. Kilimanjaro and ran further in a straight line to a point on the eastern shore of Lake Victoria and, therefore, through Bukuria The prime manifestation of the colonial presence in Bukuria when the German officials arrived at Shirati during the early years was therefore the sporadic collection of taxes by the appointed chiefs.

Ostensibly, taxation was introduced in order to meet the cost of colonial administration, but it was also used effectively to push people into labour. The construction of the railway for example opened the country to more intensive European domination, enabling the international economy to absorb indigenous economies and restructuring them to meet its needs (Iliffe 1979:135). Malcom Ruel gives a vivid account of how the Germans conquered the people on their arrival in Bukuria:

> the River Mara at Bokenye, where they were received peacefully. Spurred perhaps by the Abakenye, they attacked and raided the neighbouring province of Busweta and then moved to Shirati. From thereat various times they raided the Abatimbaru, Abanyabasi, Abakira and the Renchoka clans of the Abakuria (Ruel 1959).

In their initial stage the colonial administrators opposed the Kuria's apparently 'irrational fondness' of their herds. They argued that the Kuria spent too much time discussing, stealing, and guarding so many 'unproductive' animals, they saw that Kuria large herds would hurt agricultural yields, they were grouped as part of the 'cattle complex peoples'. Therefore, formulated some policy towards cattle industry, this they did through directly and indirectly induced changes, the direct induced ones comprised actions like the control of cattle numbers and their movements and marketing.

Indirect induced changes were aimed at breaking the hegemonic position of cattle by *inter alia* monetising bride-price, increasing taxation, destocking, and forced cattle sale. In pursuit of this objective, the colonialist sought to promote crop production while undermining the pastoral component of the Kuria economy. Ironically, by making the agriculture more profitable while undermining the pastoral component, the policy enabled the Kuria to acquire more cattle, instead of marketing their stock for example, they preferred to retain their stock by deriving the necessary cash income from the sale of crops and wage employment One man declared in the British court why he was opposed to destocking and other cattle reduction measures:

> Our cattle are our mother, our father, and our children. Would you make me kill my mother because she was old? Would you make me slaughter some of my children because they are many? The answer is no. And neither do I expect you to sell your mother for cash when you want a new blanket or slaughter a son when you have a wedding. Do you castrate your children? (Winnington-Ingram 1959:90).

Such are the sentiments that typified the meaning of pastoral life to the Kuria social relations in colonial period, and for that reason, the Kuria were not ready to abandon this mode of production. As a result of these conditions bride-price, in began to raise steadily even allowing more and women marriages to be conducted forcing the colonial government to interfere more strongly with the Kuria marital relationships beginning with regulation of bride-wealth and then woman to woman marriage whose bride-price were higher than ordinary marriages.

The Germans and later the British recognized that there were organized communities in Tanzania who had their own law-like rules of family order, of property, of crime, of government, and so on, which, while not written down, were generally known and conformed to by the local groups to which they were pertinent. Colonial governments wanted the taxes they imposed to be paid, the labor they recruited to be obedient, the roads kept in repair, and they wanted to suppress all collective violence. They often counted on 'traditional authorities' in the countryside to maintain the requisite order. But those princes, chiefs, and clan leaders were not to exceed the authority delegated to them. The scope of that authority was greatly limited and altered by the colonial presence, and they helped the settlers they invited into the colonies to acquire property as well. The laws that governed this kind of property were entirely different from the 'customary law' that applied to the African population. Those elements of local systems of normative order that were left to local communities to manage in their own 'traditional' way, came to be known as 'customary law'.

To understand the impact of the changing woman to woman marriage within this framework of the customary law and colonialism, one has to look at colonialism as a system of subjugating cultures and knowledge that were not familiar to the colonizers. In instances where the cultures and knowledge systems could not be as easily subjugated through law, the colonial masters sought to redefine the institutions of enforcement of customary law such marriage. In redefining and refashioning this institution, certain sections of the community such as women were left out. The marginalisation of women and customary law is thus symptomatic of global developments towards monolithic trends of thought and intolerance for different systems that did not fit neatly into the so-called modern way of thought.

In fact, the colonial state acted as an autonomous entity-separated from the rest of the society as it were interventionist in character and authoritarian. (Ghai & McArslan 1970). According to Ghai the creation of the colonial state was intended to 'subordinate all groups and classes in the colonized society'. So that in fact, these powers according to Fitzpatrick (1980) were used to integrate the overall colonial social formation by tying the traditional mode of production and the capitalist mode together into an operational whole'. Similar law and state operated in a coercive manner to integrate Kuria customary law into world system.

In fact, in the illustration of the structural effect of colonialism on the substance, practice and institutions of customary law in Africa, Mahmood Mamdani suggests that 'customary law' was largely a construct of colonialism, and it was therefore, a colonial authorities conspiracy to freeze 'customary law' into narrowly defined areas minus its autonomous logic (Jeppe, S. See Bibliography for URL). When we consider that the state and law are closely connected spheres. The contraction and weakening of the African state also witnesses growing claims for more recognition of cultural difference and its inscription into law.

Generally, and just like any other institution, early colonial officials completely misunderstood the woman-to-woman marriage practice's among Africans, Lugard for example, referring to a similar practice is most Africa, noted that:

> … the custom of orderly women procuring young girls whom they go through a marriages ceremony appears to be prevalent among tribes with widely different origins and customs. The purchase money as misnamed 'dowry' and the woman husband becomes absolute owner of the girl (Lugard 1965:385).

Lugard must have thought that such relationship were forms of slavery. With regard to the functions of the relationships, Lugard noted that:

> …in some cases it may be that the purchaser who wishes to assure herself of a 'wife' who will tend her in her old age, but the more usual reason is in order to claim for adultery and to gain possession of the children of such intercourse who by nature custom are property of 'husbands' who has paid dowry (Ibid).

In Tanganyika, similar views were held. For example, in 1927 the Acting District Officer, W.J. Bonavia, summoned an assembly of all North Mara Chiefs and ordered them to endorse the abolition of the practice. Having done that he then recorded that since the custom had been abolished, it would be helpful to the future colonial officials to understand its basic characteristics and further assist in bringing the custom to a final end. In the opinion of Bonavia,

> the custom permitted wealthy spinsters or windows who wished to obtain children to contract marriages with young girls whom they farmed out to chosen men for intercourse, all progeny from such intercourse was the property of the old woman. Secondly, it was the custom for husbands whose wives were barren to invite their wives to buy 'wives'. Again the wives farmed out their girl wives and obtained progeny, thereby, which became the property of the husband (Bonavia 1935).

Some years later Baker described the practice in similar terms, noting that:

> …until quite recently, it was the practice for a rich widow who was too old to attract men herself to marry a young girl whose work it was to look after her. Such were in fact slaves and took lovers in accordance with the orders of their female husband. If any children were born to the young girls, they were considered as the children of the widow and her deceased husband and used his name as their patronymic (Baker 1935:113–4).

Both colonial social anthropologists and government officials thus shared a common, though mistaken, belief concerning the nature of woman-to-woman marriage in Africa. Some thought that it was a type of homosexual relationship, while others saw it as a kind of slavery with an incipient element of prostitution. In either case the woman-to-woman marriage was considered as immoral practice which was to be discouraged and where possible abolished altogether. Christian missions viewed the practice as being opposed to basic Christian ideas on marriage and at all costs to be avoided by Christians. This negative attitude and ignorance of most Kuria institutions as explained above, made the people consistently refer to the Europeans as mad men particularly in Tarime District.

During the colonial period in Tanganyika, state intervention in the practice of woman to woman marriage was concretely expressed in the abolition of the custom starting from 1927. Like a number of other colonial attempts to regulate Kuria social relations using law, the measure was not successful. The state succeeded, however, in turning the custom into a clandestine relationship. Indeed some officials, such as Baker, (1935:113–4) even believed that it had been abandoned by the people. It is important to bear in mind this point because in the years following independence, many Kuria litigants tended to deny the existence of such relationships whenever it seemed advantageous to do so.

When considering the post-colonial state regulation of woman to woman marriage involved the transfer of property and like conventional marriages, gave rights to disputes over property rights between parties and involved children whose welfare the state was anxious to regulate. One would therefore conclude that the regulation of woman to woman marriage by the state was entirely to be expected, particularly as more disputes came out to court for adjudication.

In conclusion then, colonial occupation and the penetration of capitalist economy brought about a number of changes which profoundly affected marriage in general and the family in Bukuria. The creation of an alternative means of acquiring wealth, the acceptance of the European money as a universal means of exchange, and tax payment; and above all the creation of labour reserves, altered seriously the concept of marriage and especially that of the woman to woman marriage. However, it worked at the advantage of the women who amassed a lot of wealth in the absence of men who had taken wage labour outside Bukuria. The situation in the colonial Bukuria therefore was at best described as a 'society of women and children'.

The Post Colonial State and Woman-to-Woman Marriage: A Legal Dilemma

The independent African states inherited a dual legal system where the general law or state law co-existed with customary laws of the various ethnic groups. In some African countries customary law was reduced into codes. This process was geared towards bringing 'native' law at par with the general law which was predictable since it was written. Even where states recognized customary law as valid, there were concerted efforts at bringing all laws at par with the general law.

Issues over the right of the children borne of the woman to woman family to education particularly, was challenging since the government thought that the relationship lacked the head responsible for the education of the children. Yet, the male consorts or *abatwari* were not keen and as a matter of principle not bound by law to assume such roles, their duties were limited to biological reproduction. The newly independent government therefore, held views that the female-husbands were unable or unwilling to educate their children, therefore, continued to discourage the practice.

Similarly, post independence therefore, saw continued efforts in the unsuccessful regulation of the woman to woman marriage alongside this, Christian churches especially the Seventh-day Adventist Church (SDA), in North Mara for example decreed that all families whose such marriages were contracted, all members would be struck off their church membership although some church members preferred not to adhere to church policies at the expense of the extinction of their 'houses' and went ahead to contract the marriage.

A major factor which militated against the marriage was the development of formal education. After the 1960s there was a push for education in most districts in Kenya, facilities were expanded drastically to meet the needs of both sexes, both woman to woman relationships and early marriages were therefore, abolished by the school administration. This was particularly reinforced by the education officers in those areas that were considered vulnerable: Musoma and North Mara Districts. However, soon, it was discovered from the ministry of agriculture annual reports that bride-wealth in Bukuria were sharply increasing and the immediate reason for this was obviously thought that both women and children were extensively marrying. The trend can be shown in tabular form below:

Year	Bride-wealth in Cattle
1913-1920	10-15
1921-1927	20-25
1928-1960	25-35
1961-1971	**26-50**

Source: Lexander and Chacha (1979: 14).

To reinforce this, the traditional *inchaama* (council of elders) administered an oath in which the Abakuria swore never to receive bridewealth of less than 26 head of cattle. The African Local Council was forced to approve this recommendation (Rwezaura:100). It is interesting also, to note here that women especially those from Nyabasi, Ngureme and Butimbaru had accumulated cattle and were paying bride-wealth to marry women as were permitted by the tradition to do so. However, normally it could be agreed that Kuria being a polygamous society, there was competition for the resources from the head of the household, therefore a woman who had more girls than the other fellow wives and that her house to have access to portable wealth after the death of the household head would decide to marry.

The post-colonial state while recognizing the importance of regulating woman to woman marriages and its incidents, was somewhat ambivalent about how it should do it. If court decisions and the law can be relied upon to assess the mode of state regulation of this relationship, it seems to correct to say that ignorance of the nature of the relationship prevailed and outlived the colonial period. Was it a marriage between two women, as earlier colonial scholars and official had supposed? Or was it a unique and ingenious pre-capitalist social relationship which functioned to protect a sonless wife and ensured that the property she had helped to accumulate was usefully spent in ways which had long term benefits to her? Was it arrangement which rectified a 'biological' accident while at the same time rescuing a 'poor house' from social and meta-physical extinction? Or was it a form of prostitution and slavery? The woman to woman marriage relationship, having undergone rapid transformation in the era of capitalist penetration, tended to elude any form of casual attempt to understand its pre-capitalist characteristics and functions. As Rwezaura beautifully points out:

> Moreover, the new ruling class of the independence era were just as intolerant of practices they considered backward and out of step with 'civilised' living. These factors tended to influence the form of state intervention in woman to woman marriage during the period following independence (Rwezaura 1985).

In 1963, the Customary Law Declaration panel did not consider woman to woman marriage as one form of customary marriages. It was doubtful that its exclusion from the declaration order was accidental or based on the belief that the custom had become obsolete. However, it was manifest that the Declaration Order was intended implicitly to abolish the custom. I will use some support from court cases used by Rwezaura in his dissertation titled: 'Kuria Family Law and Change' quoting for example a 1965 case where one Nimrod Logue, visited Tarime Township in Kuria to carry out research on 'the former customary law' (the pre-Codification law) among the Kuria and other peoples of the district. He came across a case (Rwezaura 1985) in which a young woman had sued her 'woman husband' for divorce. In that case a young Nyangi was married to the house of Mugaya d/o Monanka and the latter had appointed a male consort named Siongo to act as the genitor of Nyangi's children.

But ten years later according to Rwezaura, a misunderstanding led to the institution of a divorce suit at a local primary court. According to Logue, the primary court magistrate refused to recognize the relationship, saying that a marriage between two women was illegal. He nonetheless ordered a divorce decree on the ground that Siongo did not love the petitioner (the appointed consort). On appeal, the district court overturned the lower court's decision holding that as no marriage had taken place there could be no divorce (Logue 1965: 56).

According to Logue's interview with the two magistrates who heard the case, the main reason why they refused to recognise the relationship was that the Declaration Order had abolished the woman to woman practice. Logue thought, however, that the two judicial officers, might also have thought that the custom was 'old-fashion' and decided not to enforce it. Logue's work thus presents some evidence on the views and approach of courts in the district during the period following the coming into force of the Declaration Order. Whether indeed the magistrates believed that they were bound by the Order to refuse recognition of the custom, or they were concerned to discourage it, both views are consistent with our understanding of the policy of state intervention in woman to woman marriage practices after the colonial era.

From 1963 to the passing of Law of Marriage Act in 1971, Tarime courts held the view that woman to woman marriage was not legal. For instance in 1968, Juliana Muhochi married to Robi Magwi, petitioned for the dissolution of her relationship with her at a primary court in Tarime district (Rwezaura 1985). Her main complaint was that she did not want to continue being married to a 'fellow woman'. The primary court held her favour that 'a marriage between two women (was) against the law of nature and should be dissolved' (Ibid).

In a different case, in which a legal point involving woman to woman marriage was raised, appears to have been reported 1971. It involved parties belonging to the Ngurueme Kuria clan of the Abakuria who also practice such a form of marriage. There was evidence to the effect that a woman named Patiri Magesa was married to the house of Keresa's mother and had two children before that relationship was legally terminated in accordance with Nguruimi law.

This time the claim involved the custody of the children. Kirisia, the plaintiff, sued for custody and further claimed that he was the husband of Patiri. In support of her case the defendant Patiri stated that she had never been married to the plaintiff but she was his mother's wife and that in any case the relationship had been terminated already. The court held that 'since no marriage between plaintiff had taken place, and that the ladies are now divorced, no such question could arise'.

The case of Gati Getoka v. Matinde Kimune shed additional light on the court's understanding of the relationship, and on the parties' rather tactical approach to the issues. In 1967 Matinde Kimune gave thirty-five head of cattle, three goats and forty-five shillings to Gati Getoka, being bride-wealth for marriage of the latter's daughter named Robi, to her sonless house. Both parties belonged to Kuria, of Musoma district, who also practice woman to woman marriage. After three years of marriage, Robi had not been able to give birth to a child, which failure turn caused misunderstanding between her and her 'husband'. There was no evident whether a consort had been appointed for her. Matinde Kimune's petition for divorce was dismissed by the Kiagata primary court on the ground that there was no sufficient reason for dissolving the marriage. On appeal, the Musoma district court held that although it agreed with the lower court's findings of facts and its reasoning, it was held that 'such a customary union…has meaning, if any, if only it persists by mutual consent, and it cannot be suited against a rebellious party. Here the respondent (i.e. female husband) seeks to terminate it and …Courts should readily accede'. The High Court accordingly dissolved the relationship (Rwezaura 1985).

This decision reveals that the primary court thought the 'marrying woman' was being difficult and was not giving her 'wife' sufficient time to conceive. This view was shared by the district court yet unlike the law court considered itself obliged to make a more definite intervention by disclosing the relationship. The High Court did not express its opinion as to whether the relationship was or was not slavish, not did it even decide the issue relating to the legal status of the relationship. And in ordering the refund of the bride-wealth the appellate judge simply relied on the opinion of the assessors. By 1978 the majority of High Court judges at Mwanza registry were unanimous in holding that woman to woman marriage was not a marriage at all and should not be so treated. In spite of the notoriety, this form of marriage was not recognized by the Law of Marriage Act, hence it was not a marriage at all.

Although the above mentioned decisions of the courts were considered in holding that woman to woman marriage was not a marriage, there were marked disagreements to its incidents, particularly in respect of rights to children. For example, a case involving a man named Mchele Marwa brought a claim at a local primary court for two children born during the desertion of his barren wife's 'wife'. There was evidence showing that in 1957 Mchele Marwa's wife, called Nyasanda, married a girl named Robi was pregnant by him (marwa). Thereafter, Robi returned to her parents but was brought back later when Nyasanda added to Robi's father some more cattle. On returning, Robi was not assigned another consort, but she soon became pregnant and had three children by unknown men. In 1968 Robi again escaped and went to cohabit with a man called Daniel Saraya in Musoma district. She was discovered five years later by Mchele Marwa, having in the meantime given birth to two children. It is these two children, born during Robi's desertion, who became a bone of contention.

Both the primary and district courts arrived at different decisions on the case. The primary court magistrate held that Daniel Saraya was the lawful husband of Robi and as such was entitled to the two children, while the assessors held that Nyasanda had a right to one child and the other belonged to Daniel Saraya. As a result of this difference of opinion, the case was sent to the District court for the review. At the same time, Mchele Marwa appealed to the District court where it was held that 'the relationship of 'married woman' between the respondent (i.e. Marwa and Robi) amounted to a valid marriage and that since such a marriage had not been dissolved, the children born to Robi were born in wedlock and belonged to the respondent by virtue of the provisions of (Rule) 175 of the law of Person". Danel Saraya then appealed to the High Court against this decision.

In considering the appeal, Magistrate Maganga dealt with three main issues. The first was whether Mchele Marwa, not being Robi's husband, had a legal right to calm the children. The second was whether the custom of

> a woman marrying another woman is recognized under the Local Customary Law Declaration and, if so, what rights does such a relationship confer to the 'marrying' woman and/or her husband in respect of such 'wife' and her children, during the subsistence of such relationship' (emphasis by Court).

The first issue was disposed of easily on the basis that Kuria law, which governed the parties, permitted a father-in-law to make such claim. On the second issue, the appellate judge held that the Customary Law (Declaration) Order did not

> ...provide for a marriage between a woman and another woman. Thus, although the practice of a woman marrying another woman might have been recognized among the members of the Wasimbiti tribe, it was abolished by the Declaration .... The practice therefore ceased to be binding among the members of that tribe as of the date the Declaration came into force in (Tarime) district and as such it cannot be adjusted by courts.

The appellate court, however, did not say that the practice was either illegal or unlawful. It merely expressed the view that courts would not assume jurisdiction on the matter simply because such a custom was not recognized by law and therefore not enforceable in a court of law. According to magistrate Maganga, the only remedy for people who still recognized customs concerning such marriages 'to have disputes arising from such customs settled within their tribal councils, if such councils exist(ed). They (could) not resort to the courts for remedy since such customs (were) not recognized in the Declaration.' Having held as above, the appellate judge did not dismiss the case or even require parties to go to their 'tribal councils' for settlement. Instead he went on to decide the appeal on the basis that woman to woman marriage was civil contract between the mother-in-law (i.e. Marwa's wife) and Robi's mother. According to Maganga whatever was given to Robi's father was not bride-wealth but a consideration for a contract in which Nyasanda was

...to have Robi children which she could regard as 'belonging' to her either as her own children. When she assigned Robi to her stepson, the stepson became Robi's husband. But when she paid additional cattle after the death of her stepson and decided not to assign Robi to any other man, she thereby renewed the contract between her and Robi's father to have Robi to help her and produce children for her. Such a relationship cannot be turned 'marriage'.

The above decisions, in my view, represent the current judicial understanding of woman to woman marriage. It is clear from these and other decisions that most of the judges and magistrates believe that woman to woman marriage is a physical and sexual relationship between two women. But as noted by Huber (1969:764), the term 'women-marriage' does not adequately express the meaning of the custom. 'There is no suggestion in the view of the people, in the terminology or in the wedding ritual itself that a woman assumes the role of a husband in relation to another woman'. Yet judicial officers have understood the relationship differently and it seems to me that this has to some extent influenced their attitude to the relationship.

In a more serious tone, the judge further pealed to 'authorities that be, and those who purport to champion the female cause to wake up to the indignity of these marriages'. Lugakingira no doubt represents the out spoken thinking on this point while Mfalila takes a more pragmatic stand on the matter. In his view, the 'custom has a lot of common sense in it for it safeguards the interests of women who are unable to have children of their own.' Mfalila in fact, states that although it is an error for anyone to call the custom a 'marriage', courts should both abolish 'this centuries old custom of the Wazanaki', but should be 'preserved until, as the liberation of women catches more fire, it will itself die of natural causes'.

The preceding discussion shows, therefore, that the post-colonial state unsure what policy to adopt towards woman to woman marriage. It was not explicitly abolished nor was it legally recognised. The judicial officers were also uncertain as to how to treat the woman to woman marriage. Some thought it was rather like slavery while others saw it as ancient custom which was to be preserved until the women were liberated. Underlying all this official ambivalence was the problem of understanding what the relationship entailed and the more so when it was undergoing such rapid transformation. We turn now to examine the nature of this transformation.

The Challenge of the Millennium: Woman-to-Woman Marriage and Its Dilemma

Today in modern Tanzania, the constitution permits the application of customary law to personal matters and to the devolution of property. However, the constitution contains no provision for gender as a basis for non-discrimination and as a result, even gender-biased practices are held as valid and constitutional. Women's access to economic resources in Kenya are consequently largely defined by customary laws. Inheritance is usually along the male lineage-hence, women do not inherit family property. An additional complication in the Tanzania situation is the growing number of woman -woman who found families outside of both the formal or customary legal regimes. When such unions terminate, the woman in usually left with no access to any household property nor to entitlement to maintenance from her partner or his family.

Although in Tanzania, codification has significantly modified customary practices. Customary laws are, nevertheless, held to apply to the African population unless the contrary is proved. Inconsistencies in statutory interventions leave women in Tanzania vulnerable when a marriage terminates – women are not provided with full access to household property. The Law of Marriage Act (1971), while, for example, prohibiting the alienation of the matrimonial home without the consent of the other spouse, paradoxically provides that the wife loses this right if the marriage terminates either by divorce or death. Tanzanian courts have, in order to provide the wife with some access to matrimonial assets upon divorce, used the reasoning that marriage is an economic venture. Similar to the situation facing Kenyan women, Tanzanian women do not inherit where there are male heirs. Women's access to household property and to land under inheritance laws are therefore severely constrained, underlining the urgency of the need to revisit gender in the current on-going revision of land tenure in this country.

In addition the issue of women and land ownership touches traditions and customary law. These are shaped by tribal customs and traditions which often create barriers for women to equal rights of access to land, property ownership and inheritance. History shows that Tanzanian women have been deprived of their rights to acquire, hold and own land the same as women in most other African societies (Tesha, http://tanzania.fes-international.de/Activities/Docs/landuse.html). In Tanzania, constitutionally, the land is owned by the state. Individuals can only acquire rights of occupancy.

However, the right of occupancies is acquired mainly through family transfer or through direct allocation from a state agency or by monetary transaction. In practice land ownership through family transfer is the major known way used by the Tanzanian rural people. About 90 percent of land acquisition in rural areas takes place under customary law or through inheritance. Most rural women settle on and use land which they get through family ties. Under customary laws women and girls are never beneficiaries of this type of acquisition (Chanok 1985). The acquisition and ownership of land is a monopoly of male members of a family. Such a system deprives women who are the main users of land, accounting for about 85 percent of all land users of the right to own land. The National Land

Policy of 1995 recognizes the existence of discrimination of women in matters related to access and ownership of land. It asserts the right of every citizen to have access to and to own land. It declares land to be a constitutional right. The Land Policy of 1995 was the basis for the new land legislations, namely the Land Act No. 4 of 1999 and the Village Land Act, No. 5 of 1999 (Tesha, op cit).

Woman to woman marriage is being transformed on a significant and recent development in the economic position of women. As more women who are divorced or widowed begin to establish their own homesteads away from the living lands of their former husbands or their natal homes. As they begin to acquire and accommodate inheritable property, there is the need for heirs and other dependants also. Under normal circumstances, woman to woman marriage were conducted to give sonless woman a child, but it is clear that other motives have been added. According to Kirsten women's motives appears to be no different from those of men, she states that 'female marriages have been on the increase and this has caused tension over women in Nyabasi' Kirsten Therefore, there are many other reasons why men as well as women find advantages to woman to woman marriage in contemporary Kuria society. One important reason, is the fact that a wife married to this marriage becomes a significant asset for the husband in forms of labour. She remains in her female husbands' husband (if there is any) until she losses access to it when the son (born of the marriage) establishes his own household.

As a result of harsh economic condition, today, it has been possible for a wife married to a female husband to be without a specific appointed male consort (*umutwari*) in which case, she enters into sexual relationship with lovers who may be anonymous. Such a consort is said to assume the rights of a husband in some respects (which shouldn't be the case) while disregarding a husband's responsibilities in others. He has no obligation to help the women in agricultural work, in maintaining the hut, in building granaries, and so on. In her interview in Tanzania, one woman described her consort to Tobisson:

> He buys meat and divides it between the wives on his own homestead but gives me nothing. When my children are ill, he does not contribute a cent to the dispensary fees or medicine. Yet guards me jealously and does not permit any man to cross my doorstep (Tobisson 178).

While a male consort is often referred by the mother-in-law of the young woman as 'a son of the house' implying that he is free to come and go as he pleases and may be provided with food beyond usual quality and quantity. More often however, there are cases where the behaviour of consorts renders them undesirable especially when they seem to demand more than the lady can afford, or when they keep on nagging, in fact the Ngoreme (Kuria clan of Tanzania) have embodied their deeds and nature in a series of audio recording that describes them as troublesome, the song goes:

'Abatwari baana ehegere,
Abatwari baana amangana,
Abatwari baana amakono,
Abatwari baana iking'etyo,
Hata ninyoora na agasuhu,
Taang'a ekabuti yaane ngeende,
Taang'a banga yaane ngeende…(Abatwari, recordings, 1999).

Translated as:
The consorts have problems,
They are indeed interesting,
They are often amusing,
Even with small misunderstandings [with their women],
They keep get out of their way, they get annoyed,
Saying: give me my coat, I want to leave [your house];
Give me my sword, I want to leave….

In Tanzanian courts especially those in Ngureme, have ruled out that the consort has no right to the children decreeing that if the marriage between the two ladies will still subsisting, some rights of inheritance might eventually benefit the plaintiff, but for the ladies who are divorced, no such questions could arise.

Woman to woman marriages are today mainly contracted by independent women who have accumulated wealth and who seek to protect their wealth against male relatives. According to Ruwezaura such women take on the role of men and should be looked upon as 'female husbands'. Although wealth accumulation by women may be a factor accounting for the increased occurrence of woman to woman marriages, one should be careful not to underestimate the possibility of Kuria women accumulating and controlling their wealth in their own right. Tobisson also asserts that the practices is disrupted by the increasing dependence on consumer goods in the area.

As a result of accumulation of cattle, in many areas such as Kurutiange, Masurura, Ikerege, and some parts of Bwirege on the Kenyan side, and also due to increased cattle rustling, there is an established practice of the homestead head temporarily, placing a wife and her dependant children to a safer destination with cattle dividends to assist in the rearing and supervision of the herds. It is under this circumstances that a wife decides to 'marry' a woman as an asset to supervise the cattle in the same way as would apply to her. Likewise, women whose son have married and established their own homesteads away from home and her daughters already married, find herself lonely, she may decide to contract to woman to woman marriage to add a female into her 'house'.

Among other changes, it appears also that family heads in Bukuria have been more inclined to let their wives 'marry', even when the wives are young enough to stand the chance of having sons before passing child-bearing age, or whom they have sons already. The reason for this as already indicated may be because of the need for female labour accompanying the increased market-orientation of agricultural production.

And although, the AIDS disease has not been so pervasive in Bukuria, there is fear especially of females accepting to be married into woman to woman, more so especially considering the notion of appointing male consorts to the married lady by the female husbands, seems to be disappearing since the females who accept this marriages are now selecting their own choice of lovers on the basis of mutual attraction and understanding. They now choose not necessarily from the relatives of the female husband as it was during the pre-colonial times, but now from anywhere. Furthermore, the most important aspect of this marriage is the ability of the lady to get pregnant and have children.

Even until today the Tanzanian law still does not recognize the existence of the woman to woman marriage, however, it is held and protected by the local authorities embedded in the Chiefs Act. Powers are appended to the Kuria chiefs allowing them to solve all sorts of disputes arising in the process of transactions and practice of the marriage.

Conclusion

Everything has been said concerning the significance of the woman to woman marriage and the objectives for contracting such marriages. However, one is often mistaken to assume that the social and economic changes that have occurred in consequence of colonial and post-colonial policies and measures have made the practice obsolete or even that it has been disrupted to any noticeable extent. In this paper, I have argued that the practice has become increasingly widespread over the years accompanying such changes. We have seen how during the colonial and later periods of state regulations of the marriage was exercised, first in the form of abolition, and after the colonial era, by limited recognition of it. Common to both periods, however, was the government's general ignorance of what the relationship really involved.

What is most interesting are the changes in different forms in which the marriage has been taken. Initially it was a marriage that was intended to give a sonless wife a son and, also to give barren women an opportunity of raising up a family but today, especially as a result of accumulation of wealth by women in general, we have noticed that the marriage has been contracted for various reasons including: cheap labour, house property system, security and many others.

Note

1. I wish to thank Rwezaura of Law Faculty at The University of Hong Kong for permission to use some of his selected court cases from his dissertation cited in the text. Boke O'Matiko and Benard Maroa O'sanga for collection of oral data.

References

Alsaker, K. K., 1996, 'The Belated Incorporation of the Abakuria into Modern Kenya,' PhD Dissertation, University of Bergen.

Bernstein, J.L., 1996, The Maasai and Their Neighbours: Variables of Interaction' in *African Economic History* Vol. 2.

Blackwood, E., 1984, 'Lesbian Behaviour in Cross-Cultural Perspective,' MSc. Thesis, San Francisco State University.

Blackwood, E. and Saskia E. W., eds, 1999, *Female Desires: Same-Sex Relations and Transgender Practices Across Cultures,* New York: Columbia University Press.

Chacha, B. K., 1999, 'Agricultural History of the Abakuria of Kenya from the End of the Nineteenth Century to the Mid-1970s. MA Thesis, Egerton University.

Chacha, B. Kerata, 'The Agricultural Base of the Kuria Society: Change and Continuity in Family Labour Force, 1890–1975,' Mimeo.

Chanock, M., 1985, *Law, Custom and Social Order: the Colonial Experience in Malawi and Zambia,* Cambridge: Cambridge University Press.

Evans-Pritchard, E. E., 1951, *Kinship and Marriage Among the Nuer.* Oxford, UK: Clarendon Press.

Evans-Pritchard, E. E.,1945. *Some Aspects of Marriage and the Family Among the Nuer.* Livingstone, Northern Rhodesia: The Rhodes-Livingstone Institute.

Fitzpatrick, 1980, *Law and State in Papua New Guinea,* London: Academic Press.

Ghai, Y. P. and Mc Arslan, J.P.W, 1970, *Public Law and Political Change in Kenya: Study of the Legal Framework of Government from Colonial Times to the Present.* Nairobi: Oxford University Press.

Gluckman, M., 1970, 'Kinship and Marriage Among the Lozi of Northern Rhodesia and the Zulu of Natal, in A.R Radcliffe-Brown, and D. Forde, ed., *African Systems, Kinship, and Marriage* London.

Gordon R. W. *Customary Law in Common Law Systems* in IDS Bulletin, 32:1, 2001, p. 28-34, University of Birmingham, UK

Herskovits, M. J., 1937, 'A Note on Woman Marriage in Dahomey.' *Africa* 2-3:335-41.

Iliffe, J., 1979, *A Modern History of Tanganyika.* CUP: Cambridge.

Jeppie, S., 'Regional Issues in East Africa-Islamic Law in Africa found in at www.humanities.uct.ac.za/6/regional/10.html

Krige, E. J., 1974, 'Woman-Marriage, With Special Reference to the Lovedu – Its Significance for the Definition of Marriage' *Africa* 44:11-37.

Lang S., 1998, *Men as Women, Women as Men: Changing Gender in Native American Cultures,* trans. John L. Vantine Austin: University of Texas Press.

Le Vine, R., 1970, 'Personality and Change.' In *The African Experience,* Vol 1, eds. J. N. Paden and E. W. Soja. Evanston, IL: Northwestern University Press.

Lugard, F.J., 1965, *The Dual Mandate in British Tropical Africa*. London: Blackwood.

Mc Arslan and Yash P. Ghai, , J.P.W , 1970, *Public Law and Political Change in Kenya: Study of the Legal Framework of Government from Colonial Times to the Present*. London: Oxford University Press.

Maroa, M. S., 1989, *Nihanchere Ekeganbo Geito* Nairobi, East African Publishing House.

O'Brien, D., 1977, 'Female Husbands in Southern Bantu Societies' in Alice Schlegal, ed., *A Cross-Cultural View*, New York:Columbia University Press.

Oboler, R. S., 1980, 'Is the Female Husband a Man? Woman/Woman Marriage Among the Nandi of Kenya.' *Ethnology* 19:69-88.

Peristiany, J.G, 1939, *The Social Institutions of the Kipsigis*, London: Routledge Kegan & Paul

Ruel, M.J, 1959, 'The Social Organisation of the Kuria' Fieldwork Report, Institute of Development Studies, University of Nairobi.

Rwezaura, B.A, 1985, *Traditional Family Law and Change in Tanzania: A Case Study of the Kuria Social System*, Baden-Baden.

Schmidt, Elizabeth, 1992; *Peasants, Traders, and Wives : Shona Women in the History of Zimbabwe, 1870–1939*, Portsmouth, NH: Harare, London, Heinemann, Baobab, J. Currey

Sharpe, A. 1983, 'Journey from the Shire River to Lake Mwiru and the Upper Luappula' in *Geographical Journal*, Vol. 1, 1983 pp. 524-533 and F. Stuhlmann, Deutsch-Ostafrika Berlin.

Uchendu, C. V., 1965, *The Igbo of Southeast Nigeria*, New York:Holt, Rinehard and Winston.

Tobbison, Eva, 1986, *Family Dynamics Among the Kuria Agro-Pastoralists in Northern Tanzania* Goteberg.

Wairimu, N. N. and William e. O'Brien, 1992, 'Revisiting "Woman-Woman Marriage": Notes on Gikuyu Women from *NWSA Journal* Volume 12, Number 1.

Wakefield, T. 'Notes on the Geography of East Africa' in *Journal of the Royal Geography Society*, Vol. XL

Weis, Marx, 1910, 'Die Abakulia' in *Noden Deutsch-Ostafrikas* Berlin.

9

Collaborators or Warriors?
A Sociolinguistic Analysis of the
Discourse Patterns of Men and Women
in their Claim for Space in the
Public/Formal Workplace

Felicia Arudo Yieke

Introduction

In this century, women may appear to be liberated, sophisticated and educated. In fact today, we even have radical feminist movements. Men are 'seemingly' no longer the oppressors and enemy, but partners, and women are involved in almost all the professions that were initially held by men. These professions range from engineering, to medicine, to law, to commerce, to politics, the clergy, and the list is endless. In all these professional workplaces, both men and women are supposed to be viewed as collaborators, and not warriors. We are made to believe that people are judged on an individual basis, and that everything is possible for every one, and that gender differences are nothing but a social construct. However, if we look at any society, even in Europe and America, which are about the most developed of all, we find the following scenario:

- The unemployment rate among women is still higher than men.
- Women are placed in less qualified jobs and less prestigious jobs.
- Women earn less than men, even when they are in relatively the same positions.
- There are few women in top echelons in boardrooms and middle-management positions.

- As regards this last point, it can be remarked that whereas women often encounter a 'glass ceiling' that prevents them from advancing upwards in male dominated professions, men encounter a 'glass escalator' that prevents them from remaining in lower-level positions. As Williams puts it; 'As if on a moving escalator, they must work to stay in place' (Williams 1995:127).

Women are consequently still very much aware of gender differences, as they constantly have to face disadvantages due to their biological sex. If it is true that more women today can now be found in top positions, even though we have moved on to a new century, these women have had to fight their way up the ladder. The question thus asked is this; Why is it that we have such few females chief executive officers (CEOs) and managers in and around the world? And even in cases where we have them, the pattern is usually as follows. Increasingly they are women who had just reached the 'Glass ceiling' in the mainstream organisations, and it seemed apparent that they had reached their apex, and that there was no more upward or vertical mobility, whatever their performance. Maybe out of frustration, or maybe due to being ambitious, the women who have been 'able' maybe financially, have thus moved out, and gone on to form their own companies, which they subsequently head as CEO or managing director (MD) or senior managers.

Gender and Discourse

One of the main weapons for these struggles for one's place at the workplace, and in society at large, is language. Language determines who we are and how we position ourselves in relation to others. Language creates social reality, and societal reality is transferred through it. If it is a social reality that women compared to men are disadvantaged in our societies even at the beginning of the 21st century, it has to be expected that those differences will surface in the use of language by men and women. Language is never trivial or neutral. It is an extremely powerful tool for looking at, and (re)creating reality in different ways. What is communicated is much more than an individual means of expressing how the world is viewed. It constantly reflects and helps to create the social structures and systems that control us. As a result, one comes to recognise the relationship between language and power. For researchers on discourse and gender, power relations get articulated through language.

Kendall and Tannen (1997) argue that the workplace is characterised by many constraints. The workplace is an institutional structure, in which individuals are hierarchically ranked. It also has a history of greater male participation in most work settings, and this is especially so at the higher ranking levels such as middle management and top management. The workplace has a still existing though recently permeated pattern of participation along gender lines. The workplace therefore provides a special challenge to gender and language researchers, as well as an opportunity to observe interaction in the context of these constraints (Kendall & Tannen 1997:81).

We may also look at the workplace as a 'community of practice' (Eckert & McConnell-Ginet 1998: 490), within which participants perform their various identities. The 'community of practice' in this case takes us away from the community defined by a location or by a population. Instead, it focuses on a community defined by social engagement, and it is this engagement that language serves, and not the place or the people as a collection of individuals. Gender is thus produced (and often reproduced) in differential membership in communities of practice. From our studies of interactional behaviour, we see that women do the work necessary for interaction to occur smoothly. But it is men who control what will be produced as reality by that interaction. They (men) already have, and they continually establish and enforce their rights, to define what the interaction and reality will be about (Fishman: 100).

This paper therefore looks at gender and discourse in a work place setting, and at how language is an invisible tool of discrimination, and is rarely given much thought. In most cultures, those with power may exercise the right to speak for longer in contexts such as meetings. They may interrupt others, or use joking insults as silencing devices. Because men in general more often hold positions of power in particular interactions, they (men) contribute to the construction of normative masculinity. As a group, women rather than men are more often excluded from power. With women entering the situations that were previously all male, where established norms of behaviour are based on the ways men behaved in those roles, expectations must give way; either expectations of how someone in that role should behave, or expectations of the women who move into those roles.

This paper is motivated partly by the discussions so far of the links between language, gender and power. Robin Lakoff for example explains that norms of men's discourse styles are institutionalised, and that they are not seen as 'the better way to talk, but as the only way' (Lakoff 1990: 210). Gal argues that men's discourse styles are institutionalised as ways of speaking with authority, that institutions are 'organised to define, demonstrate, and enforce the legitimacy and authority of linguistic strategies used by one gender; or men of one class or ethnic group, while denying the power of others' (Gal 1991: 186). Recent research has shown that the power and status of conversational participants has a strong and predictable effect upon the way in which these interactions are organised.

To best examine gender, discourse and power variables in the workplace setting, we need to use Critical Discourse Analysis (CDA) as an interpretative framework. CDA is very useful in moving beyond the surface level examination of discourse to the 'deep structure' subtle relations of power and inequality, and as they relate to gender. CDA sees discourse as a form of social practice. This implies a dialectical relationship between a particular discursive event and the situations, institutions and social structures, which frame it. Critical discourse studies see organisations not simply as social collectives where shared meaning is produced, but rather as sites of struggle where different groups compete to shape the social reality in ways that serve their own interests. It is not only economic resources that are issues of interests in these struggles, but also symbolic resources. Many scholars of organisations are therefore concerned with examining how these competing interests get resolved through the control of symbolic and discursive resources.

Critical discourse analysts tend to see power as already accruing to some participants, and not to others, and this power is determined by their institutional role as well as their social economic status, gender or ethnic identity (Fairclough 1992, van Dijk 1993). In this sense, social relations of power pre-exist the talk itself, 'power is already there as a regime of truth' (Foucault 1980: 131). As a result, in CDA, approaching the role of power in discourse tends to be a question of examining how those members of society who possess it, reflect, reinforce and reproduce it through the language they use; their discourse practices (Thornborrow 2001). Discourse is thus socially constitutive in that it helps to sustain and reproduce the social status quo, with an aim of transforming it (Fairclough & Wodak 1997). As critical discourse analysts therefore, we are inclined to look at the discourse structures more critically, and uncover those subtle discursive practices that ensure that women never climb to the top, but are instead always relegated to the rear.

A lot of research conducted demonstrates that women in authority in fact also face a 'double bind' regarding professionalism and femininity. Lakoff comments on the double bind in this case as follows. 'When a woman is placed in a position in which being assertive and forceful is necessary, she is faced with a paradox; she can be a good woman, but a bad executive or professional, or vice versa. To do both is impossible' (Lakoff 1990:206).

One of the sources for women's inability to be perceived as being both a good authority figure and a good woman is that, as Tannen puts it, the 'very notion of authority is associated with maleness' (Tannen 1995: 167). Women who attempt to resolve the double bind by using interactional strategies associated with men find that they are judged and treated very harshly by both men and women (ironically). Some researchers suggest that language strategies that women use to downplay their authority are drawn from the resources available to them as mothers; this may be seen as an attempt to (re)solve the double bind between professionalism and femininity.

As has already indicated, women in high status jobs are few (most of women in the workplace are in subordinate and relatively powerless roles). This suggests that it is most unlikely that they are getting a fair opportunity to contribute to discussions and decision-making. They are unlikely to be getting a fair share of the talking time; they are likely to be interrupted more often than men; and in interactions with a predominantly male group, they will get little encouragement to contribute (Holmes 1995: 211). Because boardrooms and work-based meetings among professionals tend to be dominated by male talk, it is generally male ways of interacting which predominate. Many interaction problems may thus be the result of structured inequality in the society. Power is the issue. As Henley and Kramarae (1991) put it: 'Greater social power gives men the right to pay less attention to, or discount women's protests, the right to be less adept at interpreting their communications than women are at men's, the right to believe women are inscrutable' (Henley & Kramarae 1991: 27).

The problem goes further than this. Women's ways of talking differ from men's because each group has developed interaction strategies, which reflect their societal positions. The different patterns of interaction into which girls and boys are socialised are not randomly different. Their features are attuned to the requirements of the society. They are determined by the power structure. Women are socialised to be polite; this means even being negatively polite in public; not intruding or imposing oneself, and being possibly polite in private as well as taking responsibility for the interaction, and ensuring that others are conversationally comfortable.

Troemel-Ploetz (1998) talks about this disparity in now a more familiar way, but nevertheless quite effective in showing how grave the situation is:

> Men are used to dominating women; they do it especially in conversations: they set the tone as soon as they enter a conversation, they declare themselves expert for any topic, they expect and get attention and support from their female conversational partners, they expect and get space to present their topics and, above all, themselves - their conversational success is being produced by the participants in that conversation. Women are trained to please, they have to please also in conversations, i.e. they will let men dominate...Men also exhibit and produce their conversational rights: the right to dominate, the right to self-presentation or self- aggrandisation, at the expense of others, the right to have the floor and to finish one's turn, the right to keep women from talking (by disturbance or interruption), the right to get attention and consideration from women, the right to conversational success. Women, on the other hand, have conversational obligations: they must not disturb men in their dominating and imposing behaviour; they must support their topics, wait with their own topics, give

men attention, take them seriously at all times, and above all, listen and help them to their conversational success. (Troemel-Ploetz 1998: 447.)

As we enter the public workplace, we do so with the following assumptions:

- That Power-relation(s) somehow exist and determine the course of actual concrete encounters, by focusing on the local management of talk-in-interaction.
- That power may be viewed in terms of differential distribution of discursive resources.
- That these discursive resources enable certain participants to achieve interactional effects that are not available to all, or are differentially available to others in the workplace setting.
- That the employment of Interruptions, Questions and Topic control within the turn-taking process, are examples of powerful interactional resources, which may place constraints on the discourse options, which are available to actors/agents/speakers in a discourse situation.
- That the more powerful people/speakers in a workplace situation may employ the use of these interactional resources, which may suppress and/or oppress their less powerful interlocutors.
- That the less powerful interlocutors in most cases, in the corporate world, are women.
- That the use of these interactional resources within conversations, may then be just one of the very many factors which may contribute to women not rising up the ranks within the corporate world, above that 'glass ceiling'.
- That the situation created thus far may create disparity or polarisation of men and women in the workplaces, and this may lead to further marginalisation and invisibility of women in this public sphere, and by extension, in the general society.

With these assumptions in mind, we therefore look at the discourse patterns of men and women in the workplace and analyse them using Conversation Analysis. (Huge corporate firms in Kenya were investigated. In this respect, the researcher attended and audio-recorded management committee meetings, which were subjected to intensive transcriptions and analysis.) To critically analyse gender and power within these interactions, Critical Discourse Analysis (CDA) is then used as an interpretative framework. This is very effective in uncovering the subtleties of the discriminatory discursive practices, which mark institutional discourse.

Turn-Taking and Interactional Resources as Controls

Speaker change is one of the fundamental components in a conversation. In most cases, only one speaker usually speaks at a time. This is particularly true of dyadic conversations. It can therefore be assumed that in dyadic conversations, speaker change as such is not problematic since the choice of the next speaker is limited to one person only. Points of speaker change are however more interesting. Implicit in the statement that the organisation of speaker change is a fundamental principle of conversations is the notion that if this principle is really fundamental, all speakers must have a certain skill. This skill involves the ability of the interactants to correctly 'analyse and understand an ongoing sentence' as well as to 'produce immediately a relevant next utterance'.

Interactional control features broadly have to do with ensuring that the interaction works smoothly at an organisational level; that turns at talking are smoothly distributed, that questions are asked and answered, and that topics are selected and changed. O'Donnell (1990) points out that floor holding, topic control, and interruptions are closely related with power. 'Interactionally, greater power is correlated with floor holding, topic control, and interruptions. Friendly talk among equals is more likely to be characterised by utterance completions, latchings, and casual overlaps.' (O'Donnell 1990: 211.) Zimmerman and West, and other scholars also state that 'Just as male dominance is exhibited through male control of macro institutions in society, it is also exhibited through male control of at least a part of micro institutions' (Zimmerman & West 1975:125).

In this paper, we therefore look at interactional control. The objective here is to describe larger-scale organisational properties of interactions, upon which the orderly functioning and control of interactions depends. An important issue is who controls interactions at this level; to what extent is control negotiated as a joint accomplishment of participants, and to what extent is it asymmetrically exercised by one participant. In the next sections we thus examine as interactional controls the following: Turn taking, Interruptions, Questions, and the issue of Topics. One of the controlling mechanisms in micro institutions is related to the strategy of interrupting. As men interrupt more often than women, male dominance can be established in conversations. Turns are thus claimed, as topics are initiated and maintained by men or abandoned by women.

Turn-Taking and Interruptions

The study of interruption has been the locus of scholarly interest for nearly a generation. Interruption has been studied across a broad spectrum of human behaviour in both same and mixed gender exchanges. This has been done for both children and adults, in variant contexts where power, status, topic and task have been manipulated, and controlled in laboratory setting. In the current study, interruption is done in a natural setting. It involves mixed-gender exchanges for adults in the workplace setting, and within this context, issues of power, status and gender are discussed. Interruption has also been linked with personality traits such as dominance and assertiveness (Ferguson 1977, Wodak 1981). In spite of substantial effort to explain the dynamics of interruption, there is still little consensus about what an interruption actually is, how it manifests itself in interaction, how to best measure its occurrence, and how to interpret the role and function of interruption in conversation (Hawkins 1988, James & Clarke 1993).

In this section therefore, we examine the concept of interruption. This is done under the general auspices of the turn taking process. The kind of questions that would therefore be asked could include questions such as; Who interrupts whom? Who interrupts the most? Who is interrupted the least? What kind of interruptions are we talking about? Are the rights and obligations of participants (with respect to overlaps, interruptions or silences, for example), symmetrical or asymmetrical? As a way of beginning, we classify the interruptions in order to see how they are spread across the speakers. All along as we undertake these discussions, we have to relate these concepts to power and gender, which are crucial to this study. We must determine whether communication at workplace is pegged on gender, or it is pegged on power, or whether there is a possibility of both gender and power being players in such contexts and situations.

From the meetings recorded and analysed (although I recorded seven meetings, I concentrated on only two of them), the percentage of interruptions out of the total turns was relatively the same in both the meetings, which I refer to as A and B. In most conversations, people usually interrupt without even being conscious of the action. It is sometimes taken for granted. Sometimes speakers only become aware of interruption when one specific speaker constantly interrupts his/her interlocutors. As Coates (1989) argued, talk then becomes interruptive when it infringes negatively on the current speaker, who in turn may respond with verbal or non-verbal annoyance.

From the meetings also, it became evident that the status of a participant within the larger context (of the firm) had a lot of influence on the turn-taking behaviour in the specific contexts; namely meetings in this case. It is also undeniably evident that the role of the chairperson in any meeting is quite powerful and in most situations, we will have the chair taking the most number of turns, and this is regardless of the gender of each chair. However, if we critically compare meetings, which had a female chairperson, and those which had a male chairperson in terms of their number of turns, an interesting scenario unfolded. The male chairpersons seemed to have longer turns and more amount of speech compared to their female counterparts. They also had less interruptions on their turns, but incidentally interrupted their interlocutors more than the female chairpersons did to their interlocutors.

It was found that Interruption is a more complex phenomenon than what we normally think when we first see it. It was also found that in order to analyse interruptions effectively, we had to conceptualise them, and consequently classify them. This was in view of the fact that it was noticed that not all interruptions were an indication of violation of speaking rights by the more powerful people. Less powerful people, it was observed, also used interruptions with their more powerful counterparts. We thus devised a categorisation (workable for the project) that showed Supportive interruptions, Neutral interruptions, and Unsupportive interruptions.[1] These were able to bring in both the power and gender variables.

On Gender, it was noted in both meetings that men used interruptions more than women. In meeting A, at first glance, this did not appear to be the case. This was obscured by the fact that the chair was female. It was only when the interruptions attributed to her were put together with those of the rest of the women that the women seemed to have more interruptions than men. When her contributions were subsequently removed, it was noted that the women fared rather badly compared to the males. This was even despite the fact that there were more women than men in this meeting. When both the chairpersons from the two meetings were observed, it was noted that the male chairperson in meeting B outperformed his female counterpart in meeting A. This may be an argument not just of power, but more so of the gender factor, since both these people were powerful in their capacities as chairpersons.

On the types of interruptions, it was found that whenever the women used interruptions, most times, they tended to use the Supportive type, whose principle aim was to express solidarity and interest in the interrupted persons. Women generally did not use the Unsupportive interruptions (which may be seen to violate a speaker's turns) although we should point out that the female chairperson used them occasionally. In general therefore, both men and women avoided the unsupportive type of interruptions. Whenever they used interruptions however, most times they were of the Supportive type, which were identified as being the least effective in violating speakers' rights. It was also found that after Supportive interruptions, both men and women in relatively the same fashion also used Neutral interruptions.

It was thus noted that before making conclusions on interruptions, you have to know exactly which kinds of interruptions you are dealing with. It was also noted that before you can make any judgement on the conversational behaviour of the participants as regards these discursive controls, the issue of context that featured in the discourse patterns very greatly had to be addressed. We thus had to look at among other things, the post-interruptive behaviour of the interrupted persons. At the same time, it was found that we had to look at the contextual backgrounds that the participants brought with them to the interaction process; these included the expertise role they brought with them to the meetings.

We found that whereas some speakers seemed to take the floor without a fight, others always had to struggle to do so. In terms of gender, it was generally found that men fought less to get the floor, and even when they eventually got it, the resistance they got from their interlocutors was in most cases much less, and they usually maintained the floor up to the point they wanted to exit it of their own volition. This did not always happen to the women in the meetings, of course apart from the chair in meeting A, who despite her status and position, still somehow faced some form of resistance in the form of interruptive behaviour from the male interlocutors.

When it came to power, it was also found that it was mostly the more powerful speakers hierarchically within the organisation who took the floor without a fight, and maintained it until they were through. In cases where these individuals had to fight for the floor, they always emerged as the more powerful participants in most cases, and most times they won. It was noted that the behaviour of the rest of the members in the meetings was usually less interruptive when these powerful people spoke and whenever they interrupted, it was in a Supportive way, which in most cases expressed solidarity with these people.

Turn-Taking Process and Questions

In many forms of institutional interaction, questions get asked primarily by institutional figures such as attorneys, doctors and news interviews. It is however important to mention that in most of these situations, it is the setting that makes these people more powerful, and the number of questions they ask does not quantify their immense power. Power here therefore depends on the setting, which entrusts these institutional figures with their powerful positions. Questions are however a powerful interactional resource for the simple reason that the asking of questions places constraints on the discourse options which are available to its recipients. And while individual questions constrain, sequences of questions can constrain more strongly. An example is in the courtroom discourse which Atkinson and Drew (1979) studied. The fact that the attorney is able to ask sequences of questions, which the witness is restricted to answering, gives particular powers to the attorney. Power here depends on the setting, and not really on the power pegged on the number of questions. The setting in this case entrusts the judge with a powerful position of being able to ask questions whereas the respondent can only answer them, and in most cases, is obliged to do so.

The theme of questions and questioning is an area where gender differences have been noted, in different contexts, including the public workplace. We would pose the following questions: What are questions? Who asks most questions in different contexts and why? How do they ask questions? What is the function of questions in different situations and different contexts? What types of questions are asked? One important question is whether these different types of questions are pegged on gender? Is it possible that they are also pegged on power? Still, is there a possibility of an interplay between gender relations and power/hierarchical relations in these contexts?

Generally speaking, we can divide the types of questions into two broad categories when dealing with conversational groups. Holmes (1995) says that it is useful to distinguish between response-restricting and facilitative or supportive questions according to their function in context. Response restricting questions are more often of the Yes - No answers, whereas facilitative questions are usually more than one word answer. In her study of second language learners, Holmes found that response-restricting questions were generally more frequent than facilitative questions. She also found that more men overly used considerably more response restricting questions (88 percent) as compared to women (66 percent). This she says is because females tend to use more facilitative or supportive questions than males, opening up discussion and encouraging others to participate. Males on the other hand use 'organising' questions, or questions that restrict responses to short factual statements. A further broad categorisation was identified and found relevant to this research project. The categories were thus labelled as supportive questions, critical questions and antagonistic questions. It must however be pointed out that it was sometimes difficult to determine the question type just from the surface level, until we looked at it within its contextual framework.

Supportive questions on the one hand imply a generally positive response to the content of the presentation. They may invite the speaker to either expand or elaborate on some aspects of it. Supportive questions also provide 'openings' and invite the speaker to develop a point, or expand on an area of their presentation. Critical questions on the other hand are a type of questions which are less whole-heartedly or explicitly positive, and may contain a hint of criticism. They often consist of a modified agreement, or a qualified disagreement, perhaps expressing a degree of negative evaluation or scepticism. The tone in which any question is expressed is also extremely important in interpreting its function in order to classify it accurately. This is particularly obvious with critical questions. A sceptical tone of voice can turn a superficially supportive comment into a critical one. Antagonistic questions are a type of question which generally involve challenging, aggressively critical assertions whose function is to attack the speaker's position and demonstrate that it (the position) is wrong. These antagonistic questions are clearly very face-threatening. Somehow on the women's part, it was only the chair that used them, and even so, did it sparingly.

I would however hasten to add that it was not always easy to determine whether a question was supportive, critical or antagonistic. This is even despite the fact that the descriptions of each type was so clearly laid down. What this meant was that we also had to look at the question, in its context of situation; what had come before the question, or what had prompted the question to be asked. Also to be considered was how the next speaker reacted to the question. In many cases, this next response gave an insight into the type of question at hand, especially if it may have been problematic in its description.

On Turn-taking and Questions, it was observed that questions are a normal phenomenon in any kind of verbal interaction. It is also quite central in the institutional interactions that we have analysed. It was noted that questions are a powerful interactional resource, since the asking of questions places constraints on the discourse options, which are available to its recipients. It was also noted that questions are one way of handing the floor over from one speaker to another, and yet still maintain politeness. This is in view of the fact that although they may be quite effective, interruptions may be considered impolite, so speakers who are interested in politeness would prefer to use questions. However, although questions may be an alternative, it was found that this depended on the type of questions since different questions function differently in various contexts.

In the private sphere, it has been observed that women tend to ask more questions, and sometimes actually ask more questions in comparison to men. In the formal context, of which this research is a part, it was found however that this was not always the case. In meeting A, women generally had more questions than men. However, it was found that this was due to the fact that most questions emanated from the chairperson who was female. When we separated the chairperson's questions from the rest of the women, it was found that women's contributions were pathetically low. This brings us to the power interplay even within the same gender. In meeting B however, the male participation in terms of the questions was invariably higher than for the women. The fact that the chairperson was male only magnified the numbers. However, it was also found that when both the female and male chairpersons were compared in terms of their contributions on questions, the male chairperson outperformed his female counterpart. This suggested not only the interplay between gender and power, but also the fact that gender may supersede power.

In terms of the categorisation of questions, it was found that most of the speakers often used Supportive questions whenever they asked questions. It was found that the second most used type of question was the critical kind, and antagonistic types of questions were the least used.

In terms of who used what type of questions, it was found that both males and females used Supportive questions, whether they were more powerful or less powerful within the ranks. Of course the more powerful used them more, and also more men used them compared to the females in both meetings. The chairpersons of each meeting however asked more questions than the rest of the speakers, although it was found that the chairperson in meeting B generally asked more questions than the chairperson in meeting A. When looking at Critical questions, it was also found that although both men and women speakers used them, both chairpersons tended to use them more often than the rest. At the same time, more males than females tended to use them (of course in meeting A, this is if we removed the participation of the chair). The rest of the women did not use them. Being the least used type of questions, it was hardly surprising to find out that Antagonistic questions whenever used were mostly asked by the chairpersons, and the more powerful speakers. In meeting A (with female chairperson), it is only the chairperson who used them, and also a speaker who was male, and also hierarchically more powerful. The rest of the females in this meeting refrained from using them. In meeting B, no woman speaker used Antagonistic questions at all. As for the male participation on this, all of the Antagonistic questions apart from one came from the chairperson.

In the use of and distribution of Questions across the meetings, it was noted that both gender and power seemed to have a bearing. There was usually interplay between gender and power, and in some cases observed it was found that gender seemed to be the decisive factor.

Turn-Taking and Topic Organisation

Fairclough (1992) in discussing interactional controls gives us an example of a standard medical interview, where the doctor closely controls the basic organisation of the interaction by opening and closing each cycle, and accepting or acknowledging the patient's responses. One corollary of this is that the doctor is controlling the turn-taking system in the way that the turns are distributed between participants in the interaction. The patient only takes turns when offered them by the doctor, for example when the doctor directs a question at the patient. The doctor on the other hand is not offered turns, but takes them when the patient has finished her/his response, or when he decides the patient has said enough for the purpose of the diagnosis. A further corollary of this basic organisation is to do with 'Topic control'. It is mainly the doctor who introduces new topics through his questions.

It has been suggested that the person who controls the topic is the person who controls the interaction (Shuy 1987; Walker 1987), and especially so in legal settings. Just as in the medical discourse and also classroom discourse, research on domestic discourse between female and male partners has also shown an asymmetry in the take up of topics; women offer more topics than men, but it is men's topics which are more often accepted by women than vice versa (Fishman 1983). Ethnomethodological research on topics is however based on conversation, and on an assumption of equal rights and obligations between participants. In such interactions, topics are introduced and changed only by the dominant participants, often according to a pre-set agenda or routine, which may or may not be overtly set in the discourse. What this means is that topic organisation and control in most cases is never symmetrical, although this may depend on a lot of factors such as status/power (as seen in the medical encounter), expertise, or even gender. The context also matters greatly, and when you are talking of institutional discourse in the workplace, these factors affect a great deal the manner in which topics are organised and handled.

West and Garcia (1988) studied mixed sex dyads and analysed male dominance in interaction by investigating the frequency of instances of 'unilateral topic change', or one speaker's attempt to change topic while the other speaker is still on the previous topic. They found that men were responsible for initiating more changes of topic than women (64 percent versus 36 percent). However, in contrast to the study by West and Garcia (1988), other research conducted of conversations between strangers found no gender differences in the number of topics initiated for discussion or the number of topics developed.

Pamela Fishman in her studies tried to find out why some topics by both men and women sometimes failed, and yet some others succeeded. In the private conversations that she studied (Fishman 1983:89-101), she found that women raise more topics than men, and they worked harder to develop those topics. She found that women raised 62 percent of the topics. While all the topics raised by men produced conversations, only 38 percent of the topics raised by women were successfully developed. Men thus did less work in interaction to develop topics than women did. Fishman found that women had much more trouble getting conversations going than men did. She further found in her study that she could not explain women's failures on the basis of the content of the topics, since what the women and men wanted to talk about was quite similar: an article in the paper, something that happened during the day, friends, dinner or work. She found that topics introduced by the women failed because the men did not respond with the attention necessary to keep the conversation going. In contrast, she found that the men's topics succeeded not because they were inherently more interesting, but because the women upheld their part of the conversations. Topics men initiated thus succeeded because both parties worked in a joint development, to turn the initial attempt into an actual conversation. This study by Fishman (1983) has been widely cited, but there have been no follow-up studies that attempt to replicate her results.

In working with data on the current study, it was observed that Turn-taking and Topic organisation were also central issues in interaction, especially so when one is interested in looking at the issue of power. It was noted that the person who controlled the topic was also by extension the person who controlled the interaction. Topic control was thus seen to be a crucial factor in measuring the status of a member within the interaction and also in judging how power is distributed.

Like in the other interactional controls, the role of the chairperson here was found to be crucially important. Most times, the chairperson initiated topics, and also shifted them occasionally and also closed the topics. It was found that the laying out of the agenda was always the prerogative of the chair, and this was regardless of the sex of the chair. It was also found that a great deal of subtopics flowed from the general framework of laying out the agenda, which, as has been said, was the responsibility of the chair. With regard to this, the position of the chairperson was therefore found to be very strong and unquestionably powerful. However, of the two chairpersons, it was found that the female chairperson was more flexible in her handling of the agenda. This could be seen in situations where a member deviated from the actual topic, even though there might have been a relationship with the previous topic. In such cases, it was observed that she gave the speaker audience and listened to such contributions with a lot of patience. However, the male chairperson, it was found, had the habit of dismissing the contributions of the participants as 'not ideal for the current discussion', and he would recommend that such topics could be discussed in more relevant forums or meetings. This, it could be concluded can work to discourage contributions from participants who would thus refrain from making future novel contributions.

It was also found that the male chairperson when interrupted, as in the ringing of the telephone, could resume or abandon a topic that was in progress at the time, and if he decided to abandon it, or change it, despite what the initiator of the topic did, the chair always succeeded. The female chairperson however, in all the cases where there was an interruption as in the ringing of the telephone, always went back to the topic that had been in progress before the interruption.

It was found therefore that in connection with Topic organisation, three things became clear:

- The first was that topic initiation, topic development, topic change and topic closing were all influenced by the gender of the participants.
- The second was that different occupational status and power had an adverse influence on who raised topics and how they were received and organised in the interaction.
- The third was that both gender and power were related to context, which had an influence on how the topics were organised.

Conclusions

From the findings, various conclusions were drawn. These conclusions were based on the findings related to the different interactional resources that were found within the interaction patterns in the workplace. Understanding the complex interplay of gender and discourse required careful examination of the context of social roles. The variation evidenced in these contextualised forms offered clues about a changing world and changing gender role expectations, where discourse participants are struggling to challenge restrictive notions and pursue new choices. Unfortunately, such participants also struggle with the continuing forces of traditional gender norms and the maintenance of the status quo by those who oppose the loss of their power and privilege. This is where Critical Discourse Analysis (CDA) plays a pivotal role by making those practices more opaque so that the affected know exactly what they are up against.

It was concluded that most interaction problems such as the unequal distribution of talk in public contexts are the result of structured inequality in our society. Women's ways of talking differ from men's because each group has developed interaction strategies which reflect their societal positions. Most cross-gender communication problems in public contexts are women's problems because the interactional rules in such situations are men's rules. So consciousness-raising and mutual understanding may resolve not only some problems of cross-cultural miscommunication between the sexes, but also in the real world situation. In the real world situation, the real issue is power. (There has been unequal distribution of power between the sexes in society. Changing the power structure would probably alter the patterns.)

It has often been suggested that quantitative findings on male dominance in conversation can be explained to a significant extent by the fact that males on average hold higher status positions than women; that is, it is not simply gender that causes men to dominate and women to differ. If this is true, then it should follow that:

- Where women are in a position of power they will dominate conversation in ways similar to men.
- That where men are in subordinate positions, their dominant behaviour will diminish or disappear.

From my findings however, less powerful men in my sample were still able to dominate more powerful women status-wise, although the truth is that more powerful women status-wise came out more strongly and more assertively in their conversational styles than less powerful women. On power, when you however look at the performance between the chairpersons in their respective meetings, although one was male and the other was female, the male chair seemed to have more of the interruptions, and these may be indications of gender variables outdoing status and power.

It was thus concluded that the gender based patterns tend to override status variables, so that even when a woman is in a higher status position or more powerful role, she is likely to be interrupted by even a lower status man within that hierarchy, more often than she interrupts him i.e. subordinate males interrupted higher status females in other work situations more than they did to their male counterparts. Through 'violations' of the turn-taking model, men denied equal status to women as conversational partners with respect to rights to the full utilisation of their turns and support for the development of topics. The study has provided strong evidence to suggest that the power generally assumed by males is reflected in domination of conversational interaction.

From the current study, it is also concluded that in most cases, powerful participants will be selected to speak more often than non-powerful participants. It was noted that powerful people dominate conversation; not only because of their own efforts, but also because of the support they receive from others. Powerful participants will self-select more often than non-powerful participants. Powerful participants will interrupt and overlap others more frequently than non-powerful participants. Powerful participants will be interrupted and overlapped less frequently than non-powerful participants. However, status alone as we have seen, cannot account for the results. There is thus enough evidence from the research carried out, to suggest and conclude that a significant difference exists in the way that men and women organise conversation. Also, that the power assumed by males is reflected in their domination of mixed-sex interaction and thus also in disproportionate floor holding. More powerful participants dominate conversational organisation thereby gaining for themselves a disproportionate amount of floor apportionment, and in most cases, due to societal arrangements and structures, the more powerful participants are men. In verbal behaviour within the organisation, the participants are acting out the real life situations where men dominate, and women continue to be suppressed and oppressed.

This study showed that when the two power bases of gender and occupational status are at work, then gender seems to exert the greater influence on floor apportionment. The power base of occupational status did influence the way that both men and women organised conversation (Generally, speakers in high occupational positions spent more time holding the floor than their subordinates, and more specifically in two cases, the same speakers gained more floor space in 'boss' rather than subordinate positions). Nevertheless even when women held high-status occupational positions, male subordinates still organised the interaction in a way that allowed them to dominate the floor.

Gender and power as we have concluded, are so intricately related in the way that they influence the Turn-taking behaviour of participants, although we have singled out Gender as being more deterministic in the verbal behaviour of the participants. We should however note that the patterning of specific linguistic forms may be illuminated by many more variables than just gender. These include the role taken by participants in interaction, the objectives of interaction, the participants' relative status on a number of dimensions, and many more variables. One thing to remember is that 'women' do not form a homogeneous social group. We have women from Africa, Europe, Asia etc, and they all come with differing cultural characteristics, which are reflected in their linguistic behaviour. Gender is crosscut with other social divisions, and their relative importance is affected by the specifics of the situation.

The question may thus really be who are the powerful speakers in a workplace setting. This domain, as has been discussed, had traditionally left out women, and as of today, the picture has not changed very much, and the linguistic equation may similarly follow the same pattern. However, we have slightly more women in these key powerful positions, but as compared to male representation in the same domain, this is still quite insignificant. Women in this domain thus need to work towards negotiating and struggling against the conditions of their oppression in these kinds of settings. They need to work towards making the so-called 'glass ceiling' more opaque, or shattering it altogether. Looking beneath the discourse patterns of men and women in the workplace, the two groups have been un-veiled as working as warriors in their claim for public space. This does no good to society in general. Because these practices are bound to be made more visible and opaque, men and women should now work towards being collaborators in this crucial sector if our society is to achieve maximum benefit. This would go a long way in reforming the African public sector.

Notes

* This paper forms part of my PhD dissertation, which was completed in October 2002 at the University of Vienna (Austria), Institute of Applied Linguistics. I would particularly like to thank my two supervisors; Professor Ruth Wodak and Professor Florian Menz for the guidance they offered me throughout the whole project. Any shortcomings however remain wholly my own.

1. Supportive interruptions include questions or statements, which are related to the speaker's topic. They are utterances by a listener, primarily to indicate interest, attention and concern to what the speaker is saying. They are thus acts of collabo-ration and cooperation, and encourage the development of the speaker's talk. Neutral interruptions are short statements that are not meant to challenge the current speaker in any way, or to provoke any reaction if any, especially if it is to challenge the current speaker. They may be used to repeat, repair or clarify an utterance. Unsupportive interruptions may be a violation of a current speaker's turn talking rights and may be considered interruptive, disruptive, obstructive and even dominance related. For a wider discussion on this, look at Yieke (2002b).

References

Atkinson, J. M. & P. Drew, 1979, *Order in Court: The Organisation of Verbal Interaction in Judicial Settings*, London: Macmillan.

Coates, J., ed., 1998, *Language and Gender. A reader*, Oxford: Basil Blackwell.

Coates, J., 1989, 'Gossip revisited: Language in all female groups', in Jennifer Coates & Deborah Cameron (1991), eds., *Women in Their Speech Communities*, London and New York: Longman, pp. 94-122.

Eckert, P. & S. McConnell-Ginet, 1998, 'Communities of practice: where language, gender and power all live', in Coates, Jennifer, ed., *Language and Gender. A reader*, Oxford: Basil Blackwell, pp484-494.

Fairclough, N., 1992, *Discourse and Social Change*, Cambridge:Cambridge University Press.

Fairclough, N. & R. Wodak, 1997, 'Critical discourse analysis', in T. A. van Dijk, ed., *Discourse Studies: A Multidisciplinary Introduction*, London: Sage, pp258-284.

Ferguson, N., 1977, 'Simultaneous speech, interruptions and dominance', *British Journal of Social and Clinical Psychology*, 16, pp. 295-302.

Fishman, P., 1983, 'Interaction: the work women do', in Thorne, Kramarae & Henley eds., *Language, Gender And Society*, Cambridge: Newbury House Publishers, pp.89-101.

Gal, S., 1995, 'Language, gender and power: an anthropological review', in Kira Hall and Mary Bucholtz, eds., *Gender Articulated: Language and The Socially Constructed Self*, London: Routledge.

Gal, S., 1991, 'Between speech and silence: the problematics of research on language and gender', in Michaela di Leonardo, ed., *Gender At The Crossroads of Knowledge: Feminist Anthropology in The Post-modern Era*, Berkley CA: University of California.

Hall, K. & M. Bucholtz, eds., 1995, *Gender Articulated: Language and The Socially Constructed Self*, London: Routledge.

Hawkins, K.W., 1988, 'Interruptions in task oriented conversations: effects of violations of expectations by males and females', *Women's Studies in Communication*, 11, 1–20.

Henley, N. & C. Kramarae, 1991, 'Gender, power, and miscommunication', in Nikolas Coupland, Howard Giles and John Wiemann, eds., *Miscommunication and Problematic Talk*, pp 18-43, Newbury Park, CA: Sage.

Holmes, J., 1995, *Women, Men and Politeness*, U.K: Longman Group Ltd.

James, D. & S. Clarke, 1993, 'Women, men, and interruptions: A critical review', in Deborah Tannen, ed., *Gender and Conversational Interaction*, Oxford: O.U.P., pp. 231–80.

Kedar, L., ed., 1987, *Power Through Discourse*, USA: Ablex Publishing Corporation.

Kendall, S. & D. Tannen, 1997, 'Gender and Language in workplaces', in *Gender and Discourse, R*, Wodak, ed., London: Sage, pp81-105.

Lakoff, R., 1990, 'Why can't a woman be less like a man?', in *Talking Power: The Politics of Language*, San Francisco, Basic Books.

Lakoff, R., 1975, *Language and Women's Place*, New York: Harper & Row.

O'Donnell, K., 1990, 'Difference and dominance: How labour and management talk conflict', in Grimshaw A., ed., *Conflict Talk: Sociolinguistic Investigations of Arguments in Conversations*, pp. 210–40, Cambridge: CUP.

Sacks, H., E. Schegloff & G. Jefferson, 1974, 'A Simplest Systematic for the Organisation of Turn-taking for Conversation', *Language*, 50, pp696-735.

Shuy, R., 1987, 'Conversational power in FBI covert tape recordings', in Keder Leah, ed., *Power Through Discourse*, USA: Ablex Publishing Corporation, pp 43-56.

Tannen, D., 1995, *Talking From 9-5: Women And Men In The Workplace. Language, Sex And Power*, New York, Avon.

Thorne, B., C. Kramarae & N. Henley, 1983, [1975], eds., *Language, Gender And Society*, Cambridge, Newbury House Publishers.

Troemel-Ploetz, S., 1998, 'Selling the apolitical', in Coates, Jennifer, ed., *Language and Gender: A Reader*, UK: Blackwell publishers. pp446-458.

Walker, A., 1987, 'Linguistic manipulation, power, and legal setting', in Kedar Leah, ed., *Power Through Discourse*, USA, Ablex Publishing Corporation, pp57-82.

West, C. & Garcia, A., 1988, 'Conversational shift work: A study of topical transition between women and men', *Social Problems*, 35, 551–75.

Williams, C., 1995, 'The glass escalator; hidden advantages for men in the "female" professions', in Michael S. Kimmel & Michael A. Messner, eds., *Men's Lives* (Third Edition), Needham Heights, MA, Allyn & Bacon.

Wodak, R., 1997, 'Critical discourse analysis and the study of doctor-patient interaction', in Gunnarsson *et al*, *The Construction of Professional Discourse*, New York: Longman Limited.

Wodak, R., 1997, ed., *Gender and Discourse*, London: Sage Publications.

Wodak, R., 1996, *Disorders of Discourse*, London: Longman.

Wodak, R., 1981, 'Women relate, men report: sex difference in language behaviour in a therapeutic group', *Journal Of Pragmatics*, 5, 261–85.

Wodak, R. & Meyer, M., 2001, *Methods Of Critical Discourse Analysis*, London, New Delhi: Sage.

Yieke, F., 2002a, 'Language, gender and power: The use of questions as a control strategy in workplaces in Kenya', To appear in the *Wiener Linguistische Gazette. Institut für Sprachwissenschaft der Universität Wien.*

Yieke, F., 2002b, *Language and Discrimination. A Study of Gender and Discourse in Workplaces in Kenya*, Unpublished PhD. Thesis, University of Vienna.

Yieke, F., (forthcoming), 'Gender and Discourse in the Workplace. A case of the "Glass Ceiling" Syndrome', To appear in Journal for proceedings on Gender Conference on women studies; Gains and Challenges in the 21st Century. Held in Kampala, Uganda. 21 July–26 July 2002.

Zimmerman, D. & Candance W., 1975, 'Sex roles, interruptions and silences in conversation', in Barrie Thorne & Nancy Henley, 1975, *Language, Gender and Society*, Cambridge: Newbury House Publishers, pp. 105–29.

The Publisher

The **Council for the Development of Social Science Research in Africa** (CODESRIA) is an independent organisation whose principal objectives are facilitating research, promoting research-based publishing and creating multiple forums geared towards the exchange of views and information among African researchers. It challenges the fragmentation of research through the creation of thematic research networks that cut across linguistic and regional boundaries.

CODESRIA publishes a quarterly journal, *Africa Development*, the longest standing Africa-based social science journal; *Afrika Zamani*, a journal of history; the *African Sociological Review, African Journal of International Affairs (AJIA), Africa Review of Books* and *Identity, Culture and Politics: An Afro-Asian Dialogue*. It co-publishes the *Journal of Higher Education in Africa* and *Africa Media Review*. Research results and other activities of the institution are disseminated through 'Working Papers', 'Monograph Series', 'CODESRIA Book Series', and the *CODESRIA Bulletin*.

www.ingramcontent.com/pod-product-compliance
Lightning Source LLC
Chambersburg PA
CBHW020000290326
41935CB00007B/253